FEMINISM &
THE NEW WORLD ORDER

by

Henry Makow PHD

SILAS GREEN

Published by Silas Green

Cruel Hoax : Feminism and the New World Order

Manufactured in the USA

ISBN 978-0-9687725-1-5

Copyright 2010 Henry Makow   hmakow@gmail.com

Dedicated to my Wife

TABLE OF CONTENTS

BOOK THREE: *How Heterosexuality Works*

BOOK FOUR: *Freemasonry the Illuminati & Brainwashing*

FOREWORD

Your Author

M Y FATHER recalls that I looked around the delivery room at birth and seemed to ask: "What is this place? What's going on here?" That didn't change.

For most of my life, the world made no sense. I was told there was no God but I had an intuition of immanent Design and Purpose. I half expected to be taken aside and initiated into the arcane wisdom of mankind. I couldn't believe God would go to so much trouble for this mundane existence -- like building the Roman coliseum for a game of tiddly winks (to use Malcolm Muggeridge's analogy.)

My Biggest Mistake was that I did not trust my own perception and intuition. I was actually too humble. I sought guidance from my elders in the mass media and education system. As a result, I was confused and dysfunctional.

I had a desire to write the Truth. Investigative reporters were my role models. At age 12, I wrote an advice-to-parents column that was syndicated in 40 cities. When I visited the local newspaper, the smell of ink from the presses exhilarated me. The knowledge that I would reach millions of people was intoxicating.

But I didn't know the Truth, so I pursued other careers as a stopgap. I became an academic and invented a popular board game, Scruples. Politically I was a typical left-leaning feminist and Zionist.

My breakthrough came at age 48, in 1997, when I started to question my feminist conditioning. My instincts were telling me that

I wanted to rule my own roost.

Returning to teaching part-time, I encouraged a debate on feminism in my English class. I discovered that university had changed during my absence. From a place of free inquiry, it had become a factory for feminist indoctrination.

Feminist zealots went berserk when I presented them with an alternative point-of-view. They distorted my statements and drove me from the classroom with the help of the feminist administration. I sued a local newspaper that printed their lies and won. Many female students testified on my behalf.

Feminism belongs to what Marilyn Ferguson called *"The Aquarian Conspiracy"* an occult (Luciferian) movement that tacitly dominates most government and social institutions today.

Feminists imagine they are "fighting the patriarchy" but the Rockefellers and Rothschilds wholly sponsor them. I visited the director of the Manitoba Business Council, which represents the largest corporations in the province. They fund the university.

Didn't it bother him that students were being taught to hate corporations and become homosexuals?

It didn't bother him one bit. (He pretended it wasn't true.) So much for feminists fighting the establishment.

Grasping for an explanation, I picked up James Perloff's book, *"The Shadows of Power"* and everything started to fall into place. But it took three more years to finally deprogram myself. It felt like struggling to get out of a mental wet suit. But once done, it was spiritually liberating to understand that our society is built on fraud, and does not require our deference.

I chronicled every step of my re-education on my web site www.savethemales.ca and developed a small following. A good teacher is just a student who shares his learning path.

I have not changed the world but my life has improved immensely, and I hope I have taken some readers along. My writing is a labor of love and my readers have compensated me in kind.

Here is the part of my work dealing with the sexual sabotage of society in political context. I have tried to eliminate repetition, but I beg your indulgence. Each article was originally designed to stand alone. These truths were revealed to me over time, so I returned to the same themes in different terms.

INTRODUCTION

The Assault on Heterosexual Society

WHAT I AM GOING TO SAY WILL SOUND OUTRAGEOUS AT FIRST. It will fly in the face of what you've been taught. I ask only that you hear me out, and then verify or discredit my assertions at your leisure.

This subject is so large that I can only "connect the dots". The "dots" consist of articles that first appeared on my website www. savethemales.ca When you have finished this collection, you should get the picture.

Born in 1949, my adult life coincided with a secret program of social engineering designed to destabilize society by programming straight people to behave like homosexuals. This insidious assault on heterosexuals masqueraded as the "sexual revolution", "gay rights" and "feminism."

This sounds preposterous because we think of homosexuality strictly in terms of same-sex attraction. However, homosexuality should be seen in broader terms: as *arrested development* caused by *confusion over gender identity,* resulting in *inability to bond permanently* with *a member of the opposite sex* and (usually) *establish a family.* The main symptom of this disorder is the pursuit of anonymous sex for its own sake (i.e. promiscuity.)

According to this definition, many heterosexuals can be classed as homosexuals. Indeed elite social engineers appear to be aiming at a "hetero-homo" world, i.e. where individuals are bisexual, promiscuous and bereft of family.

(Yes, a small minority of homosexuals are monogamous. Soon we might say the same thing about hetero-homos.)

The purpose of turning us into hetero-homos is to advance the centuries-old plan of an international financial elite based in the City of London to absorb the world's wealth and establish a veiled totalitarian one-world government devoted to Lucifer.

This "New World Order" is in fact the old "British" Empire repackaged. The "British" empire always represented a small Satanic largely homosexual financial oligarchy that colonized England and much of the world.

This group represents a union between Jewish finance and the British aristocracy joined by money, marriage and a belief in the occult (Freemasonry.) This may sound extreme to some, but if you dig you will find that it is true. You might start with the article on my website, *"The Jewish Conspiracy is British Imperialism."*

The "Plan" calls for the destruction of all "collective" forces capable of resistance. These forces, which support our human identity, are family, race, religion and nation-state. They are to be eliminated through a campaign of "tolerance" which erases the differences between them. If you accept everything, eventually you become nothing.

Thus we have ecumenicalism in religion, miscegenation in race, and regionalism in nation states. *You destroy family by erasing gender differences.* Their goal is one world government, one race, one religion, and ultimately one sex, the hetero-homo.

Families give people their purpose, identity and sense of belonging. They provide values and a measure of social, spiritual and financial independence. The goal of Communism and the New World Order always has been the destruction of family. This forces people to get their sense of belonging from the elite-run media, political causes or products.

We only know what we are taught, and obviously they aren't going to reveal this to us. The nature of conspiracy is that it pursues a subversive agenda while actively denying it.

For example, Arnold Toynbee told an elite gathering in Copenhagen in 1931: "I will merely repeat that we are at present working, discreetly but with all our might, to wrest this mysterious political force called sovereignty out of the clutches of the local national states of our world. And all the time we are denying with our lips what we are doing with our hands...."

Elite social engineers turn us into hetero-homos by confusing us about our sexual identity. They deny that obvious gender differences exist, and convince young women to act like men. They portray the traditional feminine role as an "artificial and oppressive social stereotype." Sex roles are artificial unless of course they are reversed. Then women can act like stereotypical men, and men can be stereotypically feminine.

Social engineers know people are lazy and gullible and prefer to do as they are cajoled rather than use their own reason or instinct. Thus, when a subversive power takes secret control, people are easily manipulated.

Heterosexual roles are not invented. They correspond to biological differences. For example, men have ten times more testosterone than women. This hormone turns men into single minded, aggressive risk takers. (See the books *"Why Men Don't Iron"* (1992) and *"Brain Sex"* (2003) by Anne Moir and David Jessel. Excerpts can be found on the Internet.)

Women's brains are different. For example, they talk three times as much and twice as fast as men. (See *"The Female Brain"* (2006) by Louanne Brizendine)

Sex roles represent cultural recognition of biological and psychological differences. When sex roles are denied, confusion results. We can't bond with the opposite sex. Our natural instincts are frustrated and arrested development and dysfunction follow.

Heterosexuality is not a "sexual preference." It is part of the reproductive cycle. Each stage (marriage, parenthood etc.) is necessary for our development and happiness as human beings. For most people, parenthood is essential to personal fulfillment. Social health depends on raising the new generation in a wholesome environment with positive values.

We are being conditioned to follow a hetero-homo pattern intended to arrest our development at the courtship stage, and make us dysfunctional, barren and docile. This is why practically all movies and music are fixated on romance, as if the whole population has been frozen at age 19-26.

THE DAMAGE

In less than 50 years, feminism and "sexual liberation" have ravaged the institution of the family. Feminism pretends to champion women when in fact it disparages feminine qualities. It has ruined the lives of millions of women (and men) who now can't find lasting love.

A damage inventory:

• The number of married-with-children households has declined by half, from 50% of the total in 1960 to 25% today.

• In 1965, 24 percent of Black infants and 3.1 percent of White infants in the US were born to single mothers. By 2007, four out of ten babies were born out of wedlock.

• The marriage rate has fallen nearly 30% since 1970 while the divorce rate has increased about 40%.

• The fertility rate has declined by almost one-half. In 1960, an average Canadian woman had four children. Today she has barely 1.5. In 2002, the US non-Hispanic birthrate was at its lowest point in history, about 1.8. Just maintaining the population requires a birth rate of 2.2.

(These stats and indeed all of my assertions can be found using Google.)

"Most of our social pathologies — crime, imprisonment, welfare, educational underachievement, alcohol and drug abuse, suicide, depression, sexually transmitted diseases --are manifestations, direct and indirect of the crack-up of the modern American family." (William Bennett *"The Broken Hearth"* p.4)

BECOMING HETERO-HOMOS

In an article in the *McGill Daily,* student Anna Montrose described how her humanities education and the mass media made her question her heterosexuality:

"It's hard to go through four years of a Humanities B.A. reading Foucault and Butler and watching 'The L Word' and keep your rigid heterosexuality intact. I don't know when it happened exactly, but it seems I no longer have the easy certainty of pinning my sexual desire to one gender and never the other."

(Michel Foucault is a major French "post-modern" philosopher; Judith Butler is a prominent "gender theorist" at UC Berkeley; and "The L-Word" is a popular TV drama about "glamorous" lesbians, i.e. the ones that don't look like refrigerators in plaid shirts and overalls.)

Montrose thinks men and women are interchangeable and marriage is mostly good for a tax deduction. She is unfit for marriage and motherhood. Unfortunately, she is becoming the rule rather than the exception.

Paradoxically, when females reject the male, they usurp the masculine role and abandon the feminine one.

According to Charles Socarides, a New York City psychiatrist who studied and treated homosexuals for 50 years, there is a plan to make the whole world gay:

"You can read an account of the campaign in Dennis Altman's "The Homosexualization of America." In 1982 Altman, himself gay, reported that more and more Americans were thinking like gays and acting like gays. There were engaged "in numbers of short-lived sexual adventures either in place of or alongside long-term relationships." Altman cited the heterosexual equivalents of gay saunas and the emergence of the swinging singles scene as proofs that "promiscuity and 'impersonal sex' are determined more by social possibilities than by inherent differences between homosexuals and heterosexuals, or even between men and women." ("How America Went Gay")

Gay or straight, people who cannot mate will be promiscuous. According to a 2003 study in the American Journal of Public Health, gays averaged seven sex partners in the previous six months, while 25% had 18 or more.

Since media-induced "sexual liberation," we have all become obsessed with sex. All human relations have been degraded to this level.

Now the educational system is actually promoting sex to children. In Winnipeg where I live, a public health teacher recently told 12-year-olds to have sex at age 13. They were taught about flavoured condoms and shown explicit pictures that appalled the children.

This action exposes the public school system as an instrument of indoctrination, corruption and yes, child abuse. When 13-year-olds are told to have sex, is it any wonder they are inviting adult predators to their homes? (See "NBC Dateline: To Catch a Predator") How long will it be before certain homosexual activists get their wish and pedophilia is legalized?

Another local school program ("RespectED") run by the Red Cross teaches ten-year-olds to fear dating. The emphasis is on recognizing "the cycle of abuse" and when they are being "terrorized."

Schools are actually teaching children to experiment with gay sex in the name of "human rights" and "tolerance." Courts are upholding the right of schools to mentally debauch children over their parents' objections. In Hungary, adults can have sex with children of 14.

All of this is designed to make the sex act and end-in-itself apart from love, marriage and procreation. Thus the habit of monogamy is lost. Promiscuous women cannot commit to one man "until death do us part" (and men can't commit to them.) Compare this to 50-years-ago when sex was consecrated for marriage and family.

Marriage is the basic building block of society. If men and women are not faithful, then there is no basis for social stability. There is no foundation for the family. Break up marriage and you break up society, rendering it vulnerable to political control.

THE HETEROSEXUAL CONTRACT (MARRIAGE)

The focus of Part Three of this book is "How Heterosexuality Works." I'll provide an introduction here.

I reached the age of 48 without understanding how to relate to a woman. I had no standard of masculinity and therefore could not find my identity. The women I met were also confused or messed up.

Predictably, I had two failed marriages and suffered from emotional arrested development. I missed my opportunity to have a normal family.

Too late I figured out how heterosexuality works. This information was culturally transmitted but it has been suppressed by feminism as "politically incorrect."

Femininity is defined by a woman's love for husband, children and home.

Masculinity is defined by power and leadership. Male power is the ultimate aphrodisiac for women.

Men naturally seek power. Women want love. Thus, the heterosexual contract (marriage) is the exchange of female (worldly) power for male power expressed as love.

Women empower men by entrusting their power to them in exchange for love. Marriage channels male power into a socially constructive path: raising and supporting a family.

Women *cannot* have it all. They must choose between love and power in the personal sphere.

This is how heterosexuality works. An ideology that equalizes power is designed to *neuter* heterosexuals. It turns women into men and emasculates men. It creates hetero homos-- two sames instead of two complements, unable to bond.

The purpose is political: The plutocracy does not want men who can defend and reform society. In 1976, an insider Harold Rosenthal, Sen. Jacob Javits' assistant, gave a famous interview:

"We have castrated society through fear and intimidation. Its manhood exists only in combination with a feminine outward appearance. Being so neutered, the populace has become docile and easily ruled. As all geldings...their thoughts are not involved with the concerns of the future and their posterity, but only with the present and with the next meal."

By exchanging power for love, I am referring to the personal setting only. I have no objection to women having careers after establishing their families. Nor do I believe all women must marry or have children. (The fact is, most want to.)

My objection is to the hidden agenda of feminism: Tricking women into having careers *instead* of families. Making women providers also ensures they make men redundant, and have fewer children.

Economist Sylvia Ann Hewlett found that 55 percent of 35-year-old career women were childless. Almost half of 40-something women with professional degrees have no children. Only 14% of these women said they didn't want children. *("Creating a Life: Professional Women and the Quest for Children" 2004)*

WHY ARE THEY SABOTAGING US?

The unprecedented decline of the family was caused by mass psychological conditioning ordered by the central banking cartel using the CIA, the Rockefeller Foundation, the mass media, government and the education system.

A privately owned international cartel based in London controls the credit of the world's nations. Essentially they create money out of thin air based on our credit i.e. our productive capacity and property. They create this money by virtue of loaning it to us.

The bankers can buy everything and anyone they want, including politicians, media empires and universities. Thus they define reality.

As Nathan Rothschild (1777 -1836) famously said: "I care not what puppet is placed on the throne of England to rule the Empire. The man who controls Britain's money supply controls the British Empire and I control the British money supply."

(The money supply is to the economy like oxygen is to a fire.)

When the government wants money, it has to petition these bankers like little children. It sells a bond to these bankers who allow it to withdraw the "money."

This "money" takes the form of a bookkeeping entry, i.e. it is produced out of nothing. Our currency represents an IOU that the government owes these bankers. It costs the bankers paper-and-ink to issue these IOU's.

Yet the government must repay the face value of this "loan" *with interest!* Remember this "money" is backed by our (the taxpayer's) credit! In the words of the homeless man's dog, "I could do this myself."

The government easily could exploit its own credit and print all the money it needed to make the economy purr, interest free. (This was the program of the much-maligned Social Credit party.) Only then would the government have real power. The people would no longer be collateral for this debt. We would be free men, not "human resources."

A former Canadian cabinet minister told me that the government only has about 50% of the power. The corporations have the rest. What he didn't say is that the Rothschild-Rockefeller cartel largely controls these corporations. The "corporations" dictate the major issues; we get to decide where to lay the sewer pipes. Thus the majority is against the Iraq war. Therefore we are in Iraq. Democracy.

In order to protect its golden goose, the banking cartel has to control us. Since the Eighteenth Century it has been scheming to create a "world government" dictatorship.

They mask this plot with talk about ending poverty and war, but they create both. World government is really designed to ensure *no country defaults on its debt or tries to escape from its bondage.* The motivation behind 9-11 and the "War on Terror" is to create the apparatus of a world police state.

A dominant faction of the rich is holding mankind hostage. About 50% of the world's wealth is owned by just 2% of the population. The richest 300,000 Americans have as much wealth as the poorest 150 million.

The bankers are responsible for most of humanity's woes. They start wars and depressions in order to distract and divide us. They create the social trends and ideologies that make us superficial and dysfunctional. They provide a list of approved politicians. They determine what we learn from the mass media and schools. It is far easier to control people who think they are free.

Much of what we consider normal is an elaborate hoax. Wars are planned years in advance and carefully orchestrated. Both sides of every war, including the Cold War and the War on Terror, are controlled. The work of people who see through the veil is suppressed.

Can we trust the mass media about anything when it gives carte blanche to the slaughter of more than 3000 Americans on Sept. 11, 2001? What happened to the passengers of those "hijacked" planes?

"COMMUNISM"

The central bankers created Communism as a dry run for the New World Order. In 1953, Ford Foundation President Rowan Gaither brazenly told (Congressional researcher) Norman Dodd that the State Department, the United Nations, etc. had for years *"operated under directives issued by the White House, ...that we should make every effort to so alter life in the United States as to make possible a comfortable merger with the Soviet Union."*

(One of Dodd's researchers actually went insane when she learned the truth.)

The bankers have ample means to create their own enemies. They give their puppets the money and publicity to eclipse any uncontrolled resistance. They call this "dialectic": creating two opposing forces which then destroy each other, leaving the bankers unscathed, richer and even more powerful.

It's called "divide and conquer." The central bankers created both Communism and Nazism and then orchestrated World War Two where they destroyed each other. The same thing may be happening in the run up to World War Three.

The aim is demoralize, brutalize and degrade humanity, and kill off the new generation of men. They are creating a new feudalism, which reduces the masses to the status of serfs (producers and consumers.) As I said, they must first destroy race, religion, family and nation. By no coincidence, this was exactly the program of Communism.

Feminism is about destroying the family. Feminist theorists have a lesbian hatred of heterosexuality and blame "the patriarchy" for all the world's problems.

Feminism is but one example of how a small sick financial elite holds mankind hostage. Other examples are the suppression of cures to cancer and sources of cheap, abundant, pollution-free energy.

FREEMASONRY AND THE ROOTS OF FEMINISM

The poet Charles Peguy said, "Everything begins in faith and ends in politics." The banking cartel needs a philosophy to justify enslaving mankind. That philosophy appears to be Luciferianism.

Look at the logo of Universal Studios. It features a globe emitting "a thousand points of light," an occult concept popularized by George H.W. Bush in 1991. It refers to the Illuminati Order, the top rung of Freemasonry.

The Illuminati are Luciferians who believe evil is good and good is evil. Thus these "points of light" are really evildoers. This is the origin of Orwell's "doublespeak." (Technically Satanists differ from Luciferians in that they know the difference and deliberately do evil.)

The central banking cartel operates through a powerful Luciferian secret society called Freemasonry. Only the Illuminati know the real agenda. They include Jesuits, who apparently control the Vatican, and leading families of England, Europe and America.

Since the "Enlightenment," Western culture has been Luciferian in nature. It is based on the denial of God. We pay lip service to God and that's all.

Freemasonry, the church of Lucifer, is the true religion of the modern world. Our "culture" is essentially pagan, dedicated to money and sex. It is predicated on replacing God with man, hence "humanism," the religion of man, sex and excrement.

Western history is punctuated by a series of "revolutions" sponsored by these bankers –English, American, French and Russian. "Revolution" means turning the world upside down, replacing God with banker, i.e. replacing the Old Order (aristocracy, church) with the New World Order. The sexual "revolution" was part of this process. Because they create money the bankers think they are God. They think they can define reality.

Lucifer, the rebel angel and "light bringer," is the symbol of the banker plan to hijack mankind for their own purposes.

[Truly, what is God? God is Reality. Even if we don't believe in God, we all have a sense of truth, goodness, justice, love, peace, and beauty. This spiritual sense and craving is our connection to God. It defines us as human.

Just as God made the natural world with exquisite design, so natural and spiritual laws also govern humanity. It's our job to discern these moral laws and live accordingly.]

In the New World Order, the Illuminati bankers turn reality upside down to serve their interests. They proclaim evil is good and lies are true as they did in the Soviet Union. They smell like skunks but they say they smell like roses and the mass media and professors sing hosannas.

Already their cabalistic magic makes such absurd claims as men and women are identical, and homosexuality is natural. Other magic tricks include the disappearing planes that crashed into the Pentagon and at Shanksville PA. and the demolition of the World Trade Centre due to "fire." Believe what we tell you, not what you see.

The Illuminati control the world through a complex network of Masonic societies that spawned Communism, Socialism, Nazism, Liberalism, feminism, Neo Conservativism, and organized Jewry (B'nai Brith, ADL, AJC, Zionism.)

Communism and Zionism are actually Masonic Orders. I'm not saying that these movements have no merit, but any good they do disguises the Illuminati's true "revolutionary" agenda.

The banking cartel rules through control of intelligence agencies, foundations, think tanks, universities, professional associations, churches, secret societies, NGO's and the mass media. (In most cases they own or fund them.) Western society functions like a secret society, circles within circles. Only the Illuminati know the real agenda.

A CONSPIRACY AGAINST GOD

We think we live in a "secular" i.e. (religion-neutral) society. In fact we can no more banish God from the world than light and not be in the dark. Secularism is a transitory stage from a civilization based on spiritual truth to one based on Luciferian bankers' occult belief. First we are weaned off religion; then we are taught the "New Age" (i.e. Luciferian) dogma.

In his book, "Marx and Satan" (1986) Richard Wurmbrand, a pastor who was imprisoned in Romania, says Communism is in essence Satanism empowered. Christians weren't just brutally persecuted and murdered; they were made to blaspheme. Communism's goal, the goal of the New World Order, is to mock God and to praise Lucifer. A Communist newspaper confessed, "We fight against God: To snatch believers from him."(77)

According to Wurmbrand, the Russian Revolution was a time when "love, goodwill, and healthy feeling were considered mean and retrograde. A girl hid her innocence, and husbands their faithfulness. Destruction was praised as good taste, neurasthenia as the sign of a fine mind. This was the theme of new writers who burst on the scene out of obscurity. Men invented vices and perversion, and were fastidious in their avoidance of being thought moral." (85)

The Luciferians portray their rebellion against God and nature as progress and freedom. This permissiveness refers only to tearing down the Divine Order. In the initiation into the Seventh degree of Satanism, the adept swears, "Nothing is true and everything is permitted." In the Communist Manifesto, Marx said all religion and morals will be abolished and everything permitted.

The goal of globalism is the same as Communism. The world's elite masks their Luciferianism in new age paganism and Gaia worship. The Lucifer Trust runs the only chapel at the United Nations and the only statue in the UN building is the pagan god Zeus.

For Luciferians, man (banker) and not God is the measure of all things. For example Gloria Steinem, a founder of second-wave feminism, said: "By the year 2000 we will, I hope, raise our children to believe in human potential, not God." (Thus the Luciferian separates the two.)

SEX CULT

The Illuminati's real agenda is to degrade people. Sex is the great leveler, the lowest common denominator. Freemasonry is in fact a sex cult. By some accounts the "G" in its emblem stands for "generation." Its obelisks are all phallic in origin. Its symbol, the dot in a circle, represents the penis in vagina, as well as the evil eye of Horus. We have all been unwittingly indoctrinated into this cult in the name of "sexual liberation" and "progress."

In 1786, defectors exposed the Illuminati Order. Many of their secrets were published. On the subject of women, one Illuminati document stated:

"There is no way of influencing men so powerfully as by means of the women. These should therefore be our chief study; we should insinuate ourselves into their good opinion, give them hints of emancipation...of standing up for themselves...it will cause them to work for us with zeal, without knowing that they do so; for they will only be indulging their own desire for personal admiration." (James Wardner, *Unholy Alliances* 1996, p.35)

Another Illuminati document, *The Protocols of the Elders of Zion* (1905) talks about eliminating the family and manipulating the masses. "By cultivating in all a sense of self-importance, we shall destroy among the goyim the importance of the family and its educational value...In this way we shall create a blind mighty force which will never be in a position to move in any direction without the guidance of our agents..." (Protocol 10-5)

PSYCHOLOGICAL WARFARE

Post-war feminism can be traced directly to the international central banking cabal. The Rockefeller network funds and controls foundations, think tanks, the Communist Party, the CIA and most intelligence agencies.

For over a century, their aims have been to decrease population, increase government power (socialism, liberalism) and control our minds. (See Rene Wormser, *"Foundations: Their Power and Influence"* 1958 and William McIllany II, *"The Tax-Exempt Foundations"* 1980.)

The Rockefeller Foundation funded the birth control and "pro choice" (abortion) campaigns, the development of the "pill" and other contraceptives, the promotion of the (homo) sexual revolution. All of these were intended to divorce sex from marriage and procreation and make sex the national pastime.

Recently Aaron Russo, the respected producer of Bette Middler's "The Rose" and the documentary *"America: From Freedom to Fascism"* confirmed this.

He reported that when Nicholas Rockefeller tried to recruit him for the CFR, he said his family's foundation created women's liberation. "He asked me what I thought of the 'women's movement,' and I told him that I support equal opportunity," Russo said.

"He looked at me and said, 'you know, you're such an idiot in some ways. We' - meaning the people he works with - 'created the women's movement, and we promote it. And it's not about equal opportunity. It's designed to get both parents out of the home and into the workforce, where they will pay taxes. And then we can decide how the children will be raised and educated.' That's how they control society - by removing the parents from the home and then raising the children as the elitists see fit."

("He also said [in 2000] there's going to be an event and out of that event we're going to invade Afghanistan so we can run pipelines through the Caspian sea, we can go into Iraq to take the oil and establish bases in the middle east and to make the Middle East part of the new world order ...that's what's going to come out of this event."

"Eleven months to a year later that's what happened.... he certainly knew that something was going to happen. In my relationships with some of these people I can tell you that it's as evil as it really gets - this is it - this is the game," stated Russo.)

Rockefeller told Russo that the ultimate goal is to control humanity through credit/debt. He admitted the bankers also want to "chip us."

If you Google "Rockefeller Foundation" and "Women's Studies," you'll get a half-million citations. Most acknowledge financial support from the Rockefeller Foundation. Many applications ask for evidence of political activism. In "Women's Studies" classes, young women are taught to be activists, i.e. New World Order "change agents."

MEDIA ERADICATES LOVE

The bankers know mind control ("education" "free press") is more effective than physical coercion.

Every facet of the mass media (movies, TV, magazines, music, commercials, the "news") is used for indoctrination and social control. The propaganda model established during World War Two was carried into peacetime. The connection between what happened in Communist Russia and America today is that the central banking cartel is asserting its totalitarian control. (On my website, see within the three-part series "*Rothschilds Conduct Red Symphony.*")

In order to arrest our development, the elite struck at the crux of heterosexual union: female trust in men. Gloria Steinem, a CIA agent, wrote:

"The most dangerous situation for a woman is not an unknown man in the street, or even the enemy in wartime, but a husband or love in the isolation of their own home." (Gloria Steinem, *Revolution From Within* p. 261)

The other feminist founder, Betty Friedan was a professional Communist propagandist. In her famous book, *The Feminine Mystique* (1963) Friedan actually compared homemakers to concentration camp inmates.

These "walking corpses" surrendered "their human identity and went almost indifferently to their deaths," she said. Strangely enough "the conditions which destroyed [their] human identity ...were not the torture and the brutality, but conditions similar to those which destroyed the identity of the American housewife...It was work that did not emanate from the prisoner's own personality...monotonous, endless [work which] offered no hope for advancement..." (305-306)

Can we compare looking after loved ones in the comfort and privacy of home with being subject to forced labor, rape, beatings and starvation? "Strangely enough" according to Friedan, this torture was nothing compared to the housewives' lack of opportunity for self-expression and advancement! Who is she kidding?

Standard psychological warfare makes such absurd and obscene claims as though they were brilliant insights. Feminists fell for this hoax-- hook, line and sinker.

Both Steinem and Friedan were alienated from love and marriage because of their families. Steinem was the product of a divorce, an irresponsible father and an invalid mother whom she had to nurse as a teenager. As a girl, Friedan hated her super critical mother for making her feel ugly and for "killing" her father. (See: *"Betty Friedan: Making of a Feminist"* within.)

In her book *"Spin Sisters,"* Myrna Blyth says the media sold women "a career in exactly the same drum banging way that the Happy Homemaker had been sold to their mothers." (Blyth was the editor in chief of *Ladies Home Journal* from 1981 to 2002.)

According to Blyth, the Illuminati-owned women's magazines undermined women's natural loving instincts with the following mantras: 1) Men can no longer be trusted. 2) Women are victims by virtue of their sex. 3) Women should be selfish. 4) Sex is not reserved for love and marriage. 5) Self-fulfillment lies in career, not family.

Thus millions of women became schizophrenic as they attempted to reconcile these messages with their natural instincts and desires. The wreckage -- broken families and dysfunctional people -- is strewn everywhere.

At the same time, as we shall see, *Playboy* magazine aimed a similar message at men. You don't need to get married to have sex. Marriage and children are a burden and a bore.

Dysfunctional isolated alienated sex starved people are politically impotent.

At my web site www.savethemales.ca you will find dozens of

articles that expose the working of the world government conspiracy throughout history.

MORE EVIDENCE

Conspirators don't broadcast their plans but over the years, word leaks out.

Sen. Jesse Helms was anything but a conspiracy theorist. But in a speech to Congress Dec. 15 1987, the future Senate Majority Leader warned that the "Eastern Establishment" was waging "systematic psychological warfare" against the American people to establish a world government. The "Eastern Establishment" refers to the Rockefellers.

At the 1991 Bilderberg meeting, David Rockefeller thanked the media for covering up elite plans for the "supranational sovereignty of an intellectual elite and world bankers." "It would have been impossible for us to develop our plan for the world if we had been subjected to the lights of publicity during those years."

In a memo to Bernard Berelson dated March 11, 1969, Frederick S. Jaffe, Vice-president of Rockefeller-sponsored *Planned Parenthood*, outlined measures to reduce United States fertility. (http://www. newswithviews.com/Cuddy/dennis84.htm)

Among the proposals were: 1) Restructure family: postpone or avoid marriage and alter ideal family size. 2) Encourage homosexuality. 3) Educate for family limitation. 4) Encourage women to work outside the home.

If this failed, he recommended the placement of "fertility control agents in the water supply." (*"Family Planning Perspectives"* Oct. 1970.)

They put the neutering agent in the cultural drinking water.

According to feminist Ellen Willis, feminism "is the cutting edge of a revolution in cultural and moral values...The objective of every feminist reform, from legal abortion...to child-care programs, is **to undermine traditional family values.**" (*The Nation*, Nov. 14, 1981)

What part of traditional family values do feminists object to? Love? Sacrifice? Devotion? Loyalty? Security? Preparing a new generation for life?

As we shall see, feminism is not about equal opportunity. These Illuminati inspired groups always pretend to espouse something like "equality" that nobody can object to. Feminism is about undermining the social fabric. Pretending to champion an oppressed "minority" is a well worn ruse.

Communist dictator Josef Stalin wrote, "America is like a healthy body and its resistance is threefold: its patriotism, its morality, and its spiritual life. If we can undermine these three areas, America will collapse from within."

The transfer of power from male to female has destabilized society and poisoned male-femail relations. Who would attempt to destroy the bond between man and woman, and mother and child?

Ladies and Gentleman, I give you Satan. We are dealing with a cosmic conspiracy, a diabolical conspiracy against God and man. They wear a friendly face and talk about rights and freedoms. But the true agenda to replace God, to further concentrate and wealth and power in the hands of the super rich, and to degrade and control the human race.

When confronted with the truth, they respond in three prescribed ways: ignore, deny and trivialize/smear. People prefer to cling to a lie than admit their lives are based on a monstrous fraud.

"Where there is no vision, the people perish," Proverbs says. I'm afraid we are well down this gangplank.

There is a Far Side cartoon in which a flea is surrounded by tree-like stalks. He is studying a sign featuring a dog with an arrow pointing to the dog's back. It says, "You are Here."

Despite the unflattering analogy, and the disturbing nature of the truth, I hope this book provides similar perspective for people.

BOOK ONE

FEMINISM, COMMUNISM
& THE NEW WORLD ORDER

BETTY FRIEDAN

"Mommy" was a Commie

> *"Comrades, you will remember the ancient tale of the capture of Troy ... The attacking army was unable to achieve victory until, with the aid of the famous Trojan Horse, it managed to penetrate to the very heart of the enemy camp."*
>
> --GEORGE DIMITROV, COMINTERN GENERAL SECRETARY, AUGUST 1935.

B ETTY FRIEDAN, the "founder of modern feminism" pretended to be a typical 1950's American mother who had a "revelation" that women like her were exploited and should seek independence and self-fulfillment in career.

Friedan (nee: Betty Naomi Goldstein) didn't say she had been a Communist propagandist since her student days at Smith College (1938-1942) and that the destruction of the family has always been central to the Communist plan for world tyranny. See "The Communist Manifesto" (1848).

Friedan dropped out of grad school to become a reporter for a Communist news service. From 1946 -1952 she worked for the newspaper of the United Electrical, Radio and Machine Workers of America, (UE) "the largest Communist-led institution of any kind in the United States." In 1947, Congress targeted the UE as a Communist front and its membership began a steady decline.

Daniel Horowitz, a history professor at Smith with impeccable liberal and feminist credentials documents all this in his book, *Betty Friedan and the Making of the Feminine Mystique: The American Left, the Cold War and Modern Feminism* (University of Massachusetts Press 1999.) Horowitz cites a union member who described how a Communist minority "seized control of the UE national office, the executive board, the paid staff, the union newspaper and some district councils and locals."

Betty Friedan doesn't want anyone to know her radical antecedents. Throughout her career, she said she had no interest in the condition of women before her "revelation." She refused to cooperate with Professor Horowitz and accused him of "Red-baiting."

Why? Because her book *"The Feminist Mystique"* (1963) would not have sold over five million copies if her subversive background were known. Communists operate by subterfuge -- pretending to be just like us. This is the "Popular Front" strategy that consisted of starting idealistic sounding movements in order to ensnare well-meaning people, usually students, workers, women, artists or intellectuals. The membership was ignorant that their organization was funded and controlled by people with a totally different agenda. This is also the principle behind Freemasonry, Zionism and Communism itself. Essentially the adherents are dupes, "useful idiots."

Willi Munzenberg, an early confidant of Lenin, organized the Popular Fronts in the 1920's and 1930's and referred to them as "my innocents clubs". He pioneered the protest march, the demonstration, the radical bookstore and publication, the arts festival, and the recruitment of celebrities ("fellow travellers.")

In the words of historian Stephen Koch, Munzenberg "was amazingly successful at mobilizing the intelligentsia of the West on behalf of a moralistic set of political attitudes responsive to Soviet needs. In the process, he organized and defined the 'enlightened' moral agenda of his era." *(Double Lives: Spies and Writers in the Secret Soviet War of Ideas Against the West,* New York, 1994, p.14.)

In a 1989 interview, Babette Gross, the wife of Willy Munstenberg, described the Popular Front modus operandi:

"You do not endorse Stalin. You do not call yourself a Communist. You do not call upon people to support the Soviets. Never. You claim to be an independent minded idealist. You don't really understand politics but you claim the little guy is getting a lousy break." (Koch, p. 220)

Friedan observed this principle when she helped start second-wave feminism, which is a classic "Popular Front." The very name, "the woman's movement" and claim to be for "equality" are a smoke screen for a diabolical crusade to destroy the heterosexual family. For example, Friedrich Engels said, "The first condition of the liberation of the wife is to bring the whole female sex back into public industry, and this in turn demands the abolition of the monogamous family as the economic unit of society." *(The Origins of the Family, Private*

Property and the State (New York, International Publishers, 1942 p.67)

The "Congress of American Women," a Popular Front organization founded in 1946 reached a membership of 250,000. It was disbanded in 1950 after being required to register as a "foreign agent" by the U.S. Government. Feminist historian Ruth Rosen writes that the "CAW's agenda prefigured much of the modern Women's Movement that emerged in the sixties." *(The World Split Open: How the Modern Women's Movement Changed America,* New York, 2000, p.28.)

The FBI kept tabs on the "Women's Movement" but found no direct connection with Soviet subversion. Ruth Rosen, herself a veteran, finds this ironic.

"Ironically, the FBI searched for signs of subversion in the Women's Movement but couldn't recognize what was truly dangerous. While they looked for Communists and bombs, the Women's Movement was shattering traditional ideas about work, customs, education, sexuality, and the family. Ultimately the movement would prove far more revolutionary than the FBI could ever imagine. Feminism would leave a legacy of disorientation, debate and disagreement, create cultural chaos and social change for millions of men and women, and, in the process, help ignite the culture wars that would polarize American society. But at the time these ideas were not what the FBI considered subversive." (260)

By attacking the social fabric, feminists inflicted more damage to Western society than Communists ever dreamed. Manufactured hysteria over domestic violence has driven a wedge between men and women. Women have been psychologically neutered. They are encouraged to pursue sex and career not marriage and family.

The feminist Trojan horse has proven extremely effective. The question is why? How could a sick subversive philosophy that openly pits women against men have been able to succeed?

The disconcerting answer is that monopoly capitalists are behind both Communism and feminism and use them to undermine the political and cultural institutions of Western Civilization.

The Rockefeller-Rothschild cartels own much of the world and naturally assume they should control it too. They own most of our politicians, media and educators. Their goal is a "New World Order" (a.k.a. "globalization") in which they remake mankind to fit their nefarious ends.

Betty Friedan, take a bow.

GLORIA STEINEM
How the CIA Used Feminism to Destabilize Society

"IN THE 1960'S, the elite media invented second-wave feminism as part of the elite agenda to dismantle civilization and create a New World Order."

Since writing these words last week, I have discovered that before she became a feminist leader, Gloria Steinem worked for the CIA spying on Marxist students in Europe and disrupting their meetings. She became a media darling due to her CIA connections. The CIA indirectly funded *MS* Magazine, which she edited.

Steinem has tried to suppress this information, unearthed in the 1970's by a radical feminist group called "Red Stockings." In 1979, Steinem and her powerful CIA-connected friends, Katharine Graham of the Washington Post and Ford Foundation President Franklin Thomas prevented Random House from publishing the information in a book, *"Feminist Revolution."* Nevertheless the story appeared in the *Village Voice* on May 21, 1979.

Steinem has always pretended to be a student radical. "When I was in college, it was the McCarthy era," she told Susan Mitchell in 1997, "and that made me a Marxist." *("Icons, Saints and Divas: Intimate Conversations with Women who Changed the World,"* 1997. p. 130) Her bio-blurb in June 1973 MS. Magazine states: "Gloria Steinem has been a freelance writer all her professional life. *Ms magazine* is her first full-time salaried job."

Not true. Raised in a dysfunctional Jewish family in Toledo Ohio, Steinem attended elite Smith College, Betty Friedan's alma mater. In 1958, Steinem was recruited by CIA's Cord Meyer to direct an "informal group of activists" called the "Independent Research Service." This was part of Meyer's "Congress for Cultural Freedom," which created magazines like *"Encounter"* and *"Partisan Review"* to herd intellectuals into a non-Communist chic left-liberal pen. Steinem attended Communist-sponsored youth festivals in Europe, published a newspaper, reported on other participants and helped to provoke riots.

One of Steinem's CIA colleagues was Clay Felker. In the early 1960's, he became an editor at Esquire and published articles by Steinem that established her as a leading voice for Women's Lib. In 1968, as publisher of *New York* Magazine, he hired her as a contributing editor, and then editor of *Ms.* Magazine in 1971. Warner Communications put up almost all the money although it only took 25% of the stock. Ms. Magazine's first publisher was Elizabeth Forsling Harris, a CIA-connected PR executive who planned John Kennedy's Dallas motorcade route. Despite its anti-establishment image, Ms magazine attracted advertising from the cream of corporate America. It published ads for ITT at the same time as Pinochet was torturing women political prisoners in Chile, after an ITT/CIA-inspired coup.

Steinem's personal relationships also belie her anti-establishment pretensions. She had a nine-year relationship with Stanley Pottinger, a Nixon-Ford assistant attorney general, credited with stalling FBI investigations into the assassinations of Martin Luther King, and the ex-Chilean Foreign Minister Orlando Latelier. In the 1980's, she dated Henry Kissinger (See Dave Emory,http://www.geocities.com/CapitolHill/8425/ST-CIA.HTM).

Our main misconception about the CIA is that it serves US interests. In fact, it has always been the instrument of a dynastic international banking and oil elite (Rothschild, Rockefeller.) It was established and peopled by blue bloods from the New York banking establishment and graduates of Yale University's secret pagan "Skull and Bones" society. George W. Bush, his father and grandfather fit this profile.

The agenda of this international cabal is to degrade the institutions and values of the United States in order to integrate it into a global state run by the United Nations. In its 1947 Founding Charter, the CIA is prohibited from engaging in domestic activities. However this hasn't stopped it from waging psychological war on the American people.

The domestic counterpart of the "Congress for Cultural Freedom" was the "American Committee for Cultural Freedom." Using foundations as conduits, the CIA controlled intellectual discourse in the 1950's and 1960's, and continues to do so today. In *"The Cultural Cold War,"* Francis Stonor Saunders estimates that a thousand books were produced under the imprint of a variety of commercial and university presses, with covert subsidies.

The CIA's "Project Mockingbird" involved the direct infiltration of the corporate media, including the direct takeover of major news outlets. "By the early 1950's," writes Deborah Davis, in her book *"Katherine the Great,"* the CIA owned respected members of the *New York Times, Newsweek, CBS* and other communication vehicles, plus stringers, four to six hundred in all."

In 1982, the CIA admitted that reporters on the CIA payroll have acted as case officers to agents in the field. Philip Graham, publisher of *The Washington Post*, who ran the operation until his "suicide" in 1963, boasted that "you could get a journalist cheaper than a good call girl, for a couple of hundred dollars a month."

I was born in 1949. Idealists in my parent's generation were disillusioned when the Communist dream of universal brotherhood turned out to be a disguise for a brutal despotism. My own generation may discover that our best instincts have also been manipulated and exploited. There is evidence that the 60's drug counter culture, the civil rights movement, and anti-war movement were, like feminism, CIA directed.

For example, the CIA has admitted setting up the National Student Association as a front in 1947. In the early 1950's the NSA opposed the attempts of the House Un-American Activities Committee to root out Communist spies. According to Phil Agee Jr., NSA officers participated in the activities of SNCC, the militant civil rights group, and Students for a Democratic Society, a radical peace group.

According to Mark Riebling, the CIA also used Timothy Leary. The agency distributed LSD to Leary and other opinion makers in the 1960s. Leary made a generation of Americans turn away from active participation in society and seek fulfillment "within." In another example of the CIA's interference in domestic politics, Gary Webb describes how in the 1980's, the CIA flooded Black ghettos with cocaine.

I won't attempt to analyze the CIA's motivation except to suggest what was the result: They demoralized, alienated and divided Americans. The elite operates by fostering division and conflict in the world. Thus, we don't realize who the real enemy is.

Feminism has done the most damage. There is no more fundamental yet delicate relationship in society than male and female. On it depends the family, the red blood cell of society. Nobody with the interests of society at heart would try to divide men and women. Yet the lie that men have exploited women has become the official orthodoxy.

Man loves woman. His first instinct is to nurture ("husband") and see her thrive. When a woman is happy, she is beautiful. Sure, some men are abusive. But the vast majority have supported and guided their families for millennia.

Feminists relentlessly advance the idea that our inherent male and female characteristics, crucial to our development as human beings, are mere "stereotypes." This is a vicious calumny on heterosexuals. Talk about hate! Yet it is taught to children in elementary schools! It is echoed in the media. Lesbians like Rosie O'Donnell and Ellen DeGeneres are advanced as role models.

All of this is calculated to create personal confusion and sow chaos among heterosexuals. As a result, millions of American males are emasculated and divorced from their relationship to family, the world and the future. The American woman has been hoodwinked into investing herself in a mundane career instead of the timeless love of her husband and children. Many women have become temperamentally unfit to be wives and mothers. People, who are isolated and alone, stunted and love-starved, are easy to fool and manipulate. Without the healthy influence of two loving parents, so are their children.

Feminism is a grotesque fraud perpetrated on society by its governing elite. It is designed to weaken the American social and cultural fabric in order to introduce a friendly fascist New World Order. Its advocates are sanctimonious charlatans who have grown rich and powerful from it. They include a huge class of opportunists, liars and moral cripples who work for the elite in various capacities: government, education and the media.

Women's oppression is a lie. Sex roles were never as rigid as feminists would have us believe. My mother had a successful business in the 1950's importing watchstraps from Switzerland. When my father's income increased, she was content to quit and concentrate on her children. Women were free to pursue careers if they wanted to. The difference was that their role as wife and mother was understood, and socially validated, as it should be.

Until Gloria Steinem and the CIA came along.

RED FEMINISM

American Communism
and the Origins of Women's Liberation

"Rape is an expression of ... male supremacy ... the age-old economic, political and cultural exploitation of women by men."

DOES THIS SOUND LIKE A MODERN RADICAL FEMINIST? Guess again. It is from a 1948 American Communist Party pamphlet entitled *"Woman Against Myth"* by Mary Inman.

In a recent book, *Red Feminism: American Communism and the Making of Women's Liberation,* (2002) feminist historian Kate Weigand states: "ideas, activists and traditions that emanated from the Communist movement of the forties and fifties continued to shape the direction of the new women's movement of the 1960s and later."(154)

In fact, Weigand, a lecturer at Smith College, shows that modern feminism is a direct outgrowth of American Communism. There is nothing that feminists said or did in the 1960's-1980's that wasn't prefigured in the CPUSA of the 1940's and 1950's. Many second-wave feminist leaders were "red diaper babies," children of Communists.

Communists pioneered the political and cultural analysis of woman's oppression. They originated women's studies, and advocated public daycare, birth control, abortion and even children's rights. They forged key feminist concepts such as "the personal is the political" and techniques such as "consciousness raising."

In the late 1940's, CPUSA leaders realized that the labor movement was increasingly hostile to Communism. They began to focus on women and African Americans. They hoped "male supremacy" would "bring more women into the organization and into the fight against the domestic policies of the Cold War." (80)

Communist women who made up 40% of the party wanted

---

more freedom to attend party meetings. After the publication of *"Women Against Myth"* in 1948, the CPUSA initiated a process of "re-educating" men that we recognize only too well today.

For example, in the party newspaper *"The Daily Worker"* a photo caption of a man with a young child read, "Families are stronger and happier if the father knows how to fix the cereal, tie the bibs and take care of the youngsters." (127)

The Party ordered men who didn't take the woman question seriously to undergo re-education ("control tasks involving study on the woman question.") In 1954 the Los Angeles branch disciplined men for "hogging discussion at club meetings, bypassing women comrades in leadership and making sex jokes degrading to women." (94)

A film *"Salt of the Earth,"* which critic Pauline Kael called "Communist propaganda", portrayed women taking a decisive role in their husbands' labor strike. "Against her husband's wishes, Esperanza became a leader in the strike and for the first time forged a role for herself outside of her household... [her] political successes persuaded Ramon to accept a new model of family life." (132) Portrayals of strong assertive successful women became as common in the Communist press and schools as they are in the mass media today.

Communist women formalized a sophisticated Marxist analysis of the "woman question." The books *"In Women's Defense"* (1940) by Mary Inman, "Century of Struggle" (1954) by Eleanor Flexner and *"The Unfinished Revolution"* (1962) by Eve Merriam recorded women's oppression and decried sexism in mass culture and language. For example, Mary Inman argued that "manufactured femininity" and "overemphasis on beauty" keeps women in subjugation. (33)

The founder of modern feminism, Betty Friedan relied on these texts when she wrote *The Feminine Mystique* (1963). These women all hid the fact that they were long-time Communist activists. In the 1960, their daughters had everything they needed, including their parents' example of subterfuge, to start the Women's Liberation Movement.

Feminism's roots in Marxist Communism explain a great deal about this curious but pernicious movement. It explains:

- Why the " woman's movement" hates femininity and imposes a political-economic concept like "equality" on a personal, biological and mystical relationship.

- Why the "women's movement" also embraces "equality" of race and class.

- Why they want revolution ("transformation") and have a messianic vision of a gender-less utopia.

- Why they believe human nature is infinitely malleable and can be shaped by indoctrination and coercion.

- Why they engage in endless, mind-numbing theorizing, doctrinal disputes and factionalism.

- Why truth for them is a "social construct" defined by whomever has power, and appearances are more important than reality. Why they reject God, nature and scientific evidence in favour of their political agenda.

- Why they refuse to debate, don't believe in free speech, and suppress dissent.

- Why they behave like a quasi-religious cult, or like the Red Guard.

It is hard to escape the conclusion that feminism is Communism by another name. Having failed to peddle class war, Communism promoted gender conflict instead. The "diversity" and "multicultural" movements represent feminism's attempt to forge "allegiances" by empowering gays and "people of colour." Thus, the original CPUSA trio of "race, gender and class" is very much intact but class conflict was never a big seller.

The term "politically correct" originated in the Russian Communist Party in the 1920's. It usage in America today illustrates the extent society has been subverted. Feminist activists are mostly Communist dupes. We see this subversion in the dismantling of the liberal arts curriculum and tradition of free speech and inquiry at our universities. We see it when feminists push the elite "global warming" hysteria. In government, business, the media and the military. This could only happen because the financial elite in fact sponsors Communism.

"Political correctness" has dulled and regimented our cultural life. Betty Granger, a Winnipeg school trustee running for parliament referred to house price increases as due to "the Asian invasion." Granger was pilloried mercilessly in the press. People sent hate letters and dumped garbage on her lawn.

At a school board meeting, the chairman acknowledged that she is not a racist. He acknowledged that Asians have married into her family. Nonetheless, Granger was censured because, and I quote, "appearances are more important than reality." This slippage from the mooring of objective truth is the hallmark of Communism.

The atmosphere at the meeting was charged. Mild mannered Canadians, all champions of "tolerance" behaved like wild dogs eager to rip apart a wounded rabbit. Betty Granger *repented* and voted *in favour of her own censure.*

These rituals of denunciation and contrition, typical of Stalinist Russia or Maoist China, are increasing in America. These show trials are supposed to frighten everyone into conforming. We have "diversity officers" and "sexual harrassment officers" and "human rights commissions" and "sensitivity training" to uphold feminist shibboleths. They talk about "discrimination" but they freely discriminate against heterosexuals, especially white males. They use phoney charges of "sexual harassment" to fetter male-female relations and purge their opponents.

In 1980, three women in Leningrad produced 10 typewritten copies of a feminist magazine called *Almanac.* The KGB shut down the magazine and deported the women to West Germany. In the USSR, feminism has largely been for export. According to Professor Weigand, her "book provides evidence to support the belief that at least some Communists regarded the subversion of the gender system [in America] as an integral part of the larger fight to overturn capitalism."(6)

In conclusion, the feminist pursuit of "equal rights" is a mask for an insidious Communist agenda. The Communist MO has always been deception, infiltration and subversion. The goal is the destruction of Western Civilization and creation of a New World Order run by monopoly capital.

Kate Weigand's *Red Feminism* demonstrates that the Communist agenda is alive and well and living under an assumed name.

COMMUNISM

Wall Street's Utopian Hoax

BELLA DODD WAS A LEADER of the Communist Party of America (CPUSA) in the 1930' s and 1940's. Her book, *"School of Darkness"* (1954) reveals that Communism was a hoax perpetrated by financiers "to control the common man" and to advance world tyranny. Naturally this important book is out-of-print and not in any used bookstores. (I found it through interlibrary loan.)

Bella Dodd was born Maria Asunta Isabella Visono in Italy about 1904. A brilliant and dedicated woman, she graduated from Hunter College and NYU Law School. She became head of the New York State Teachers Union and was a member of the CPUSA's National Council until 1949.

Dodd describes Communism as "a strange secret cult" whose goal is the destruction of Western (i.e. Christian) Civilization. Millions of naïve idealists ("innocents") are tricked by its talk of helping the poor, but it cares only for power. For example, Dodd found there was no social research at party headquarters. "We are a revolutionary party, not a reform party," she was told. (163)

CREATING "HUMAN BEINGS THAT WOULD CONFORM"

The Communist Party operates by infiltrating and subverting social institutions like the churches, schools, mass media and government. Its aim was "to create new types of human beings who would conform to the blueprint of the world they confidently expected to control." (162)

For example, Dodd reveals that the CPUSA had 1100 members become Catholic priests in the 1930's. It also subverted the American education system by taking over the teacher's unions and learned societies. Only people who accepted the "materialistic, collectivistic international class struggle approach" advanced. (98)

Involving women in the war effort fitted the long-range program:

"The party did all it could to induce women to go into industry. Its fashion designers created special styles for them and its songwriters wrote special songs to spur them.... War-period conditions, they planned, were to become a permanent part of the future educational program. The bourgeois family as a social unit was to be made obsolete." (153)

There was to be no family but the party and the state. Dodd helped organize the *Congress of American Women,* a forerunner of the feminist movement.

"Since it was supposedly a movement for peace, it attracted many women. But it was really only a renewed offensive to control American women... Like youth and minority groups, they are regarded as a reserve force of the revolution because they are more easily moved by emotional appeals." (194-195)

SUBVERSION OF U.S. COMPLETED IN THE 1930'S

When FDR recognized Russia in 1933, he deliberately turned a blind eye to the CPUSA's massive program of espionage and subversion. Liberals denied that this took place and complained about a "witch hunt."

Guess what? The "loony right" was correct. A new book *The Secret World of American Communism,* (2003) based on newly opened Kremlin archives, confirms that CPUSA was a puppet of Moscow and the Roosevelt administration was practically run by Soviet agents, Alger Hiss, and Harry Dexter White to name a few.

The war years saw the CPUSA actually renounce the class struggle and join the so-called "Roosevelt camp of progress" which included "progressive capitalists."

"The Communist Party now assumed the responsibility of establishing a rigid discipline over the working class. No employer was more effective or more relentless in checking strikes among the workers, or minimizing complaints...while wages rose a little during those years, they did not compare with the rise in profits and in monopoly control of basic necessities...war production was chiefly in the hands of ten large corporations...the Communists carefully muted such information." (153)

The war years saw amazing coordination between the Communist Party and America's financial elite. The elite financed a sophisticated propaganda agency called the Russian Institute located on Park Ave. across 68th Street from Rockefeller's Council on Foreign Relations. Here "famous names like Vanderbilt, Lamont, Whitney and Morgan mingled with those of Communist leaders." (153)

At Roosevelt's insistence, Stalin "dissolved" the Comintern in order to make the CPUSA look like an American party. The CPUSA leader Earl Browder achieved national prominence and consulted with senior Roosevelt cabinet ministers.

The joint US-Russian war effort was to be the basis of the New World Order. But, inexplicably, the policy changed and Browder instantly became a non-person. Apparently the financial elite had decided the time wasn't right for world government. A Cold War would be much more lucrative. Dodd was told that in the future, the party would often find itself opposed not only to the government, but also to U.S. workers.

"I now saw that with the best motives and a desire to serve the working people... I and thousands like me had been led to a betrayal of these very people.... I had been on the side of those who sought the destruction of my own country." (229)

Like frightened mice, the CPUSA membership scurried to adopt the new party line. Dodd tried to quit but was told: "No one gets out of the party. You die or you are thrown out." (197)

Eventually Dodd was expelled and smeared as "anti-Negro, anti-Puerto Rican, anti-Semitic, anti-labour and a defender of the landlord." (220). Sound familiar? After more than 20 years of tireless sacrifice, she was without family or friends. The party had been her family. Its "hates had become my hates."

"This is the key to the mental enslavement of mankind. The individual is made into nothing ... he operates as the physical part of [a] higher group intelligence... he has no awareness of the plans the higher group intelligence has for utilizing him." (158)

"A SECRET WELL-ORGANIZED WORLD POWER"

Bella Dodd is circumspect about the people behind the Communist Party. She once was told to phone two multi-millionaires who live in the Waldorf Towers if she lost contact with Moscow. Elsewhere, she refers to "a secret well organized world power." She is obviously afraid to be candid. She suspects that one CPUSA leader's "suicide" was in fact murder. (172)

But she does drop a possible clue. She says that each of the nine floors of the party-owned headquarters at 35 E. 12th St. was devoted to CPUSA business. The Sixth Floor held "the publication offices of the Yiddish newspaper, the Freiheit, and the "Jewish Commission." (162) Indeed Jews were prominent among Communist dupes.

"What now became clear to me was the collusion of these two forces: the Communists with their timetable for world control, and certain mercenary forces in the free world bent on making profits from blood." (229)

As "one piece of the puzzle that finally became a picture," Dodd tells the story of the ship "Erica Reed" typical of "hundreds of other stories." During the Spanish Civil War, Americans donated money to load the ship with medical supplies and food for Spain. The Communists diverted the ship to Russia instead. (89)

Censorship is crucial to Communists, Dodd says. "I have often seen leaders pull books from shelves in homes and warn members to destroy them."(223)

Communism is essentially a deceitful system of international elite control. It was not suppressed during the McCarthy era. Rather it morphed into the New Left, Counter Culture, Civil Rights, Anti War and Woman's Liberation Movements, and later into a plethora of elite-sponsored NGO's, and media, Democratic and Republican party factions, Liberal, Zionist, Labor, feminist and Gay Rights groups. Like the CPUSA itself, these groups are controlled from the top so their memberships are unaware of being used.

To the objection that some of the above mentioned groups oppose globalization, Dodd refers to examples where the CPUSA ostensibly supported causes they wished to sabotage. (205)

In conclusion, Communism was/is a plot designed to substitute for the rule of God, a cabal of the superrich. It is a utopian fraud hatched by the rich to thwart the dreams of ordinary people and stunt human progress. The same cabal is behind most wars including Iraq.

A precursor to the New World Order, Communism espouses brotherhood, peace and equality in order to deceive us. It has taken over society's eyes, ears, mind and spirit. Much of what passes for truth in the media and schools is part of this monstrous con job. Our politicians are mostly dupes or traitors.

Feminism is Communist both in origin and spirit. It pretends to champion women but in fact neuters both sexes and destroys the basic social unit, the family. The promotion of homosexuality as a "lifestyle choice" for heterosexuals is also part of this brazen elitist fraud designed to "create new types of human beings who would conform..."

Western Civilization is like a ship floundering in a sea of evil, yet the passengers are too duped and distracted to realize it. Bella Dodd had the courage to sound the alarm 50 years ago. It is never too late to begin to resist tyranny.

THE VAGINA MONOLOGUES

Feminism's Dead End

WHILE BOMBS RAINED DOWN on Afghanistan in Oct. 2001, theatregoers in Washington D.C. were paying $50-70 at the National Theatre to see Eve Ensler's play *"The Vagina Monologues"*. This play partly exemplifies why radical Islam may have declared war on America. The play pretends to be about women's rights. In fact, it is little more than a public reading of explicit lesbian pornography. *"The Vagina Monologues"* is a celebration of lesbianism that is being produced in 25 countries, including Turkey and China. We are exporting homosexuality and the social disintegration that goes with it.

Muslim fundamentalists believe their culture is threatened. They are fighting to preserve their wives and children who are the future. If their wives are infected by our homosexuality, they will insist on becoming "independent" like men. Their birth rate will plummet, as has ours, and their families and culture will disintegrate. In countries with minimal government social safety nets, families and children are also essential for survival.

"The Vagina Monologues" presents a sad picture of life at the dead-end of feminism. It is an anguished cry for male love by a generation of women who were deceived by feminism, and now have no choice but to become lesbians. For women who are literally starved for love, the play provides a steamy experience of sexual intimacy. For young women who don't know any better, it is an initiation into lesbianism.

Based on interviews with women who talk about their vaginas, the play purports to rescue the female genitals from "cultural neglect." For example, the play describes a workshop in which women examine themselves with hand-mirrors. "It reminded me of how early astronomers must have felt with their primitive telescopes," says Ensler.

They give their vagina nicknames; dress it up in imaginary outfits, and imagine what it would say if it could talk (e.g. "Where's Brian?"). At one performance at the Madison Square Gardens, 18,000 women were whipped into a frenzy of shouting "cunt" over and over.

They should have been shouting "penis" because this really is about the loss of male love. Having lost their youth and femininity, having rejected or emasculated men, millions now are left sexually high and dry.

Both sexes need validation. Men these days don't like feminists and feminists know it. Every time we turn on TV, a man is being beat-up, berated or outdone by a woman. Men resent that women have usurped the male role and deserted the feminine one. I believe this is what Ensler is actually experiencing when she says: "Our self-hatred is only the internalized repression and hatred of the patriarchal culture."

Women are justified in feeling unloved and unfulfilled. Ensler says that women want to be used for babies: "My vagina helped release a giant baby. It thought it would be used more than that. It's not." The result is a profound sense of emptiness and need. "My vagina wants to go deeper. It's hungry for depth. It's hungry for kisses, kindness. It wants to stop being angry. It wants everything. It wants to want. It wants."

It appears that only a man can staunch this wound. Ensler describes a boyfriend, Bob, who loved to gaze at her genitals for hours and made her feel good about herself for the first time. She doesn't say what happened to Bob. The only other men in the play are Ensler's first husband, a philanderer, and some rapists in Bosnia.

Thus, *The Vagina Monologues*" quickly becomes a steamy chronicle of lesbian sex. In the first place, a fixation on female genitals by women is pure homosexuality. Forgive me for what follows but I am trying to convey the pornographic flavor of this so-called play.

The author interviews a former tax lawyer who has become wealthy as a lesbian gigolo. "There are so many unfulfilled women," she says. "Women pay me to dress up like a man and dominate them." She follows with a precise description of her art ("there are four fingers inside me, two are hers and two are mine") that turns Ensler on: "Come on," I said. "Come in."

A 12-year-old girl describes how her mother entrusted her to the care of a beautiful, worldly 24-year-old woman who then betrayed this trust by having sex with her: "She transformed my sorry-assed coochie-snorcher into a kind of heaven."

Ensler regresses with children's stories of the "I'll show you mine if you show me yours" variety. She asks a six-year-old girl to say what her vagina smells like (snowflakes?) She informs us that the clitoris has twice the number of nerve fibres as the penis: "Who needs a handgun when you've got a semiautomatic?" She describes finding her clitoris for the first time: "It was all warm and pulsing and ready and young and alive." I could go into more detail but you get the idea.

A measure of our cultural timidity, depravity and self-delusion is that no major media critic has named this play for what it is. "Ensler is an impassioned wit," says the *Los Angeles Times.* "A compelling rhapsody of the female essence," says the *Chicago Tribune.* "Spellbinding, funny and almost unbearably moving," says *Variety.* The play has been performed in hundreds of American cities and universities, and in countries from Rumania to Zaire. Celebrity guest performers include Meryl Streep, Jane Fonda, Calista Frockhart, and Angelica Huston.

Ensler and her entourage try to position this pathetic lesbian primer in the mainstream. Gloria Steinem writes "men as well as women will emerge from these pages feeling more free within themselves and about each other."

Ensler has "come out" as yet another survivor of sexual abuse by her father. She has tied the play to the politicized cause of violence against women. Her hatred of heterosexuality is evident by her choice of Valentine's Day, as "V-Day" or anti-violence day, when her play will be performed. She told Molly Ivens in TIME that the patriarchal (i.e. nuclear) family is "a deadly institution." This is redolent of Communist methodology.

The nuclear family is the primary institution of heterosexuality. Before the "sexual revolution," women insisted on marriage and family, which is heterosexual behaviour. This satisfied the profoundest psychological needs of both sexes and provided a safe context for raising healthy children. After the sexual revolution, men and women engaged in promiscuous sex, which had been more typical of homosexuals. Women, increasingly independent and self-righteous, were unable to form permanent marriages. Taught that they could "have it all", they are now frustrated and bitter.

The irony of *"The Vagina Monologues"* is that feminists who regularly complain about sexual objectification embrace the play.

There is no mention of love in it. Another irony is that feminists apparently think that, when lesbians do it, an adult having sex with a 12-year-old child is OK. They also think that they can violate the natural innocence of a 6-year-old girl with invasive questions.

Finally, need I mention that the play outrages and destroys the mystery, modesty and reserve that is the essence of mature femininity? Like feminism itself, *"The Vagina Monologues"* masquerades as an affirmation of women. In fact, it is a sickening bludgeoning assault on women.

DOMESTIC VIOLENCE

Dawn of the Feminist Police State

IN 1931, Clark Gable's acting career took off after he decked Barbara Stanwyck in the movie *Night Nurse*. He got 10,000 fan letters from breathless females.

Today male and female superheroes routinely slug it out on the big screen but if ordinary men and women so much as shove, they can be arrested for "domestic assault."

Men risk jail, legal bills, and the loss of family, house and job if they so much as argue with a woman.

This is the result of the widespread "zero tolerance" policy that defines domestic assault as any physical contact, no matter how innocuous. The charge is laid by the state even if the victim objects, and no harm has been done.

Ostensibly this policy protects women but its real purpose is to emasculate men and persecute heterosexuals in general. It's another front in the Rockefeller-elite's campaign to degrade society, destroy family and decrease population by making heterosexuality unworkable.

THE DANGER ZONE

Couples all experience stress, especially if they have children. Now a woman can have a tantrum and incarcerate her husband simply by dialling 911. She can hold this threat over his head.

The policy undermines male leadership. A husband called his wife "lazy." A neighbor urged her to "teach him a lesson." So she called the police and falsely charged him with slapping her.

"Now she needs help with the children and but we have to live apart," he said outside court. "She is very upset and sorry."

"Women make false charges like crazy," a Legal Aid lawyer said.

There is no penalty for doing this.

A male said his common law wife falsely charged him in order to get him out of the house. From the back of the police car, he saw her standing on the lawn with her boyfriend.

Another man heard the 2 a.m. "knock on the door" after breaking up with his girlfriend earlier the same night. She charged him with holding her arms (to prevent her from pummelling him.) He had a hefty legal bill and risked losing his job.

The majority of these cases are "stayed" after many court appearances because the women won't testify or it's his word against hers.

WELCOME TO THE NEW WORLD ORDER

The policy accustoms people to the interference of police in their personal lives, which is the hallmark of dictatorship.

Having an argument is now a crime. "The walls are thin," one couple said. They were arrested after a neighbour heard voices raised. A witness vouched they didn't touch each other but the cops have no discretion.

People lose respect for the law. "It's supposed to be a free country but it don't seem free any more," a man told me.

The policy is a grotesque boondoggle for police, social workers, therapists, prisons, courts and lawyers. It swells the ranks of the bureaucracy, which has an economic stake in the elite's New World Order.

In Winnipeg where I live, half the 1200-man police force is dedicated to domestic violence. "To me that statistic is staggering," police Chief Jack Ewatski, told the *Winnipeg Free Press* "It puts a significant stress on our ability to police the city in other areas."

More than half the inmates at the overflowing "Remand Centre" are husbands. Special facilities have been built at a penitentiary to house 200 more "domestics." Most of these men have yet to be convicted of anything.

NINETY PERCENT TRIVIAL

I have interviewed about 65 people charged with domestic assault outside the courtroom. Most of these people have limited means. Their fights are usually trivial, harmless and involve alcohol.

I met only one person who fits the profile of a "battered woman."

Even she wanted the choice of charging her abuser or not. She felt she could handle her situation.

A veteran lawyer who specializes in domestic violence confirmed that only 10% of his cases fit the profile of chronic wife beater.

Most people call the police to help defuse a tense situation. Instead, they are arrested, finger printed and jailed. They miss work and sometimes lose jobs. They cannot return to their homes.

"Sometimes I deserve a smack," one male said. "She gave me one. I pushed her out of the way and left. We're fine. We're a normal couple. We had one rough night. No one was hurt. No one charged anyone."

I do not condone or encourage domestic violence of any kind. But most of these incidents should not involve criminal charges. Police should charge only when someone has been injured or complains. They should be given discretion over whether the complaint is serious.

When two men in a bar get into a fight, there is a mediation process. No charges are laid for a first offence. Why are lovers treated differently?

Finally, I have seen only one same-sex (lesbian) couple in 20 courthouse visits although domestic violence is reputed to be fairly common among homosexuals.

WOMEN FAVORED YET ALSO VICTIMIZED

A lawyer said: "The women call the shots." Police often refuse to accept a man's charge. When a wife bit his husband's finger, the cop told him: "What was your finger doing in her mouth?" Another man was told to "take it like a man."

Yet the system is capricious. Women are often victimized. One mother of four on social assistance slapped her common-law husband when he said he didn't care about the children. He pushed her against a wall and she called police.

They arrested only her. "That's what I get for being honest," she said. "I don't know why I'm being persecuted."

Another woman slapped her boyfriend when he made light that she was pregnant with his child. He called the police and she was arrested. Legal fees: $1200.

Another woman said: "My ex boyfriend called me from jail. He was out in two days and bothering me again. What's the point of calling the police? It's not worth the trouble."

In the crush of trivial cases, women in genuine danger are overlooked. Feminist activists don't really care about women. They are "sleeping with the enemy." Feminists are using a few endangered women to get cushy jobs and to advance the elite's lesbian agenda.

A MOCKERY OF JUSTICE

The zero tolerance policy makes a mockery of the principles of justice. A real crime (i.e. injury) must take place before someone is arrested and jailed. There should be a presumption of innocence. There should be evidence and not just one person's word.

Domestic violence was not a problem before feminists and their elite sponsors invented it. It isn't a problem today. For example, according to the 1999 *Canadian General Social Survey,* only 7% of people married or common law experienced "some type of violence" within the previous five years. These are almost evenly divided between men and women.

The rate of spousal homicide for wives is 7 per million in Canada. In the U.S., the murder rate for wives/girlfriends is between 1 and 4 /1000th of one percent depending on race.

CONCLUSION

Something fundamental has gone awry when half the police force is dedicated to marital spats.

Heterosexuals should wake up and smell the coffee. We have been under sustained attack for over 40 years. It is no accident that the roles of wife and mother have become stigmatized and men have been demonized. It's no accident that, as with people who have a terminal disease, we hear little discussion of our collective future.

Society is victim to an insidious campaign of elite social engineering and political persecution. It's time we told our Lucifer-loving financial elite, "Enough."

THE ILLUMINATI

Conspiracy Too Monstrous to Conceive

"The individual is handicapped by coming face-to-face with a conspiracy so monstrous he cannot believe it exists."

--J. Edgar Hoover

THE WORLD IS IN THE MALIGNANT GRIP OF A SATANIC CULT. People recoil at the suggestion but proof stares us in the face every day.

George W. Bush, President of the "Free World" is a member of "Skull and Bones" a chapter of the Illuminati order. His father, grandfather and uncle are also members.

In his autobiography, *"A Charge to Keep"* Bush writes, "My senior year I joined Skull and Bones, a secret society so secret I can't say anything more." In Aug. 2000 he said his "heritage is part of who I am."

Isn't this a conflict of interest?

Hello! Can a man hold any public office, let alone the most important, and belong to a "secret society"? If this society were benign, would it have to be secret?

What a secret society it is! The Illuminati is the hidden hand behind all modern cataclysms, including the French and Russian Revolutions, Communism, the Depression and Nazism. To affect the course of history only takes money. The people behind the Illuminati have plenty.

It's time we faced reality. Murphy's Law applies to humanity. "If it can go wrong, it will." It has. The world is ruled by a satanic cult.

THE ILLUMINATI AND THE SKULL & BONES

The Illuminati originates in the Jewish Kabala, Babylonian mystery cults, the Templars, Freemasons and assorted interests dedicated to Satan worship and absolute power. On May 1 1776, Adam Weishaupt, a professor at the University of Inglestadt in Germany, founded "The Order of the Illuminati." Weishaupt was sponsored by Prince William of Hesse Casel and his banker Meyer Amschel Rothschild, the wealthiest man in the world.

The Illuminati's goal was to destroy Western Civilization and to erect a new world order ruled by them. Its method was to dissolve all social ties (employer, nation, religion, race, family) by exploiting social discontent and promising a golden age of "human brotherhood."

Attracted by the promise of power and change, people served without realizing who or what they were supporting. Weishaupt urged his followers to "practise the art of counterfeit." New recruits were told the Illuminati expressed the original spirit of Christianity. Weishaupt marvelled that even churchmen could be gulled. "Oh! Men, of what cannot you be persuaded?" (Nesta Webster, *World Revolution,* 1921, p. 27)

The Illuminati had a hand in every so-called "progressive" movement of the past 200 years. In 1832, William Huntington founded the "Skull and Bones" (Chapter 322 of the Bavarian Illuminati) at Yale University. The members wore a death's head on their chests and were sworn to secrecy on pain of death. "The Order" became the preserve of the leading New England families, many wealthy from the Opium trade. These include the Whitneys, Tafts, Buckleys, Lowells, Sloans, Coffins, and Harrimans. The Bush family was dependent on these interests.

For over 150 years, "Bonesmen" have run the world from positions in banking, intelligence, media, law and government. Members included Presidential handler Averell Harriman, anti-war leader William Sloan Coffin, Time-Life magnate Henry Luce, Truman war secretary Henry Stimson (responsible for dropping the atomic bomb), pseudo conservative William F. Buckley and many more.

"THE BATTLE IS NOT BETWEEN LEFT AND RIGHT"

In the 1960's Dr. Anthony Sutton was a Fellow at Stanford's Hoover Institute when he discovered that, in spite of the Cold War, the US was supplying the USSR with technology, including weapons used against American soldiers in Vietnam. Sutton dug deeper and discovered that Wall Street had sponsored both the Bolshevik Revolution and the rise of Nazi Germany. The resulting books, which are on line, cost Dr. Sutton his academic career.

In 1983, Dr. Sutton received a list of Skull and Bones members and immediately recognized the names of many men who controlled American policy. He published a book entitled *"America's Secret Establishment: An Introduction to the Order of Skull and Bones"* (1986). He updated and republished this book just before his death in 2002. Here are some of his conclusions.

- "The Order" is "a purely American phenomenon with German origin." Dr. Sutton compares it to the Round Table, Cecil Rhodes' secret society at Oxford also known as "The Group." The American and British entities consist of 20-30 dynastic families each. Jewish banking interests connect them.

"The links between 'The Order' and Britain go through Lazard Freres and the private merchant banks... 'The Group' links to the Jewish equivalent through the Rothschilds in Britain... 'The Order' in the US links to the Guggenheim, Schiff and Warburg families." (23)

As Dr. Sutton notes, the "Order" had definite anti Semitic tendencies but by the 1960's, many Jewish names started to appear among the 15 annual inductees.

- Dr. Sutton believes the "left" versus "right" split is fraudulent and used to control the debate and condition citizens to think along certain lines. Left-wing magazines like the *"The Nation"* and *"The New Republic"* and right-wing magazines like *"The National Review"* were "artificially set up." The former were financed by Whitney money while the latter by Buckley. Both are "The Order."

Dr. Sutton states: "Sooner or later people will wake up. First we have to dump the trap of right and left. This is a Hegelian trap to divide and control. The battle is not between right and left; it is between us and them."

Similarly, in the international field, Left and Right are artificially constructed and collapsed in the drive for one-world synthesis, i.e. authoritarian socialism controlled by monopoly capital.

College textbooks present war and revolution as spontaneous conflicting forces. This is nonsense, says Dr. Sutton. They are created and financed by Wall Street to create a new world order. But you won't read this in history books.

"Our Western history is every bit as distorted, censored and largely useless as that of Hitler's Germany or the Soviet Union or Communist China..." (122)

• Dr. Sutton believes The Order has many weaknesses resulting from an inbred gene pool, a shallow power base and a limited worldview. In any future conflict between the authoritarian state and the individual, he believes opposition will take "a million forms."

"No one is going to create the anti-The Order movement. That would be foolish and unnecessary. It could be infiltrated, bought off, or diverted all too easily. Why play by the rules set by the enemy?

The movement that will topple The Order will be extremely simple and most effective. It will be ten thousand or a million Americans who come to the conclusion that they don't want the State to be boss; that they prefer to live under the protection of the Constitution. They will make their own independent decision to thwart The Order and it will take ten thousand or a million forms." (55)

COGNITIVE DISSONANCE

Bizarre as it sounds, our world is the product of a multi generational satanic conspiracy. When we compare this disturbing conclusion with the comforting picture purveyed by Illuminati controlled-mass media and education, we experience "cognitive dissonance," or psychological stress. This is usually resolved by evading reality, dismissing it as "conspiracy theory."

One reader, stirring in his sleep, wrote: "You sir are T-TOTALLY the biggest story teller I have ever heard. If I ever get really bored I will read some of your concockions."

In fact, conspiracy is very plausible. People who control a grossly disproportionate share of the world's wealth will take measures to consolidate their position. They will destabilize the public by inciting a series of wars and other mind-boggling hoaxes (Communism, feminism, multiculturalism). They will subvert faith in a loving God and promote violence and depravity (Satan) instead.

The government-inspired 9-11 atrocity proves a satanic cult controls the US. Bush and his accomplices are criminals, traitors and impostors. But don't look to the Democrats for salvation. Leading contender Sen. John Kerry was also Skull and Bones (Class of 1966.) The "Order" controls both parties.

The "War on Terror" is obviously designed to forestall domestic opposition and condition people to further subjugation in the New World Order. What can we do?

Antony Sutton had it right when he said opposition should be individual in character. It should "take ten thousand or a million forms."

SEXUAL LIBERATION

Illuminati Subversion

THROUGHOUT MODERN HISTORY Illuminati bankers have used "sexual liberation" to subvert society and establish their subtle tyranny. As Masonic revolutionary Guiseppe Mazzini said, "we corrupt in order to rule."

The Illuminati bankers need to introduce "world government" to translate their unjust monopoly over credit into total world control. They realized that they couldn't take control until they destroyed the family. This was a central plank of the Communist Manifesto in 1848.

Every major "revolution" in modern history has increased Illuminati banker control and the sexual revolution is no exception.

The bankers have encouraged sexual dissipation using their various "progressive" fronts: liberalism, feminism, socialism and communism.

The great appeal of left wing movements has always been the lure of "free" sex (i.e. free of the restraints of love & marriage.) How is free sex subversive?

A healthy society is concerned with its survival and the propagation of its values. This requires that the new generation is born and raised in a healthy manner, i.e. in a nuclear family. In a healthy society, women are honored for nurturing and educating the young, a role for which they are naturally suited.

Thus, the bankers set out to undermine and disparage women's role as wives and mothers.

They extolled "sexual liberation" because promiscuous women are less dedicated to family, and less suitable as wives and mothers. Furthermore, if sex is freely available, men have much less incentive to marry or be faithful.

Women were brainwashed to think they were being "exploited" by their family and should seek fulfillment in career instead.
The bankers used paid subversives like Betty Friedan and Gloria Steinem and the mass media to make it seem that feminism was a spontaneous occurrence.

At the same time, they severed sex from marriage and procreation and exalted romance as the main source of fulfillment. Hollywood practically has angels singing hosannas when the stars have sex. It created this bogus religion.

THE TRUTH ABOUT SEX

Sex is a natural function like eating food. If we didn't have food, we would think about nothing else.

Because of the gender confusion (caused by feminism) many people are sex starved and are obsessed with it. As a result, society suffers from arrested development manifested as an obsessive adolescent preoccupation with bodily functions, genitals, pornography and homosexuality.

If we have plenty, we know that divorced from love, "sex is the biggest nothing in the world." (Andy Warhol)

Similarly, romantic love is mostly infatuation based on the expectation of some great advantage (usually sex or security.) I have seen businessmen generate the same kind of heat while making a lucrative deal. But, like AOL-Time Warner, romantic mergers often go sour.

A marriage based on sexual attraction is like a chair with one leg. True love is based on character, personality and trust, tested over a long period of time.

YOUNG WOMEN

The inflated status of fertile young women is another characteristic of our Illuminati-induced dysfunction. These women remind me of poker players recklessly overplaying their hand. They have lost the capacity for love, and sex is a paltry substitute.
Their dependence on their sex appeal is very risky. The shelf life is short and the competition is fierce. Jaded males look at 1000's of practically identical naked women on the Net these days without being turned on.

Increasingly they need drugs to respond and I suspect disgust with women is the unconscious reason. Viagra and Cialis sales are in the billions.

Does it make sense to use these drugs?

Socrates said that when he no longer had a sex drive in old age, he was "released from the jaws of a wild beast." Why would any man take a drug in order to be captive once again?

Hormones generated by the testes cause the male sex drive which takes control of our minds. How powerful are these hormones?

Most young men would agree that their sisters are barely tolerable. However, other men's sisters are an endless source of wonder and fascination.

What's the difference? Sex of course.

Are there harmless drugs that could suppress the production of these mind-altering sex hormones? Perhaps they could be made widely available to young men.

Then women, deprived of their magical spell, could be seen clearly and men could concentrate on something else. When a man finds love with a total human being, he could go off the drug.

Of course, a better solution is for men and women to marry (or establish a long-term loving relationship) at a much younger age (i.e. 18-20) like they used to.

People decry marriage because sex declines in importance over time. I thought that was the purpose of marriage.

Sex belongs to an age-and-stage, i.e. courting and procreation. We weren't meant to be obsessed with it for our whole lives. There are much more important and interesting things to do.

CONCLUSION

Modern women are the victim of a monstrous hoax perpetrated by the Illuminati bankers and their lackeys in media, government and education.

Women have been defrauded of a secure and essential social role, that of wife and mother. In exchange they have accepted the role of sex objects and worker drones.

They tart it up with terms like "freedom" and "independence" but many are lonely, bitter and increasingly desperate. They have been cruelly duped by an evil power. Consequently, to varying degrees they have betrayed themselves, their husbands and their children.

Sex is used by the Illuminati as a *reductio ad absurdum*. Everything good in life, all relationships, culture, love, caring, justice, beauty, and intelligence; is flattened by what has become a sick societal obsession.

The Illuminati use sex to corrupt and debase. The pornography that floods our in-boxes is part of a widespread campaign to degrade us. A morally degraded people are a weak people, and a weak people are easily disinherited.

HELEN GURLEY BROWN

Turning Wives into Corporate Whores

IN 1965, Helen Gurley Brown, the editor of *Cosmopolitan,* said that a housewife was "a parasite, a dependent, a scrounger, a sponger or a bum."

Brown accused the wife of being a parasite but not a whore. Brown respects whores. She is one.

In her latest book, *"I'm Wild Again"* (2000) she tells us right off that in 1941, at age 19 she joined an "escort service" and made out with a 50-year-old man for $5.

"Why wasn't I revolted? I was a little but not utterly. I think even then I was a practising realist.... I tried to do whatever you needed to do to survive." (4) (That didn't change.)

She got a secretarial job on the understanding that she would sleep with her married boss and he would "take care" for her in return. This arrangement lasted for a few years. She describes the routine:

"After cocktail hour we did go to my flat to make love. The lovemaking? ...This was two people copulating -- he seemed to have a good time...Moi learned to fake often and well." (15)

Brown's excuse is that she was a helping a mother and invalid sister back in Arkansas. Right.

She laments she never really got the promised financial payoff for being a mistress: "I needed somebody to tell me how to treat a man in this situation, how to flatter and cuddle and coo. I should have done it better." (19)

Helen Gurley Brown became that "somebody to tell me how to treat a man in this situation."

She taught women how to be mistresses, corporate and

---

otherwise, instead of wives and mothers. She helped to transform the female mentality from one of devotion and love to one of a calculating predator.

Here is how she got her husband to marry her.

"You get the hook in. Darling, charming, delicious, sexy you, has to have sunk into him so seriously, the hook [is] buried so deep he can't get it out without severe pain, i.e. can't live without you. You then close in and deliver your ultimatum. I had to deliver mine twice."(27)

While Brown claims she was loyal, she thinks adultery is just fine. The man's wife is to blame if he strays. Sex, Brown says, "is a physical feeling" "it feels good... one of the best things we have...." not to be subjected to "a moral imperative."

[A La Marquis de Sade, the Illuminati motto is "Do what thou wilt.]

Suffocating a sexual urge can lead to "twitches, tension or depression" and driving "off a cliff some night." (52) But, like a practised madam, she cautions "never sleep with someone who has less money or more troubles than you." (225)

Office romances and even sleeping with the boss is just fine as long as you're discreet. (107) She tells her readers to make the boss "look good," let him take credit for their work, and don't complain about putting in extra hours.

Feminism, it seems, has stolen wives and mothers from families, and put them to work for corporations. Instead of following husbands who love them "until death do thee part," women now obey bosses who pay for their services and fire them in a downturn.

In Brown's view, if a loving husband provides for a devoted wife, she is a "parasite." But if she is a corporate slave or mistress, then she is "independent" and "liberated."

CREATING A FEMINIST ICON

In 1952, the Rockefellers annually controlled $250 million dollars of media advertising. Their newspapers and networks hyped Helen Gurley Brown's 1962 book *"Sex and the Single Girl"* and the movie by the same name. Millions of single women were told to pursue careers and have sex outside marriage. At the same time, the Rockefellers were funding and lobbying for population control and social engineering.

As editor of *Cosmopolitan* (1965-97), Brown was a role model and "teacher" for career women in America and around the world (36 foreign editions.) She married at age 37 and remained childless.

"She is arguably one of the most influential women of the decade, perhaps even the century", one women's website gushes. "She instructed, helped, advised, cheered for, encouraged, liberated, and promoted women, giving them new role models to emulate and a new manual for the sexual revolution. Armed with the pill, she showed women how they ...could take advantage of ... their sexual destinies."

Along with Communist activist Betty Friedan and CIA agent Gloria Steinem, Helen Gurley Brown belongs to the triumvirate of modern feminist "pioneers."

LAMENT

"My Inner Feminist is Hurting"

LAST WEEK, a young feminist mentioned my web site in her web journal. A traditional woman recommended it to a friend who told her about it.

"It seems to be a bunch of paranoid, ranting conspiracy theories about feminism and communism." This didn't faze her.

What bothered her was that the woman "has a boyfriend who agrees with much of the site...She now also subscribes to these beliefs."

The woman told her friend she is now "living the 'ideal' life described by that site, as she moved across the country to be with her boyfriend, stays at home and cleans, while he works and brings home the income."

She also encouraged the friend to have children explaining, "why not wanting to have children is wrong."

This "hit a nerve" because "people in my family give me a hard time for not being in a hurry to find a husband and breed, as if it is something I am obligated to do."

She is saddened that the traditional woman's son will grow up with these values and be deprived of the company of "some really wonderful and smart, independent women."

Even worse, if this woman has daughters, "they will be raised to believe that their entire role in life is to get married, have babies, and 'serve their husbands' ...that girls weren't supposed to show their intelligence...be outspoken, opinionated, funny etc. That it wasn't 'feminine' to be all these things."

Our young feminist has had some "self esteem problems, but I can't imagine spending my life being ashamed of, well, being a *real* person."

She used to feel guilty for being the "bright, sarcastic, creative girl I am. It's times like these when I'm really glad I embraced those qualities...some really wonderful people are my friends because of those qualities."

She concludes: "So yeah. My inner feminist hurts. But at least I love myself."

THIS GIRL HAS BEEN BRAINWASHED

This girl is a typical of millions of young women who have been psychologically neutered by feminism.

Homosexuals refer to heterosexuals as "breeders." Here is a once normal heterosexual woman using the same term: "find a husband and breed."

She expects to be loved for being " bright, sarcastic, creative, intelligent, outspoken, opinionated, and funny."

All that's very good but wake up girl! A man isn't looking for a "really wonderful and smart, independent woman" who is focused on herself. ("At least I love myself, " this one says.)

People love people who love them. People love people who sacrifice themselves for them. You don't get permanent love for having a witty comeback. You get it for keeping the faith even when your lover is in the dumps, for not asking about disappointments.

THE FEMINIST PARODY OF MARRIAGE

Since when is a wife and mother not a "*real* person?"

No one is suggesting that a woman should devote her life to just *any* man. She chooses a man worthy of her, someone with ability and vision. She gives up her "independence" in exchange for his love. This is how she expresses her love, and how two people become one.

He must be loyal and devoted or the deal's off. A lengthy courtship is necessary to ensure she makes the right choice.

When you love someone, having a baby feels natural. Both mother and father get immense pleasure from raising this new being.

Believe me there is nothing sexier than intelligence in a woman. When she doesn't compete with him, a man naturally wants his wife to express herself. I love that my wife is so intelligent and capable. Why wouldn't I? She is my right arm.

I do not dominate my wife. She doesn't even read my writing. Naturally I try to nurture and see her thrive. "Independent" women are missing this male nurturing.

Is this girl a slob? Doesn't she clean for herself? Then why is it such an ordeal to do it for her family? Making your home comfortable and inviting is not demeaning. It's uplifting. I'm not saying women can't have careers; just that family is more important.

Only a tiny minority of careers are truly satisfying. Feminists assume women are too vacuous to live rich and rewarding lives unless they have a *job*. This is very Communist. Most women work to support themselves not to find fulfillment. They find fulfillment from their family lives.

CONCLUSION

"My inner feminist is hurting," this girl says. Don't be a martyr. You are not sacrificing yourself for a better world. You are ruining your life.

Instead of listening to your "inner feminist," listen to your own soul. If your ideology is making you miserable, it's time to change it. Your soul doesn't lie.

FEMINISM CAN BE CURED

If Diagnosed Early

I'VE HAD MANY EMAILS from young feminists cussing me out for things I never said. So I was surprised to hear from "Meaghan" who actually read my web site and understood it. She realized feminist indoctrination had made her dysfunctional and she wanted help.

> *"I am a woman, 20 years old, who is grossly independent, and grew up with a "no boy can be better than me" complex. I was very capable in school, which my environment encouraged, pushing me to always be smarter, better, faster; having heard all this from such a young age, nothing seemed out of place. An eating disorder, troubled marriage, broken relationship with my mother and other problems later (which the few female friends I have managed to keep also share), it's obvious I need to rethink certain elements of my life: your work has found words for the silent, internal chaos which plagues especially my generation.*
>
> *It is ironic to think that people, after having reached full physical maturity, could still need to READ to learn to become something as basic as the gender they were born with--but if we've been raised to be broken, we have to start somewhere.*
>
> *I've noticed that ... you say [feminists] are lost causes. For all of the lost causes out there, you may want to consider publishing an essay or some material which points to the road of redemption: God knows there are a lot of us, and I'd hate to have the opportunity to heal, written off as "too late," and nothing more."*

Meaghan, congratulations for being so wise and articulate for your years. Here are some ideas:

1. Find a feminine woman, a wife and mother, who is willing to act as your role model. This is a woman who has built her life around her husband and children and is glad she did. You might find such a woman in traditional settings, church or ethnic community centre. This may be an opportunity to learn about Islam or Hinduism or

Christianity. Get the pastor-person to help you find a role model. Obviously you will decide whom you like.

2. My mother-in-law advised my wife: "Find a man to look after you, but be able to look after yourself." In other words, make husband and family your first priority while pursuing your career interests. If you go to university/college, focus on acquiring marketable skills. Humanities are indoctrination in feminist Masonic dysfunction. Ideally you will marry and start a family before going to university, if you go at all.

3. Don't sleep with anyone unless you are in a loving long-term relationship hopefully leading to marriage. Consecrate yourself to your future husband and children. Date men five-or-more years older who want to get married. For intimacy you must have exclusivity and permanence. Sex is an act of possession. You cannot be possessed by many men and ever belong to one. The ability to love/trust dies. Your womb is not some stranger's sperm-urinal.

4. Stop being "smarter, better, faster" than the men you meet. To some extent, a woman self effaces and lives through her husband and children. Find a man you naturally look up to, respect and trust. Don't waste time with boys. Men want power; women want love. Heterosexual union involves the exchange of the two: female power (in the worldly sense) for male love (his power expressed as love.) A woman loves a man by acquiescing and trusting, not challenging and competing. She gives him the power to grant her wishes (i.e. love her). Of course he will consult her. Find a man with a powerful positive vision of life with a central place for you. There is an implied message here for men. Men have to know what they want, provide leadership and earn trust.

5. Two people don't become one by fighting over the same territory. Generally speaking, the man "makes the house, the woman makes the home." This division of labour is natural and complementary. Women are designed to have and nurture children. They need men to support them. Learn how to be a homemaker and mother. Develop your personality and skills to be more desirable as a wife and companion.

Once the power-for-love arrangement is established, sex roles don't have to be rigid. The key is that a wife is willing to be First Mate to her Captain because he loves her, looks after her interests and is totally loyal. After that, who does what can be dictated by respective preferences, abilities and practical considerations.

6. Check out Helen Andelin's book *"Fascinating Womanhood"*

which reminds you that femininity is an art. Not everything will be relevant to you, but it has many useful hints. Also check out sites like "Surrendered Wife" and "Ladies Against Feminism." See also this website about healthy womanhood and homemaking. (www. homeliving.blogspot.com) There are a dozen more here: http:// www.outofthenestandbeyond.com/links_womens_interest.htm

In conclusion, the Rockefellers trick women into forgetting that they are part of a natural cycle, and the ages of 18-25 are critical to starting a family. In the same way as the apple tree blossoms in the Spring, young women need to marry and have children when nature intended. The Rockefellers want women and men to miss the opportunity to start strong families that will protect them from enslavement.

See ten pages of feminists vomiting over this article at http:// feministing.com/archives/006098.html ...proof that once neutered, there isn't a cure for most.

∽ ∽

BOOK TWO

∽ ∽

HOMO &
HETERO-HOMOSEXUALITY

FOOLING THEMSELVES & US

Is this Gay Behaviour Sick?

IMAGINE THAT AN ORGANISM IS SICK. Imagine that the sick cells convince the organism that they are healthy, and the healthy cells they are sick. The gullible organism would just get sicker.

This is the relationship between society and homosexuals today. Gays argue that same-sex behaviour is no different than being left-handed. On the other hand, they say heterosexual behaviour is not natural, but socially conditioned and "oppressive for women."

Heterosexual society and family are taking heavy casualties. Our opportunistic and craven leaders have betrayed us. We don't even know we are under attack.

Let's decide who, in fact, is sick.

Let's look at gay behaviour as defined by two gays, Marshall Kirk and Hunter Madsen Ph.D., authors of *"After the Ball: How America will Conquer its Fear and Hatred of Gays in the 90's."* (1989).

In Chapter Six, they outline "ten categories of misbehaviour," drawn from their own experiences, wide reading and thousands of hours of conversation with hundreds of other gays. Their contention is that the gay lifestyle, (not gay sexuality mind you), "is the pits." They want gays to improve their image by addressing "what is wrong with a lot of gays." (276)

What follows are some highlights. As you read this, ask yourself if there is another human community including the Mafia that could make these generalizations about itself. Ask yourself if heterosexuals haven't caught this disease, or at least the sniffles.

The authors say "a surprisingly high percentage" of pathological liars and con men are gay. This results from a natural habit of self-concealment, and leads to a stubborn self-deception about one's own gayness and its implication.

They say gays tend to reject all forms of morality and value judgments. Gay morality boils down to "I can do whatever I want and you can go to perdition. (If it feels good, I'll do it!)" If a gay feels like seducing a trusted friend's lover, he'll do it, justifying it as an act of "sexual freedom" and the friend be damned.

They say gays suffer from a "narcissistic" personality disorder and give this clinical description: "pathological self absorption, a need for constant attention and admiration, lack of empathy or concern for others, quickly bored, shallow, interested in fads, seductive, overemphasis on appearance, superficially charming, promiscuous, exploitative, preoccupied with remaining youthful, relationships alternate between over idealization and devaluation."
As an example of this narcissism, the authors say "a very sizable proportion of gay men" that have been diagnosed HIV positive continue to have unprotected sex.

They say the majority of gays are extremely promiscuous and self-indulgent. They must continuously up the ante to achieve arousal. This begins with alcohol and drugs and includes such "forbidden" aspects of sex as wallowing in filth (fetishism and coprophilia) and sadomasochism including violence.

They say many gays have sex in public bathrooms and think it is anti-gay harassment when it is stopped. Many think they have a right to pursue straight males, including children.

Many gays are "single minded sexual predators" fixated on youth and physical beauty alone. When it comes to the old or ugly, gays are "the real queer bashers." Disillusioned themselves, they are cynical about love.

"Relationships between gay men don't usually last very long." They quickly tire of their partners and fall victim to temptation. The "cheating ratio of 'married' gay males, given enough time, approaches 100%."

Even friendships are based on the sexual test and are hard to sustain. Unattractive gay men find it nearly impossible to find a friend, let alone a lover.

The authors say gays tend to deny reality in various ways: wishful thinking, paranoia, illogic, emotionalism and embracing crackpot ideas.

Is there any doubt that this behaviour is sick? I feel no malice

70

toward gays. I feel the same way about people who have the flu. I want them to get better and I don't want it to spread.

Unfortunately, even the authors of this book are deceiving themselves. They claim that it is the gay lifestyle and NOT gay sexuality that is "the pits." Who are they kidding? The two are inseparable.

The authors believe "our problem is fundamentally one of bad image with straights." Again, whom are they kidding? The problem isn't image.

The book details "a comprehensive public-relations campaign that should go a long way towards sanitizing our very unsanitary image:

"Desensitization": flooding straight America with advertising presenting gays in the "least offensive manner possible."

"Jamming": Advertising that equates fear of gays with hatred of Jews, Blacks and women.

"Conversion": Presenting images of gays that look like regular folks. "The image must be the icon of normality."

They say "it makes no difference that the ads are lies" because "we are using them to...counter negative stereotypes that are every bit as much lies." Huh? They just said the truth was even worse than the stereotypes.

This book was written in 1989 and obviously this campaign has taken effect. Read what the authors say about it:

"By Conversion, we mean something far more profoundly threatening to the American Way of Life [than subversion] ...We mean conversion of the average American's emotions, mind, and will, *through a planned psychological attack, in the form of propaganda fed to the nation via the media. We mean...to turn their hatred into warm regard whether they like it or not.*" (My emphasis, 153)

Thus gay activists want Americans to learn that something they naturally and justifiably regard as a disorder is in fact healthy. Thus Americans will be less able to resist their overtures whether in parks, barracks, bathrooms, classrooms or legislatures.

It is a measure of the authors' cynicism and self-deception that THEY quote psychologist M. Scott Peck, who in *"People of the Lie"* characterizes people who suffer from extreme or "malignant" narcissism simply as "evil."

Evil people, Peck says, have "an unshakable will to be right and will not consider the possibility that they are wrong...Their main weapon, interestingly enough is the lie with which they distort reality to look good to themselves, and to confuse others." (297)

Gays can continue to fool themselves. But they won't fool us. Some of these people are evil. Their behavior is sick. And it's contagious.

ARRESTED DEVELOPMENT

Playboy and the (Homo) Sexual Revolution

WHAT KIND OF MAN READS PLAYBOY? He is fastidious about his appearance, his home and his possessions. He wants as much sex as possible and chooses sexual partners mostly on the basis of appearance. He is self-absorbed and doesn't want emotional involvement or commitment. He thinks a woman and children would be a burden.

Does this sound like many gays? It is also the masculine ideal purveyed by Playboy magazine to men since the 1950's.

The essence of manhood is to lead and support a family. But in 1972, three out of four male college students got their ideas about masculinity from *Playboy,* at an incalculable cost to themselves, women, children and society.

The similarity between the *Playboy* and homosexual ideal is no coincidence. *"The Kinsey Report"* (1948) shaped current mainstream attitudes to sex. It championed unfettered sexual expression and became the manifesto of the counterculture. It inspired Hugh Hefner to start *Playboy* in 1953.

Essentially *"The Kinsey Report"* said that aberrant sexual behaviour was so common as to be normal. Thanks to Dr. Judith Reisman, we now know that Alfred Kinsey was a homosexual and the *"Kinsey Report"* was based on fraudulent data.

He cruised Times Square looking for subjects. More than 25% of his sample consisted of prostitutes and prison inmates including many sex offenders. Kinsey said 10 per cent of American men were gay when in fact only two per cent were.

To prove that children have legitimate sexual needs, Kinsey and his fellow pedophiles either abused 2,000 babies and children themselves and/or relied on data obtained in Nazi concentration camps. (Judith Reisman, "Kinsey: Crimes and Consequences," 1998, p. 312)

Alfred Kinsey pretended to be a Conservative family man. In fact, he died prematurely of orchitis, a disease associated with masturbation, impotence and self-mutilation. He seduced his male students and forced his wife and associates to perform in homemade pornographic films. ("orchitis" Reisman, p. 278)

Reisman concludes: "America's growing libidinous pathologies... taught in schools...and reflected in our fine and popular arts, the press, law and public policy largely mirror the documented sexual psychopathologies of the Kinsey team itself."

Sponsored by the Rockefeller Foundation, Kinsey's goal was "to supplant what he saw as a narrow pro-creational Judeo Christian era with a promiscuous "anything goes" bi/gay pedophile paradise." (Reisman, *Crafting Gay Children: An Inquiry,* p.4)

HEFNER'S HERO

Hugh Hefner said the Kinsey Report "produced a tremendous sexual awakening, largely because of media attention..." This shows how the elite orchestrates social change using media hype and the power of advertising (in *Playboy.*) (See Reisman, Kinsey, p.307)

With messianic fervor, *Playboy* took its gospel of sexual freedom to the American male who in the 1950's-1960's still consecrated sex for marriage. Playboy's aim, the aim of all pornographers, was to hook men on the glossy fantasy. To do this, they had to prevent them from finding true satisfaction in marriage.

In Reisman's words, "Playboy was the first national magazine to exploit college men's fears of women and family commitment. Playboy offered itself as a reliable, comforting substitute for monogamous heterosexual love." (Judith Reisman, *"Soft Porn Plays Hardball,"* p 47)

Supposed enemies, Playboy and radical feminists, found common ground in hatred of the nuclear family. As a result, society now suffers from epidemics of family breakdown, pornography, impotence, child sexual abuse, sado-sexual violence, teen pregnancy, a cocktail of STD's and, of course, AIDS.

HOMOSEXUALITY

I define homosexuality as a developmental disorder caused by an inability to establish a permanent bond with a member of the opposite sex. Psychologist Richard Cohen, in *"Coming Out Straight:*

Understanding and Healing Homosexuality" (2000) argues it is caused when a male child fails to bond with his father. By having sex with men, the adult gay is trying to compensate for father-love denied in adolescence.

Dr. Charles Socarides confirms that "most men caught up in same-sex sex are reacting, at an unconscious level, to something amiss with their earliest upbringing- over controlling mothers and abdicating fathers. Through long observation I have also learned that the supposedly liberated homosexual is never really free. In his multiple, same-sex adventures, even the most effeminate gay was looking to incorporate the manhood of others, because he was in a compulsive, never-ending search for the masculinity that was never allowed to build and grow in early childhood." ("How America Went Gay")

Psychiatrist Jeffrey Satinover has pointed to another cause of homosexuality. A 1990 survey of 1000 gays shows that an older or more powerful partner physically assaulted 37% of them before the age of 19. (*"Homosexuality and American Public Life,"* 1999, p.24) In addition, according to Anne Moir in *"Why Men Don't Iron,"* some men may be "born gay" due to foetal hormone imbalances. They seem to be a minority.

For many decades, gays were told that they were "sick" and cruelly persecuted. The gay activist solution: convince the world that, in fact, it is heterosexuals who are sick. In 1973, they bullied the American Psychological Association into pronouncing homosexuality normal. It was no longer a disorder but a healthy and normal "sexual preference." Psychiatrists who felt otherwise were ostracized. Their lectures were cancelled; their books and articles rejected; their promotions denied. Is this the way science should work? (See on line "How America Went Gay")

SPREADING THE SICKNESS

Together with feminists, gay activists began to dismantle all heterosexual institutions: masculinity, femininity, marriage, the nuclear family, the boy scouts, sports, and the military.

Backed by the financial elite, gay activists and their supporters now largely dictate our cultural sensibility. They are partly responsible for the puerile pornographic obsession that pervades television, music videos and the Internet. Now we all suffer from the homosexual disorder, which I believe is arrested development.

Gay liberation manuals talk about "normalizing" their sexuality and "de-sensitizing" straights by flaunting it. I was livid when I took my 10-year-old son to see Adam Sandler's movie *"Billy Madison"* and heard one teenage male youth in the film casually ask another: "Would you rather bone Pamela Anderson or a young Jack Nicholson?"

Last week, on TV's "Will and Grace," Jack who is gay dons an apron that says "Kiss the cook" pretending he thought the second "o" was a "c". Just as Communists once conned do-gooders to think radicalism was chic, gay activists define trendy for gullible liberals today.

Gay and feminist activists think traditional morality was invented to perpetuate an unjust status quo. In fact, morality is the accumulated wisdom of mankind regarding what is healthy and ultimately fulfilling. Perversion is deviation from what is healthy.

Heterosexual morality places sex in the context of love and/or marriage because it is healthy and human. It ensures that the most profound and intimate physical act between two people expresses a corresponding emotional-spiritual bond. Promiscuous sex is a desperate plea for love. Love and marriage answer that call and provide for the natural and necessary outcome of sex, children.

CONCLUSION

With Hugh Hefner's help, Alfred Kinsey detached sex from love and procreation. Homosexual activists champion anonymous sex: a majority of gays have over a dozen partners each year. In less extreme form, heterosexuals have adopted this model. Recently a social columnist enviously described straight friends whose relationships have ended: "they're out partying, having the time and the sex of their lives."

In conclusion, the "sexual revolution" was really a triumph of an elite program of arrested development. Courtship and sex fixation represent a stage of life. After marriage we move on to more important things. The elite agenda is to make sex a lifelong preoccupation.

In 40 short years, almost all sexual constraints have dissolved and heterosexual society is on the defensive. Cultural and social breakdown will only worsen unless there is a counterrevolution.

GAY MARRIAGE

Heterosexual Society is Under Siege

HETEROSEXUALS ARE UNDER ATTACK in many places. In Canada, the government has changed the legal definition of marriage in order to allow gays to marry. To satisfy marriage-minded gays, less than .5% of the population, the meaning of the central heterosexual sacrament has been altered. This is an obvious sleight-of-hand designed to undermine heterosexuality. They could have given gays a separate but equal-to-marriage status. Instead, they are telling heterosexuals that they are the same as homosexuals.

Marriage is a heterosexual institution designed to join a couple for life and begin a family. Imagine if, in the name of "equality," heterosexuals had "gay pride" parades? What if Muslims started celebrating Passover? People have a right to protect their institutions from outsiders who wish to co-opt and change them.

In 1994 gay activist Michelangelo Signorile advocated seeking gay marriage and benefits in order to "redefine the institution completely... and radically alter an archaic institution." (*Out* Magazine, Dec-Jan 1994 p. 161.)

The campaign to change the heterosexual norm is intensifying. Straights need to realize that they are under siege from big government and big business.

In Vancouver, parents narrowly blocked homosexual activists from placing their books on kindergarten curriculum. In the U.S., the American Psychiatric Association came under heavy pressure to remove pedophilia (sex with children) from its list of mental disorders. Newsweek featured same-sex couples attending their high school proms. "Instead of sparking controversy, schools are saying, what's the big deal?"

The majority of homosexuals are good people who want to be left alone. However, elite foundations and corporations fund homosexual organizations to destroy the heterosexual fabric of society.

THE HIDDEN AGENDA

Gay activists pretend they are seeking "tolerance" and "equality." But privately they admit to a hidden agenda: To reshape society in their own image. They don't care how much harm they do.

"The end goal of the feminist revolution is the elimination of the sex distinction itself," says Shulamith Firestone (*The Dialectic of Sex,* 1972, p.11)

"Heterosexual hegemony is being eroded," writes Gary Kinsman. "The forms of sexuality considered natural have been socially created and can be socially transformed." (*The Regulation of Desire: Sexuality in Canada,* 1987, p.219)

"In a free society, everyone will be gay," says Allen Young, a pioneer of the Gay Liberation Movement. (John D'Emilio, *Intimate Matters: A History of Sexuality in America,* p.322)

"In one sense the Right is right," says gay historian Jonathan Katz. "If gay and lesbian liberationists ever achieve full equality, they will do away with the social need for the hetero/homo division.

"The secret of the most moderate, mainstream gay and lesbian civil rights movement is its radically transformative promise (or threat, depending on your values)." (*The Invention of Heterosexuality,* 1995, p.188.)

GAY-FEMINIST ONSLAUGHT

Gay and feminist activists find common ground because they insist male-female distinctions are artificial, ignoring all scientific evidence. While many heterosexuals might consider themselves "feminists", feminism is a homosexual movement. It believes that men and women are the same and only social conditioning makes us different. Homosexuality is love of the same.

Today, gay and feminist activists want "people" to make love to "people" regardless of their sex. They depict normal heterosexual behaviour as pathological. Men are inherently abusive and the heterosexual family is oppressive. The way to social justice is to abolish heterosexuality altogether. (Isn't *this* "hate"?)

Illuminati-Marxism spawned both the Gay and Woman's liberation movements by transferring Marxist class conflict to gender. The "patriarchy" (male-dominated heterosexual family) is the root of all evil and must be destroyed ("transformed"). Women (the proletariat) and anyone "oppressed" (gays, certain favored minorities) must be handed position and power on a silver platter.

The Illuminati's "revolutionary" goal is the "New World Order" or authoritarian socialism run by monopoly capital. It is big government in the service of big business, the Left in the service of the Right.

PASSIVITY

Why have straights endured this attack passively?

1. The gay-feminists have waged their war with impunity by claiming a bogus victim status. Straights can't even defend their own sexuality for fear of accusations of "homophobia" and "sexism." These days anyone who does not want to be gay is considered homophobic.

2. Typical of Communists, they practice deceit. They attracted widespread support by pretending to champion women when in fact they always had a revolutionary homosexual agenda. Now politicians and media are in massive denial because they have put these radicals in charge of education. The situation is comparable to the liberal refusal in the late 1940's to admit the government was riddled with Soviet spies. This was the same phenomenon: Rockefeller Communism.

SOVIET-STYLE INDOCTRINATION

Many public schools virtually "break the ice" for gays. For example, the Grade Seven curriculum in Ontario introduces 12-year-old children to oral and anal sex.

Phyllis Benedict, president of the Ontario Elementary Teacher's Federation said the union is "trying to promote a more positive [homosexual] environment in schools." (*National Post*, Aug.16, 2001)

This extends to undermining the heterosexual family by reading books like *"Aasha's Moms"* and *"Two Dads, Brown Dads, Blue Dads."*

On the other hand, heterosexuality is virtually a taboo. Our children's textbooks have been rewritten to eliminate any hint that men and women might be different, live in traditional families, or behave in "stereotypical" ways.

As a university lecturer, I tried to teach novelists like D.H. Lawrence who portrayed male-female love in positive terms. I was accused of "sexual harassment" by feminist activists and lost my job. (Sexual harassment is now defined as anything that makes a radical feminist uncomfortable.)

As heterosexuals, we cannot explore our sexuality because homosexuals may be "uncomfortable." This has led to the demoralization of society. We cannot celebrate men as masculine and women as feminine. We do not celebrate heterosexual love, the greatest gift that life offers us.

This daily denial of our sexual identity amounts to persecution. It used to be 'live and let live.' Now illuminati-sponsored gay and feminist activists will not let us live.

MASS MEDIA MOLDING

In an episode of the TV show *Friends*, Rachel avoids paying a speeding fine by flirting with the handsome traffic cop. Ross takes the steering wheel and is stopped for driving too slowly. Ross tries to flirt with the male cop. The message is that we can all go both ways, even the cop. This is the reality behind the gay activist demand for "equality". Tolerance was never the real objective; we must be like them. It doesn't matter if we are comfortable as long as they are.

In Rochester, N.Y., Rolf Szabo a 23-year employee of Eastman Kodak Co. was fired solely because he objected to a pro-homosexual office memo. He did not adhere to the company's so-called "Winning & Inclusive Culture" designed to promote "diversity." This example of Soviet-style thought crime is not isolated.

Homosexual behaviour makes straights uncomfortable. Most men find the sight of two men kissing viscerally repulsive.

Gay families are not the same as ours. The adoption of straight children by gays denies the children's natural instincts and will probably affect their psychological development. Heterosexual children need heterosexual role models. In 20 years these children will be suing the government for millions of dollars.

THE HETEROSEXUAL CLOSET

Heterosexuals are being brainwashed to function "on the quiet," "out of the public view," so that we don't "offend" our gay brothers and sisters. There are exceptions but generally speaking our lifestyle and rituals are not celebrated in the movies or on TV. Instead they are portrayed in a jaundiced way.

Certainly, there is an obsession with male-female sex but mostly in homosexual terms, i.e. promiscuous and public. Heterosexuality is being part of the natural life cycle; it is not a sexual preference.

Non-gays, especially women, are naturally monogamous and private because heterosexuality ultimately is about exclusivity, intimacy, trust and procreation.

Heterosexual norms and institutions are routinely ridiculed and affronted in the media.

For example, in opening scene of the hit movie, *American Wedding,* (2003) which is aimed at impressionable teenagers, the future bride performs fellatio on the groom from under a table in a crowded restaurant.

At the wedding reception the groom's unruly friend accidentally has sex with the groom's *grandmother* in a dark closet. He thought he was making it with the bride's sluttish sister. The grandmother is so satisfied that she removes her objection to her grandson marrying a shiksa. In the final scene, another friend performs cunnilingus on the unruly friend's mother in a bubble bath.

This cultural assault on heterosexual norms is part of a long-term program by the financial elite to decrease population, destroy the family and destabilize society.

Far-fetched you say?

I have written more than two-dozen articles about how heterosexuality works. They resound with many people.

Agree or disagree with me, I haven't had a single interview or mention in the mainstream media. This is not sour grapes. It merely illustrates that our "free and open" society is bogus. We have freedom of speech. Being heard is another matter.

I urge you to read Dr. Charles Socarides' book *"Homosexuality: A Freedom Too Far"* to understand the true nature of homosexuality and the insidious campaign to mainstream it. I also recommend the web site of NARTH, a body of medical professionals dedicated to a correct understanding and treatment of homosexuality. There is a wealth of information and wisdom here.

The cry of "equality," "tolerance" and "diversity" is the classic underhanded Communist- elite method of subverting society. They champion some minority whom they portray as victims. They divide and conquer, putting their minority agents in power. They call this "progress" when in fact it is social disintegration.

CONCLUSION

It's time to recognize that homo and heterosexuality are in fierce competition. The gay model does not fit heterosexuals and vice-versa. *There can only be one model.* The issue is: will ours be a heterosexual society that tolerates a 4% gay minority?

Or, will it be a homosexual society that persecutes a 96% straight majority? History has many examples of minorities that have persecuted majorities. Take Communism for example.

If straights don't establish the norms, gay activists will. When gay/feminist activists demand "equality," they are demanding that their unisex model fit all. They are saying that we are the same. We are not.

Rejecting the homosexual model is not "intolerance" or "hatred." It is defending our natural birthright and our families.

Heterosexual society is the victim of a most insidious form of persecution, psychological warfare. The real "haters" are gay-feminist activists, and the politicians, media, corporations and foundations that sustain them.

FEAR OF GAY PREDATORS

Confessions of a "Homophobe"

I'M "COMING OUT" as a homophobe and I urge people who agree with me to do the same. I am defining "homophobe" as someone who is afraid of homosexual activists, hence the suffix "phobia." Gay activists use this term to bludgeon opponents. Let's embrace it instead.

I had always accepted the mass media's portrayal of gays as a colorful minority who have a special "sexual orientation." They meet each other at their bars and do their thing. As long as they kept it within their own community, what did I care?

I recently learned that most gays prefer heterosexual males. My source is a book, *"The Caricature of Love,"* (1957), by Dr. Hervey Checkley, a clinical professor of psychiatry at the Medical College of Georgia. A gay friend also confirmed this fact to me. That would explain why a recent Google search of the term "straight men" turned up over a million links. At least half are homosexual in character.

Many gays also prefer youths or adolescents. These experiences often turn victims into homosexuals and distort or destroy their lives. In a survey by the gay magazine *"The Advocate,"* 21% of respondents said an adult sexually abused them by age 15. This seems to be the way that homosexuals "propagate." My source is an extraordinary research paper by Dr. Judith Reisman entitled *"Crafting "Gay" Children: An Inquiry"* p. 9.

According to Reisman, the 1991 US Population Statistical Abstracts indicate that between 1-2 million gay males (2% of the adult male population of 90 million) abuse 6-8 million boys. The ratio is 3-5 boy victims to one gay male compared to one girl victim per eleven straight males. This is based on data on 33 million boys and 32 million girls under the age of 18. Reisman says that since 100% of the gay males do not sexually assault boys, the 2% homosexual population harbors a vast pederast subculture committing multiple repeated child sex offences. (8)

Before I continue, I want to say that I have known an older gay friend since I was 11-years-old, and not once in 40 years did he make an improper gesture. No doubt, there are many gays like him who behave with dignity and have no predatory agenda, personal or social.

Nevertheless lesbian feminist and gay activists, by their own admission, are dedicated to recasting society in their own image. The mainstream media is suppressing all negative information about gay life: data on gay violence against children, child pornography, sex rings, serial murders, and inter-gay domestic battery.

THE BOY SCOUTS

Another example of media complicity is the Boy Scouts' ban on gay scoutmasters. There was no mention that about 100 cases of sexual molestation by Boy Scout leaders occurred every year. According to the *"Washington Times,"* (June 15,1993) between 1973 and 1993, 1,416 scout leaders were expelled for sexually abusing boys.

The Boys Scouts' action belatedly recognized their obligation to protect their wards. Is there any question they are liable? Yet amazingly the Scouts have come under scathing attack for "discriminating" against gays.

The pederast magazine *"Palaver"* advises pedophiles to take positions like Boy Scout leader: "If you want to spend your time with children you must have a legitimate reason for doing so; as a teacher helping children learn... as a play or youth leader helping children to enjoy their leisure time" (*"Crafting Gay Children: An Inquiry,"* p.19).

In 1992, the North American Man/Boy Love Association" (NAMBLA) specifically targeted the Boy Scouts. They passed a resolution calling on the Boy Scouts "to cease in its discrimination against openly gay or lesbian persons in its appointment of scoutmasters" in order to "permit scouts to be exposed to a variety of lifestyles." (See "The Nazis in America" in *"The Pink Swastika"* by Scott Lively and Kevin Abrams). In their literature, gays portray adult advisors as playing a hands-on role in initiating the young to homosexuality.

According to *"The Pink Swastika"*, the moral courage exhibited by the Boy Scouts of America is not shared by all youth organizations. The Girl Scouts allows lesbian leaders in its organizations and has expelled at least one heterosexual leader who refused to keep this policy a secret from parents.

"Big Brothers" and "Big Sisters" actively recruit homosexuals in many cities and lobbied the Boys Scouts to do the same saying "non traditional volunteers can serve the best interest of children." And of course, all of this mirrors the push into public schools where youth are prematurely introduced to sex education and introduced to homosexuality as "a lifestyle option."

"Gay rights" activists have targeted the Boy Scouts. An ostensibly "spontaneous" outcry against the Boy Scouts has arisen across the country, led by the United Way Agency, which pulled its BSA funding in many cities. Homosexuals at the highest rank of the US government attempted to intimidate this organization.

Former Surgeon General Joycelyn Elders used her post to castigate Scout officials (*USA Today* June 2, 1994) and Interior secretary Bruce Babbitt signed an order prohibiting Boy Scouts from volunteering in national parks (*"Washington Times,"* May 28,1993). As of June 2001, at least 359 school districts in 10 states have forbade the Boys Scouts from using their facilities, according to a gay organization quoted in the *"Washington Times,"* Nov. 1, 2001.

CONCLUSION

Homosexuals, both feminists and gays, have gained incredible power by successfully disguising their true character and their true agenda. This is how subversive movements such as Nazis and Communists function. Under the guise of being a persecuted minority seeking human rights, homosexuals are actually using the state to persecute heterosexuals. They are waging successful war against all the institutions of masculinity, femininity and the nuclear family.

Their goal is to supplant Judeo-Christian heterosexual values with their own. Society is in a state of denial about this vicious subversion, which takes practical form in the actual seduction of heterosexual youth.

As a father of a son, I am afraid of the power of gay activists and predators. I guess that makes me homophobic.

LITERARY PROPAGANDA

A Streetcar Named "Straight Bashing"

THE FEMINIST BELIEF that society is sexist and homophobic in fact masks a subversive elite campaign against heterosexuals. One of the most celebrated plays in American Literature, *A Streetcar Named Desire* (1947) depicts men as "subhuman", and heterosexual family and society as frauds. The play, produced by Irene Selznick, contributes to the "modern" sense that human life has no inherent dignity, value or purpose.

There is also a startling similarity between Tennessee Williams' homosexual perspective and the modern feminist one. Guilt and self-loathing seem to motivate both.

Feminists have made common cause with homosexuals by promoting a gender less society. In *"The New Victorians"* (1996), Rene Denfeld writes that feminists regard heterosexuality as the source model for oppression per se and homosexuality as the remedy:

"For many of today's feminists, lesbianism is far more than a sexual orientation, or even a preference. It is, as students in many colleges learn, an ideological, political and philosophical means of liberation of all women from heterosexual tyranny..." (45)

MALE AS "SUBHUMAN"

Long before feminists portrayed all men as rapists, Tennessee Williams depicted the male icon Stanley Kowalski in these terms. Stanley drives his sister-in-law Blanche DuBois insane by raping her while his wife Stella is in the hospital bearing his son. Blanche is portrayed as a tragic heroine; Stanley as the symbol of a brutal male-dominated society, and the traditional family as a fraud.

Blanche DuBois has been banished from her hometown for her immorality. Sick and broke, she takes refuge with her sister's archetypal traditional family.

Stanley, carrying the "red stained package from the butcher's" is the male protector and provider (Signet, p. 13). The pregnant Stella, nurturing and malleable, is the epitome of the feminine. She believes in her husband: "it's a drive that he has" (50). The couple is madly, sensually in love.

Nevertheless Blanche/Williams is determined to make heterosexuality appear pathological. Immediately on arrival, Blanche refers to Stella's home as "this horrible place." (19) She reproaches Stella for not helping to save the plantation: "Where were you? In bed with your Pollack!" as if this were wrong (27). When Stanley and Stella exchange blows, Blanche is like a counsellor at a womyn's shelter. She urges Stella to leave her husband, open a shop, and become independent. (67)

Stanley is genuinely repentant for hitting Stella, although today this would be discounted as part of "the cycle of violence." In fact, Blanche has made the pregnant Stella criticize and defy her husband for the first time. Now like her feminist sisters, the envious Blanche hopes the resulting violence will shatter the family altogether.

Stella ignores Blanche's appeals, and while cleaning says: "I'm not in anything that I want to get out of." (65). But Blanche persists: "Stop! Let go of that broom. I won't have you cleaning up for him!" (66)

The feminist tone is again heard in Blanche's dehumanizing of Stanley. "There's something downright bestial about him! ... He acts like an animal, has animal's habits! ... There's even something subhuman something not quite to the stage of humanity yet! Yes, something ape-like about him, like one of those pictures I've seen in anthropological studies."(71)

Can you imagine a modern play in which a man says this of a Jew, a woman, a Black or a homosexual? But the white male is fair game.

Stanley overhears this conversation, yet this supposedly ape-like creature does not react violently. He patiently tolerates Blanche although she has been mooching from them in a two-room apartment for six months.

Blanche, a demented pitiable woman, appeals to progress and civilization. "God! Maybe we are a long way from being made in God's image, but Stella my sister; there has been some progress since then! ... In this dark march toward whatever it is we're approaching

. . . Don't hang back with the brutes!" (72)

At the end of the play, Williams has achieved his unconscious goal: destroying the heterosexual male and family. Stella must ignore her sister's claims of rape in order to preserve her family. "I couldn't believe her story and go on living with Stanley," she says (133).

Nevertheless, her family is bereft of moral legitimacy. In the movie version, Stella becomes a single mother. She leaves Stanley vowing never to return.

HOMOSEXUAL SELF HATRED

There is more to this picture than meets the eye.

First, Tennessee Williams often said that *he was Blanche DuBois*. The similarities are clear. Like Blanche Dubois, Tennessee Williams was neurasthenic, lusted for Stanley, and was very promiscuous. In the play, Blanche warns herself not to seduce the newspaper boy, "I've got to be good and keep my hands off children."(84)

Second, Tennessee Williams hated himself. Gore Vidal who knew the playwright said: "He is still too much the puritan not to believe in sin. At some deep level, Tennessee believes that the homosexual is wrong and the heterosexual is right. Given this all pervading sense of guilt, he is drawn in life and work to the idea of expiation, of death."(Ronald Hayman, *"Tennessee Williams: Everyone Else is an Audience,"* 1993. p.xviii)

The guilt-ridden Williams/Blanche wants to be destroyed by Stanley to expiate his sins. (Blanche calls Stanley "my executioner" before she even knows him.) But, in this psychodrama, Williams doesn't have the integrity to confess his guilt feelings and admit his death wish. He postures as a hero by identifying Blanche's defeat with the cause of goodness and culture. Thus he transfers to Stanley and society the hatred he feels for himself.

Robert J. Stoller, an eminent psychiatrist and UCLA Professor, described this process in his book, *"Perversion: The Erotic Form of Hatred"* (1975).

"Homosexuals, taught self-hatred in childhood, persist in attracting punishment because in part they agree with the cruel straight society; they provoke attack in order to be humiliated . . .Revenge energizes aspects of many homosexuals' behaviour, erotic and otherwise. In order to salvage a sense of value from the foci of despair, they must strike back at all who have qualities like old enemies of their childhood." (201-202).

CONCLUSION

Tennessee Williams' *Streetcar Named Desire* is an example of how the financial elite used a homosexual playwright to discredit the family and twist the way heterosexuals think about themselves and society. Since heterosexuals have derived their meaning from family roles for millennia, Williams contributed to the malaise that characterizes the modern era.

Williams' example indicates that this destructive impulse, which feminists seem to share, may spring from a deep sense of envy, failure, self-loathing and hatred. Having missed the streetcar of life, they want to blow up the tracks.

THE GAY AGENDA ON CAMPUS

Here Come the Lesbian Rangers!

UNIVERSITY STUDENTS continue to face a bizarre government campaign to make them homosexuals.

Last week at the University of Winnipeg, co-eds were invited to participate in a lesbian "Reorientation Week."

They were asked to become "rangers" with the "Lesbian National Parks and Services," the brainchild of local "performance artists" Shauna Dempsey and Lorri Millan.

This is the lesbian equivalent of the university and government hiring two middle-aged males to recruit co-eds to go camping and have sex.

The two womyn had a "field office" in the university art gallery, staffed by a university employee in ranger uniform. They took part in pancake breakfasts, barbecues and interviews on campus radio. "Lesbian Rangers salute and welcome you!" their brochure said. "Here you will encounter new, even life-changing lifestyles and ideas. These may challenge you in uncomfortable ways."

The university art gallery, the Manitoba Arts Council and the Canada Council, sponsored this spectacle to the tune of $10,000. This doesn't include thousands of taxpayer dollars already expended on their promotional video and "Field Guide" which includes examples of lesbian "flora and fauna."

Their message: "Homosexuality is natural. Question the heterosexual model. Heterosexuality is a social construct."

When I went to university, students learned to question authority.

Today, they learn to question their gender.

Does the LNPS actually exist? This is social engineering

masquerading as art, propaganda disguised as parody. It is a shock tactic. Eventually the outrageous becomes accepted. Often, what begins in the imagination occurs in reality.

The Lesbian Rangers don't actually work in any parks. But the artists claim to have hundreds of junior members called "Eager Beavers."

Their video (online) is full of such *double entendres* and sexual innuendo. The two "bush women" leave "no stone or lesbian unturned." It's a "lesbian-eat-lesbian-world." Knots are practiced in various bondage positions. Their website is called www. fingerinthedyke.ca

Yet, in the video, they fine a heterosexual male $100 for wearing a lewd T-shirt ("Blow me") and intimidate him when he protests. He is reprimanded for "threatening the lesbian environment." Rangers are urged to make "citizens' arrests."

Lesbians are just a few grants shy of having a paramilitary organization, a cross between the Girl Scouts and Hitler's Brown Shirts. Its function: Persecute heterosexuals.

In the video, they "rescue" a straight female from drowning. She is enchanted by her hairy-legged saviours and "sees the world through brand new eyes."

LESBIAN PLAYGROUND

If the University of Winnipeg is an indication, universities are playgrounds for lesbianism. It makes sense. Enrolment is already 2-1 female.

In June 2001, the University of Winnipeg made headlines when high school students attending a summer art history course complained they were shown lesbian porn and instructed to use zucchinis instead of seek male companionship. The instructors were not removed.

The following year, the "Women's Centre" sponsored an event where co-eds had casts made of their breasts! Imagine if heterosexual males sponsored such an event.

Each February, the gay-dominated student council sponsors a "Question Your Gender" week.

The "Sexual Harassment Officer" stated that the university takes a grim view if only one student is made "uncomfortable." Apparently this rule only applies to the discomfort of feminists, gays and lesbians. The claim of "victimhood" masks an aggressive destructive ideology.

In Women's Studies courses, co-eds learn to be feminist "change agents" and harass professors who step out of line. Women's Studies originated in the training schools of the US Communist Party in the 1940's.

IS LESBIANISM NATURAL?

I have no problem with lesbians, many of whom are my neighbors. They seem to be nice people who want to live and let live. But their activists are funded to depopulate and destabilize society in advance of "world government." Their message is that lesbianism is not a developmental disorder but a natural alternative for women.

Unfortunately, many ex-lesbians disagree. In her book, *"Restoring Sexual Identity"* Anne Paulk surveyed 265 ex-lesbians like herself and conducted numerous personal interviews. She found that "same-sex attraction is seldom really driven by sexual needs; it is driven by an unconscious desire to be loved and to trust another person. It is also frequently driven by a desire to reconnect with the feminine but in the wrong way."

"Childhood trauma, poor self-image, anger at men, poor relationships with either or both parents, and pro-homosexual media propaganda are several key elements in women developing an attraction to other women."

In the "classic development of lesbian attraction," Paulk discovered that these women had ... domineering, critical, detached, or weak mother; and/or ... a father who was detached, critical or abusive."

"In many cases, the mother was viewed as weak or was cruelly dominated by her husband. Seventy-five percent of the women viewed the male as a more favorable role model for their lives--with a rejection of their own gender and pursuit of male characteristics."

"An astounding 90 percent experienced some form of abuse themselves. This abuse was not just sexual but included emotional abuse (70 percent), sexual (more than 60 percent), and verbal abuse (more than half of those surveyed.) "

CONCLUSION

As far as I could tell, University of Winnipeg students mostly avoided the Lesbian Rangers. But there are many feminist or lesbian professors who are harder to avoid. They make their dogma of male oppression of women (i.e. divide-and-conquer) a prerequisite for a good grade.

Let's not mince words. Orwell's "1984" has arrived. The government and universities are foisting a developmental disorder caused by dysfunctional families on our children.

Dempsey and Millin try to be campy and nice but they are really obnoxious hypocrites. Like fellow lesbian Irjad Manji, they are New World Order "change agents," cultural agitators highly paid to subvert the young. Destruction of the family is a main tenet of the Illuminati's Communist Manifesto.

The LNPS motto is "Treat a Lesbian as you would like a Lesbian to Treat You." I ask, do they want to be treated like they are treating straights? What if straight society launched a comparable campaign teaching them that their deepest life desires are not natural but a "social construct"? Do *they* want to be converted?

It's ironic that they refer to lesbians as an endangered species. Heterosexuals are the real endangered species. They are the ones who conceive and nurture the young in nuclear families. And when they disappear, so will the human race, as we know it.

IRSHAD MANJI

Lesbian Muslim Reformer is New World Orderly

(Note: Since the event described below, Manji has attended the 2005 Bildersburg meeting near Munich and rubbed shoulders with such luminaries as David Rockefeller.)

MUSLIM "REFORMER" AND LESBIAN ACTIVIST Irshad Manji, 35, symbolizes the globalist push to extinguish true religion and enslave humanity.

Her book *"The Trouble With Islam: A Wake Up Call for Honesty and Change"* is being translated into a dozen languages.

Last week, for the second time in six months, Manji spoke here in Winnipeg.

The Asper Foundation and the Jewish Women's Federation sponsored her. The Aspers (Canwest Media) own a TV network and the largest chain of newspapers in Canada. Manji charges $7500 an hr.

In her speech, Manji called on Muslims to return to their ancient tradition of "ijtihad" which encouraged them to scrutinize their social and religious institutions and make their own decisions about how to live.

As far as I could tell, there was only one Muslim in the audience of about 800.

The title of the lecture *("Why I Support Women, Jews and Pluralism")* may have been a factor. Most of the people present were Jews (some out of social obligation) with a smattering of lesbians and globots. (globalists)

It was comical to listen to Manji exhort Muslims to challenge their tradition in front of an audience composed mainly of Jews, a community not noted for welcoming constructive criticism.

Ever heard of a book (or lecture) entitled *"The Trouble with*

Judaism: A Wake Up Call for Honesty and Change?"

The globalist elite peddles Manji a Toronto writer who emigrated from Uganda as an infant, as a herald of necessary change in Muslim society.

Oprah Winfrey and *Maclean's* magazine have honoured her. She has spoken at Oxford University, the United Nations press club, the World Presidents Organization, the International Women's Forum, and the Pentagon. *The New York Times* described her has "Osama bin Laden's worst nightmare." You get the picture.

The wonder is that Manji and her audience actually think they are bucking the establishment. Many are anti globalist!

SELECTIVE DIVERSITY AND TOLERANCE

In the Q & A session, the sole Muslim present at the Winnipeg event said she had flouted her family by having a Black child out-of-wedlock. She also adopted two aboriginal children so her family was "a regular United Nations."

She was heartily applauded for her rebellion and presented as an example of racial tolerance.

I doubt if any of these Jews would have applauded had this woman been *their* daughter.

Organized Jewry seems to promote "tolerance" for other people (like Muslims) but does not embrace it itself.

For example, I asked Manji to comment on Israel's policy of forbidding Palestinians who are married to Israelis from living in Israel. Manji evaded my question and the moderator didn't remind her of it.

Jews (and homosexuals) have no idea how they are being used to create the New World Order, only to be cast aside or made a scapegoat later.

A cabal of Masonic dynastic families based in the City of London control the New World Order. They decided to use Jews to colonize the Middle East long before the birth of "Zionism." The US invasion of Iraq is the latest phase in this satanic plan for "world government." Yes Virginia, there is a Conspiracy.

EMASCULATE MUSLIMS USING FEMINISM

In her talk, Manji alluded vaguely to women's oppression in Muslim societies. She advocated "micro business loans" for women (not men) so they could become "entrepreneurs."

Muslim men then would be "working for their wives," she said. In other words, deprive men of their social role as protectors and providers.

Muslims are the only men resisting the New World Order precisely because they haven't been gelded like "men" in the West.

In Muslim society women are cherished and loved for their service to their families. Manji would export the West's family breakdown and plummeting birthrate by "liberating" women from this place of honor. How like a lesbian activist.

Globalists hate nothing more than a woman devoted to her husband and family. She is dangerous. They can't control her. She might have a healthy happy family with independent values. This could spread!

Manji said some women in Afghanistan are using these small business loans to start schools for girls (not boys.)

"They believe that if you educate a boy, you educate only him," she said. "But if you educate a girl, you educate the whole family." Huh? Don't fathers have any role in educating their children?

This unsubtle attempt to exclude fathers is typical of the hateful underhanded attack on the heterosexual family made by self-described "women of conscience" and "champions of human rights" who say they are opposed to "marginalizing any group."

These pious self-serving dupes define "human rights" selectively. The vast heterosexual majority of European or Muslim origin, males in particular, evidently are not entitled to human rights. They can be attacked mercilessly and if they resist, they are accused of bigotry.

Many homosexuals and Jews have this in common: they feel they are "outsiders" socially and metaphysically. While most are content to live and let live, organized Jewry and gay activists like Manji must convince their constituencies they are being persecuted in order to advance their hostile agenda: to shred the social fabric.

These activists are financed and promoted by the financial elite whose goal is to control society by destabilizing it.

CONCLUSION

The political ramifications of Manji's crusade became clear when she referred to Israel's occupation of the West Bank and Gaza as a "double occupation."

She acknowledged that indeed there was a military occupation. But she spoke of how Palestinians are "occupied ideologically" by their religion, which made them reject Israel's "many generous peace offers."

She related a conversation she had in Gaza City with the political chief for Hamas. He told her most suicide bombers are very successful in life and because of their religion, consider it an honor to sacrifice their lives.

She cited this as an example of Islam's fanaticism. Without condoning Hamas' tactics, clearly there would be less resistance in general if Muslims were stripped of their religion and culture.

What better way to disinherit Muslims than encourage them to become "free thinkers" like all the courageous and independent "free thinkers" for hire here in the West.

These days the champions of freedom, diversity, human rights and tolerance wear a deceptive face. One such face belongs to Irshad Manji.

HUGH HEFNER

Why All Porn is Gay

IN 2004, a woman revealed details of Hugh Hefner's sex life. If the Playboy founder is any indication, a life dedicated to porn and free sex leads to homosexuality and impotence. In old age, the former symbol of suave masculinity is a grotesque self-parody.

Hefner, 79, pays a bevy of whores $2000 a week to be his girlfriends and have sex with him every Wednesday and Friday. He uses Viagra and watches male gay porn to stay erect while as many as ten concubines mount him in succession. The other girls simulate lesbian sex to arouse him.

"He doesn't really do anything," says Jill Anne Spaulding, author of the book *"Upstairs."* He just lies there with his Viagra erection. It's just a fake erection, and each girl gets on top of him for two minutes while the girls in the background try to keep him excited. They'll yell things like, "F-k her daddy, f-k her daddy!" There's a lot of cheerleader going on!"

No one becomes a playmate without having intercourse with Hefner. The "girl next door" is a whore; and Hefner's maudlin example of arrested development is the fitting epitaph for the Playboy Philosophy.

Playboy was not a spontaneous phenomenon. It was social engineering designed to foster homosexuality and family breakdown. This is why Spaulding's revelations get little publicity.

DEFINING HOMOSEXUAL AND HETEROSEXUAL

The "establishment" agenda is to destabilize and neuter us by encouraging homosexual behavior. They redefine "homosexual" as a "sexual preference" or "lifestyle choice" in order to entrap us. Never mind that the vast majority of homosexuals come from dysfunctional families or suffered sexual abuse as youths. Our reluctance to embrace homosexuality is considered "bigotry."

In response, let's take liberties with these definitions ourselves. Having the right paradigm is the key to healthy behavior.

Forget about what you normally think of gay or straight (same-sex, opposite sex etc.) Think of heterosexuality as *monogamous* and concerned with love and reproduction. Think of homosexuality as *promiscuous* and concerned with sterile sex without for its own sake.

Heterosexuality involves bonding permanently with a *member of the opposite sex* for love and usually procreation. It is participating in the natural life cycle, reflecting the intrinsic meaning of life in every stage. Personal and societal health depends on heterosexuality.

Homosexuality is arrested development due to an inability to form a heterosexual bond. As a result, homosexuals apparently compensate using sex as a surrogate for love.

In these terms, society has become more homosexual because heterosexuals now fail to permanently bond. Normally, heterosexuals marry and put sex in perspective, focusing on more important things.

A perceptive reader recently wrote: "If heterosexual sex outside of marriage is acceptable, if we eliminate the procreative aspect from sex, are heterosexuals any different from homosexuals in regards to the sexual activity?"

Our attitude to children is also homosexual. Children are viewed as a burden and nuisance rather than as an extension of ourselves, organic growth, and a source of love and joy.

Cheating is cheating, even when it's same-sex. In the movie "Brokeback Mountain", the two men betray their wives and children in the most egregious fashion. Yet the movie ends on a nostalgia note recalling the glory days having sex on Brokeback Mountain. In our Illuminist-controlled culture, self-indulgence will always trump personal and social responsibility.

I do not disparage gays. According to my definitions, the majority of homosexuals are actually "heterosexuals" like Hugh Hefner. And a small minority of homosexuals are monogamous and partake in some heterosexual values.

HOW SEX BECAME AN ACT OF HATE

The movies are even more effective in fostering homosexuality. Sex is no longer reserved for a loving relationship. Often it is something you do with *your enemies.*

Recently I saw *"Dr. No"* (1962) again. The fashionable James Bond has sex with a woman even after he realizes she tried *to kill him.* After they have sex, Bond has her imprisoned.

In the movie *Munich* (2006), the Israeli assassins confront an attractive woman who killed their colleague. She bares herself and suggests her death would be "a waste of talent." She shares our reality and thinks they might have sex with a woman they intend to kill.

Human beings are malleable and take their standards from movies. There is nothing so destructive to human society as the separation of sex and love and procreation. It reduces men and women to dogs.

The Illuminati agenda is to degrade humanity. It wishes to harness sex in the interests of hate. Love is the enemy of hate and must be destroyed.

ALL PORN IS GAY

According to our definition of homosexuality, (i.e. promiscuity outside of love and/or procreation), all pornography is gay. The porn consumer is engaged in a promiscuous masturbatory fantasy. He is not focused on his marriage and progeny.

From what I have said, it should be clear that homosexuality is incompatible with heterosexuality, just as promiscuity is incompatible with monogamy. Gay activists admit their goal is to destroy heterosexuality.

Pornography is poisoning heterosexuality. There is a place for tasteful nudity as a stopgap while seeking marriage.

But as you know, pornography has reached epidemic proportions. "Adult Video News" predicts revenue of $12.6 billion this year. The Internet has four million porn sites. TV and pop music increasingly are pornographic.

Pornography warps the way a man sees all women and girls. Many sites include girls as young as 14. Young females learn they are useful for one thing only and try to get love the only way they know.

I hate to burst the bubble on a billion dollar industry: Young naked women are practically identical. They have the same equipment. Do men need to see literally thousands of examples?

There is something addictive here. Why don't men get sick of it? Why don't they suffer from gynaecologist's fatigue? The plethora of breasts and splayed legs takes the wonder out of sex and causes impotence. Maybe this is the point: new drugs will keep people running on empty.

We take another step to becoming robots.

At various times, Communists in the USSR considered "nationalizing" women, making them a public resource. Pornography does this. The most intimate pictures of millions of women are available to all and sundry.

The satanic aspect of the sexual revolution and pornography lies in the acceptance of anonymous sex: seeing human beings as commodities.

BETTY FRIEDAN

The Making of A Feminist

IN THE 1950's, the founder of modern feminism had a serious inferiority complex.

At parties she would introduce herself: "I'm Betty Friedan -- and I graduated Summa Cum Laude from Smith."

Friedan's mother had made her feel inadequate. She compensated by rejecting femininity and convincing women to adopt the male role instead.

In her candid autobiography, *"My Life So Far"* (2000) Friedan (born, Betty Naomi Goldstein) says that no matter what she did, her mother made her feel "messy, clumsy, inadequate, bad, naughty, ugly." (26)

Friedan spent years in psychoanalysis "talking endlessly about how I hated my mother and how she had killed my father." (121) "All mothers should be drowned at birth," she used to say in her 20's. (131)

Her mother, Miriam Horowitz Goldstein was the spoiled daughter of a doctor who at 20 made a loveless marriage to "an older Jewish businessman" a jeweller almost twice her age. She was ashamed he had "no formal American education and a heavy Jewish accent." He could do nothing right. (17)

But, instead of seeing that her parent's marriage was the problem, Betty Friedan chose to blame the traditional feminine role. She attributed her mother's unloving behavior to her lack of a satisfying career.

Also ostracized by her classmates, Friedan vowed that "they may not like me" but one day "they are going to have to look up to me." (25)

In other words, Friedan was a classic social misfit, the kind that the elite use to undermine society.

Fame and fortune came her way with her book "The Feminine Mystique," (1963) which devalued the traditional feminine role and stripped women of their "mystique."

Husband and children need the gracious love of a young wife or mother. This nurturing feminine charm was a woman's "mystique." Women don't mind sacrificing if it is appreciated.

In her book, Friedan said family-oriented women had no identity of their own and family was "a comfortable concentration camp." She devalued the countless priceless things a real woman does for her children and husband.

With the help of the elite media, Friedan convinced women to deny their natural identity as wife and mother and seek it from jobs and employers.

Friedan projected her trauma over her personal ugliness and lack-of-mother-love on other women, at incalculable cost to society.

FRIEDAN AS LATENT LESBIAN

In the "Naked Ape," Desmond Morris describes the origins of homosexuality as follows. (I will modify to emphasize the lesbian outcome.):

"If, in the parental situation, the offspring are exposed to an unduly masculine and dominant mother, or an unduly weak and effeminate father, then this will give rise to considerable confusion... If when they become sexually mature, the [daughters] seek mates with the behavioural rather than anatomical qualities of the [father,] they are liable to take [female] mates rather than [males.] For the [sons] there is a similar risk in reverse." (p.86]

Friedan's mother was dominant and had the male role. That's why Friedan wanted her to have a career. Possibly feminism was her attempt to make women do the same thing, act like her mother, ie. the man she wanted her father to be.

FRIEDAN'S MARRIAGE

In her autobiography, Friedan portrays herself as a devoted housewife who wanted to avoid her own mother's mistakes. But in fact she emulated her mother and threatened to castrate her husband.

When she claimed to be "a battered wife," her ex, Carl Friedan, started a web site (now discontinued) to give his side of the story. He said she was unstable and often attacked him. Her bruises were due to his self-defense. His injuries were worse. He even cites a police report as proof. In another case, he writes: [WARNING FOUL LANGUAGE]

"Quite vivid in my mind is a midnight in about 1967 - a year or so before Betty and I separated for good. We were living at our Dakota apartment then - Betty disagreed with something I said (that's all it took), went into one of her raging uncontrollable fits, screaming, her face twisted in hate and insane anger, "You fucking no good prick you, you no-good bastard, you fucking bastard, " meanwhile sprinting into the kitchen. Back she came straight at me brandishing two large kitchen knives. "You fucking Goddamn sonuvabitch, I'm going to cut your fucking cock off - your big cock it doesn't mean a thing to me." At this, I calmly picked up a kitchen chair, nailed her to the wall like a lion-tamer and took the knives away. And that was just a minor incident during that period when her explosive personality was further inflamed by amphetamines she was taking for weight loss, reinforced by alcohol."

Carl Friedan, who had an advertising agency told the NY Post that Betty's image as a typical housewife was a ruse:

"She didn't know what I was doing," he claimed. "I won prizes and had full-page ads in all the New York papers. She didn't care."

According to Carl, Betty was no stay-at-home mom.

"We had a full-time maid during our entire [19-year] marriage. That's who took care of the [three] kids, cooked - everything," he said. "I would say as a housewife, on a scale of 0 to 10, she was a 2."

Carl Friedan's memories are not motivated by politics. He is proud of his ex-wife's accomplishments:

"She changed the course of history almost single-handedly. It took a driven, super-aggressive, egocentric, almost lunatic dynamo to rock the world the way she did. Unfortunately, she was that same person at home, where that kind of conduct doesn't work. She simply never understood this."

OTHER SOURCES:
FRIEDAN'S "JUDAISM" AND COMMUNISM

When Betty was preparing for her "Bat Mitzvah" (like a Confirmation) at age 13, she confessed to her Reform rabbi that she did not believe in God.

Instead of giving his young ward a sense of what God is, this impostor said: "All right, but keep it to yourself until after confirmation." (22)

Friedan's Judaism amounts to a sense that "I have to use my life to make the world better, have to protest, step off the sidewalk and march against injustice." Because she was rejected as a Jew by the rich country club set in her hometown of Peoria, she "now identified with the working class, also oppressed by the masters of the universe..."(71)

People like Friedan prefer to "change the world" than heal themselves. They tend to do very well by "doing good." While writing this book, she received a one- million-dollar grant from the Ford Foundation. Aren't they the "masters of the universe?" The Friedans of this world just want to be members of this club.

Doesn't it occur to these socialists, feminists and Communists that if they were really a threat to the establishment, they wouldn't be hauling in $120,000 salaries as full professors? Don't they realize they are brainwashing the young, destabilizing society and setting the stage for a totalitarian state?

Friedan was a lifelong Communist. In the book, she tries to distance herself from Communism, describing it in terms of youthful idealism. We'll never know if she was a conscious agent or a dupe. She knew Kurt Lewin who had been in charge of social engineering at Tavistock. (45)

The elite media hyped Friedan to the heavens because the Lucifer-loving bankers wanted women to have jobs instead of families. It's possible Friedan was perfectly sincere. With her history, she would want to destroy what she didn't have, the "Feminine Mystique." She poisoned the well of femininity and sent the family into a death spiral. Women traded sundresses for overalls and business suits.

In our upside-down world, failures and crazies like Betty Friedan become "prophets".

DOWN & DIRTY

How Feminism Killed Courtship on Campus

THANKS TO FEMINISM, co-eds today do not endure the daily humiliation of courtship. They don't worry about young men offering flowers or asking them out for dinner or a movie.

The days of dating when young men sought them as friends, and possible wives and mothers are gone.

Thanks to the humanizing influence of feminism, young women can deaden themselves with alcohol and immediately give their bodies to strangers without any awkward "get acquainted" period. They can engage in degrading sex acts without fear of repressive and outdated "patriarchal" morality.

This is the picture of college sexual mores in an article "*Sex and Scandal at Duke [University]*" by Janet Reitman in a recent issue of Rolling Stone magazine. It typifies the scene at most universities.

"Whatever sex goes on, the girls say, is done in the context of the "hook up" which describes anything from making out to full-on intercourse. Much to the disappointment of many students, female and male, there's no real dating scene at Duke -- true for a lot of colleges."

"I've never been asked out on a date in my entire life -- not once," says one stunning brunette. Nor has a guy ever bought her a drink. "I think that if anybody ever did that, I would ask him if he were on drugs," she says.

Rather, there's the casual one-night stand, usually bolstered by heavy drinking and followed the next morning by -- well, nothing, usually. "You'll hook up with a guy, and you know that nothing will come out of it," says Anna. The best thing you can hope for, she says, "is that you'll get to hook up with him again." Some girls they know have managed to score a regular hook up -- meaning consistent sex

-- but others play the field, bouncing from one guy to the next."

The phrase "whatever sex goes on" is an understatement.

"Traditional intercourse is common, and oral sex nearly ubiquitous, regarded as a form of elaborate kissing that doesn't really mean very much. "Everybody gives blowjobs now," says Naomi.

"Before," she adds -- meaning a pre-Monica/pre-Britney "before" -- "it used to be you'd have sex and then give one." But now, girls give them freely -- on their own initiative, she says. (They also tend to get as much as they give, at least according to Duke men.)"

If this article is any indication, feminism has done nothing for young women's self esteem. Even though these girls get A's and are beautiful, they vie to give their body to high status males, (athletes and fraternity men.)

The reason? Other women are so sexually available; this is the only way they can get status and attention.

"I found myself falling into this thing," says Allison. "It made me very uncomfortable and unhappy, because it's not a way to live. But if I didn't do these things and he broke up with me for some reason, two days from now he'd have somebody else. That's just how it works...If my mother knew; she would smack me across the face. I was not brought up in this kind of environment."

In the past, the requirement of courtship and marriage for sex actually empowered women. Marriage was like a trade union. Want sex? Get married. Now all young women are like scabs. They perform and get nothing in return. The market has collapsed. The girls are desperate.

Young men treat them with contempt as illustrated by one male Duke blogger. (Please excuse the language.)

"These delightful young ladies deal with their massive insecurity by getting fucked by frat boys. Lucky for us guys, frat boys treat sorority girls like shit. As soon as Sally Pi Phi thinks she has secured Johnny Soccer Player, Johnny is off boning Chrissy Tri Delta . . .. All of this leads to unhappy, insecure girls all fighting to get rammed by someone of status."

This is the fruit of "equality." Young women express their "independence" by seeking status from males and being promiscuous and aggressive. "Sometimes, girls will be like, 'I'm just horny and I want to have sex,'" one says...."It's our decision if we're going to allow ourselves to be subjected to negative treatment. It's all framed by the way [other] girls behave."

Feminism depicts traditional women as " chattel" oppressed by their husbands. But by undermining the morality (fidelity, chastity) inherent in family roles, feminism has robbed women of their natural identity (wife, mother) and degraded them more than ever.

In the heterosexual contract (love/ marriage) women surrender power (symbolized by sex) in exchange for male love, which a man must first demonstrate through patient courtship. Take away that contract, and women get nothing in return for their power (which is symbolized by intercourse.).

Needless to say, young women who prostitute themselves for status are less likely to have successful marriages. How often can a woman be possessed before it becomes meaningless? Can a woman who jumps from bed to bed take a vow of "for better or for worse?" Can a man?

This trend is part of a gradual process of eliminating marriage and family by imposing the male homosexual model on society. Studies indicate that less than 10% of male gays form permanent relationships, and that the vast majority are promiscuous with 43% of them having more than 500 sex partners in their lifetime.

Using feminism as a lever, elite social engineers are foisting this model on society as a whole. Aldous Huxley warned us about it in *Brave New World* (1932) where promiscuity was encouraged, marriage and family proscribed and children born in state-sponsored hatcheries. This is where sexual behaviour at elite universities like Duke is leading. These are the "women's rights" our decadent society is fighting to impose on the Muslim world.

GIRLS ADRIFT

The Young Lady is a Tramp

IN DEC. 2003, a baseball player was sentenced to 45 days in prison for having sex with minors.

Cass Rynes, 19, from Prince Edward Island received oral sex from two local girls age 12 and 13. He maintained they pursued him, and he thought they were older.

This unusual case has drawn attention to a disturbing social phenomenon: pubescent girls from all social strata think it's a sign of maturity to dispense blowjobs.

A 2002 Health Canada survey found that one-third of all Grade Nine students (age 13) and more than half of all Grade Eleven students (age 15) report having oral sex.

Freelance writer Sara Wilson talked to typical girls and found that oral sex is not uncommon when teens gather without supervision.

Apparently girls will do just about anything to be loved (i.e. "popular.") Oral sex is considered "cool." Often they don't even know the boys and don't see them again.

The following is from Wilson's article "Good Girls Do" (*Globe and Mail*, Feb 7, 2004)

Typically, "the guy will just use the girl," says Vanessa, 13. She bears the full weight of a nasty double standard, being labelled a "slut," "whore" or "ho" while he gets praised by friends.

Still, those labels aren't as disparaging as they once were. For young girls, even negative attention can be extremely attractive. "Even if they're talking about you poorly, they're still talking about you." She adds, "To get the name 'slut', at least that means…you're like older."

Whereas a girl's first period used to signal her entrance into womanhood, now "you're a woman if you ...fool around with lots and lots of people," Leslie says.

Kate agrees: When she and her girlfriends performed oral sex, "we were pretty proud."

Wilson concludes that feminist empowerment has led to female debauchery: "Ever since the advent of Girl Power, being aggressively sexy has practically become a political statement. Pop-culture figureheads such as Christina Aguilera or Beyonce play out every bump-and-grind signal of sexual availability..."

(In homosexual culture, aggressive sexuality and promiscuity are also viewed as a political statement.)

Sex education classes also may be to blame. They actually encourage young girls to engage in oral sex, ostensibly to "cut down on pregnancies." According to one UK report, schoolchildren, particularly girls, who received such training, developed a 'more mature' response to sex.

OUR DECEITFUL LIBERAL MIND SET

We are taught to equate self-discipline with repression. Self-indulgence, on the other hand, is equated with liberation and self-expression.

In fact, the opposite is true. Dedication to an ideal makes us powerful and free while dissipation weakens and enslaves us to temptation or peer pressure.

We are taught to think it courageous to defy traditional social mores. The stodgy "establishment" wants to prevent us from having fun and discovering ourselves.

In fact, the real establishment consists of a well-organized network of superrich criminals, pedophiles, Satanists and drug dealers. See the book, *"The Franklin Cover-Up"* by John De Camp.

Their goal is to consolidate their dominant position in a global fascist police state that they call the New World Order. They are waging a secret war against humanity to destroy our "sources of natural and social energy, and physical, mental and emotional strength." *("Silent Weapons for Secret Wars.")*

The message teenage girls get from music videos and sex education classes is designed to make them unfit for marriage and motherhood. Our secret masters think of humanity as cattle.

Promiscuous girls are not defying the establishment or affirming themselves. They are falling into a trap and ruining their chances for a happy life.

ANOTHER EXAMPLE: SLUT POWER

A spate of new books exhorts women to overcome their inhibitions about casual sex.

Typical is *"Happy Hook-Up: A Single Girl's Guide to Casual Sex"* (2005) which counsels women to proudly embrace the labels "whore" and "slut." It has been excerpted on ivillage.com

Authors Alexa Sherman and Nicole Tocantins pretend to be offering women "options" (as with careers.) Typical of feminists, their real agenda is coercive and subversive, to prevent women from getting married and starting families.

"Cultural norms will catch up with us *if we give them no choice,"* the authors write.

"We, as females, need to show the world that sex without commitment is absolutely our prerogative... Say, "I'm a slut I'm a whore! I love sex!" and mean it. Society needs to change and begin to encourage women to find pleasure for pleasure's sake."

Pleasurable sex in the context of a loving marriage isn't mentioned as an "option."

Women are naturally monogamous. Surveys indicate they do not find casual sex satisfying and mostly regret it. Thus "Happy Hook-up" is devoted to helping women overcome their natural instincts.

Women are instructed not to get to know their sex partner too well. "Try not to discuss too much about your past or future or his. That said, it never hurts to inquire about his sexual history [and] gauge what risks are involved. Then, focus on the action and the action alone."

They are told to terminate the relationship after one or two trysts and distract themselves with work or hobbies.

Don't think about "what's going to happen next, whether he's going to call you, want you and be your everything. It's just not going to happen honey. At least don't expect it to. Stay in control... accept that that's it. Finito. The end. Flip him over. He's done."

Unbelievable! There is no such thing as casual sex. As a male friend said to me, "I've known this woman in the most intimate way possible and I don't especially like her. It feels unnatural."

GOOD MEN DON'T MARRY SLUTS

A young woman's charm is her capital. She must invest it wisely rather than squander it.

This requires that she make marriage and family her primary focus. Otherwise her romantic and maternal instincts will be frustrated, and she will be alone and unhappy.

A young woman's beauty reflects her physical and spiritual innocence. Men find innocence very attractive; it balances them emotionally and spiritually. A hard and cynical woman is not attractive to men.

A young woman must consecrate her innocence for the man whom she will eventually love and marry. Her thoughts should be focused on him and on her future children. She should prepare herself to be a worthy wife and mother.

There is no more beautiful sight than a young mother looking after her children. The other day I saw a tall lithe young woman in the park playing with twin daughters on the swing. What a rare sight these days when governments herd children into soulless daycares and women into fluorescent-lit offices.

"Are those children yours?" I asked.

She affirmed they were. She was glowing.

"Congratulations," I said. "They're beautiful!"

How much affirmation do these women get in popular culture? Zip. Rather girls and young women are encouraged to squander their innocence. Who can doubt that the devil's servants are coordinating this disgrace?

ORGANIZED EVIL

We're Being Brainwashed to be Gay

I WANT YOU TO COMPARE THE MESSAGES you are getting about two very different groups: homosexuals and nuclear families.

HOMOSEXUALS:

According to many psychiatrists, homosexuality is a state of arrested development caused by having an unloving father, and a controlling overbearing mother. As one gay acquaintance said, referring to his father, "I always wanted the love of a man."

Gay behavior is often characterized by extreme promiscuity (100's of partners); anonymous sex (typified by the "glory hole"); wallowing in feces and urine; and sadomasochism. This behavior may increase the frequency of AIDS. The powerful gay lobby's refusal to allow preventive measures has resulted in a deadly epidemic. And because some gays insisted on donating blood, many hemophiliacs and others became infected. (See "A Radical Holocaust" in *The Politics of Bad Faith,* 1998, by David Horowitz)

What is the message government and media give us about this self-destructive behavior? We're told that we are bigots and hate mongers to question it. We're told that AIDS is a sexually transmitted disease that affects everyone equally. We must all practice "safe sex" and teach it to children in schools. This is a lie. Seventy five per cent of AIDS fatalities are gay. The rest get it from infected needles or blood transfusions. (See *The Myth of Heterosexual Aids,* (1990) by Michael Fumento) We are told that homosexuality is like left-handedness. It is "a sexual orientation" as normal as heterosexuality. It is a matter of socialization. If a baby boy is given dolls or dressed in pink, he'll act like a girl. There is no such thing as biological sexual instinct. (For how untrue this is, see *"As Nature Made Him: The Boy Who Was Raised as a Girl"*, 2000, by John Colapinto)

NUCLEAR FAMILIES:

Unlike homosexuals who are normal, nuclear families are almost always dysfunctional. Have you ever seen a positive portrayal? The worst offender is the "patriarchal" father, who labors to provide for his wife and children. After consulting with his family, he may insist on providing leadership. In times of war or danger, he may sacrifice his life. But don't be fooled. He is usually a violent alcoholic who beats and sexually abuses his wife and children.

Almost as evil as the patriarchal father is the poor dupe called the "wife," "homemaker" or "mother." This is a woman who actually feels a profound connection to her husband and child. She calls it "love." Because of it, she will nurture her child herself, which is very bad for her career. Inevitably, government sponsored programs or the media will teach her that she is a victim of "oppressive stereotypes" and she will divorce.

CONCLUSION:

People who generally fornicate like rabbits, may wallow in shit and may spread deadly epidemics are normal. People who sacrifice their lives for love, who nurture and create the next generation, are "oppressors" "doormats", or "old fashioned." This campaign to make heterosexuals act like homosexuals is not an accident.

Powerful forces in government, corporations, media and education are brainwashing us. Daily, they assault our identities as males and females, husband and wives, fathers and mothers. Ninety per cent of marriage breakups are due to women being brainwashed to seek "equality" which in practice means controlling and emasculating their husbands.

Gay and feminist activists pretend society is oppressing them when in fact heterosexual society is the victim. This is passive aggressive. They are clubbing us over the head and then calling us homophobes for reacting. But gay and feminist activists are just pawns, empowered and manipulated by greater forces. The ultimate purpose is some kind of "New World Order" where emotionally starved people who have no culture or identity can be manipulated by sexual signals.

To understand how sinister this is, read Dr. Judith Reisman's article about the Hepatitus B vaccinations of normal American children. Hepatitis B is venereal disease which is rarely found in children unless they are infected by their birth mother. It is not a threat to the vast majority of American children. But it is a threat to pedophiles because it identifies a child who has been sexually abused. According to Reisman, in order to protect pedophiles, more than 80% of newborn American children are being injected with this vaccine, which may have dangerous side effects. Reisman writes: "Government justifications for imperilling the health of all healthy American newborns as a means of protecting a largely antisocial adult sex and drug subculture is without historical or scientific precedent."

In conclusion, we are lulled into believing that we are in a Golden Age, the "end of history." But events like Sept. 11 are a rude reminder that the passions and perversions that shaped the past will shape the future. Judeo Christian civilization is being overthrown and replaced with a new fascist totalitarianism. The plan requires the destruction of our sources of individual strength and meaning, the nuclear family. We must organize and act. We must bombard politicians, media and corporations with the message that we are on to them, and they will pay.

"How America Went Gay" by Dr. Charles Socarides
can be found at http://www.leaderu.com/jhs/socarides.html

Book Three

How Heterosexuality Works

HOW I BECAME A "MENSCH"

After Feminism Stole My Identity

WHEN I WAS 21, and living in Israel, I received a letter from my mother. She had taken my savings and invested in a town house.

"Now, you are a mensch," she said.

What did she mean? How did owning a house make me "a man?" I wanted to be defined by character, not by my real estate.

I came of age at a time (the 1960's) when youth was "looking for identity." I was searching for it in Israel. Later, I became a Canadian nationalist. In neither case did I find identity in "community."

For centuries, men have defined their identities *in terms of masculinity.* Why was I so clueless?

I had a strong patriarchal father who was an excellent role model. He built a successful career, and supported his family well.

"Work is the backbone of a man," he would tell me. A man's most important decision is finding a profession he enjoys. A wife is the second.

But for some reason, his example didn't register. Why not?
I was a feminist.

THE ERA OF MIND CONTROL

I grew up in an era that swallowed the feminist lie that men and women are identical. In our culture, women are encouraged to do everything men do, and vice-versa. I believe in equal opportunity but feminists act as if *equal* means *identical* and this retarded my personal development by 25 years. I doubt if I am alone.

"Identical" made me look for myself in a mate. I was literally attracted to lithe young women with cropped boyish haircuts: my

Jungian persona.

I sublimated my search for identity in love for a woman. I idealized her. Love would give me my soul, my *self*. Some young women were immediately repelled. Others enjoyed the adulation for a while but eventually lost respect.

What I needed was someone quite different, my feminine complement; a helpmate, not a soul mate.

It hasn't hit us yet, but eventually feminism will be recognized for what it is: a subversive, anti-feminine, anti-heterosexual ideology that neuters both men and women so they cannot bond permanently. It diverts women into careers and promiscuity, and men like me into the dead end of idealization.

Women have usurped the masculine identity, and in the process both sexes have lost their own. Unbelievably, the destruction of heterosexuality is the stated goal of many feminists. They believe gender differences are not only unnatural but also *the source of all injustice.*

The leading feminist thinkers, including Betty Friedan and Simone de Beauvoir, were Communists, and many also were lesbians. But they wouldn't have succeeded had they been up front about their bizarre "revolutionary" goal: Destroy the heterosexual family.

Talk about "equality" and "choice" is a ruse. If feminism were really about *choice,* it would not coerce women to enter the work force and become "independent." It would not demonize men, heterosexuality and family.

Feminism is not about choice. "No women should be authorized to stay at home and raise her children," said Simone de Beauvoir. "Women should not have that choice, because if there is such a choice, too many women will make that one." (*Saturday Review,* June 14, 1975)

Feminism is lesbian in the sense that lesbians have always hated the female role and coveted the male role. It is based on Marxist notions of "equality" and class conflict that have no relevance to a mystical and biological phenomenon such as love.

Feminism is a cheap swindle designed to cheat both women and men out of family. People are so naïve.

We don't find wholeness by incorporating masculine and feminine in ourselves; but by uniting with our complement. Heterosexual love is the attraction of opposites. Indeed, as heterosexuals we define ourselves in terms of these differences. If we are male, we are not female, and vice-versa, like darkness and light. Because I denied these differences, I didn't know who I was. I didn't understand women, and I didn't know how to relate to them.

FINDING MASCULINE IDENTITY

I was almost 50-years-old before I solved the riddle. A book *The Flight from Woman* (1964) by psychiatrist Karl Stern confirmed what my instincts were telling me. My mother had been right all along. *The man makes the house; the woman makes the home.*

According to Stern, masculinity is defined by power. Men provide the physical, social and cultural context for the private world of family. Men are protectors and providers. They are the risk takers, adventurers and builders.

Femininity is defined by "loving relationships." Feminine psychology is based on nurturing husband and children, and being needed and loved in return. Women circulate love in the family much like the heart pumps blood through the body. Their self-sacrifice starts love on its circuit.

Femininity comes from love of husband, children and home. While men define themselves by deeds, women simply "are" beauty, grace, faith and goodness. Men tend to be rational and objective, women subjective, intuitive and emotional.

The idea that traditional sex roles are "oppressive" is wrong. For most people, a flexible interpretation of traditional roles is essential for happiness and fulfillment.

I extrapolated from Karl Stern's distinctions.

If men want power and women want love, then heterosexual love must be an *exchange of the two.*

A woman surrenders her power, in trust. This is how a woman expresses her love: by trusting. In this way, women actually *empower* men. If a man betrays this trust, the contract is broken. He loses his power.

In return for accepting his leadership, a woman gets what she really wants: a man's power expressed as intense, undivided love for her. He includes her in his sphere of self-interest. This is how two people become one. She is part of him. Her happiness is his happiness.

Women want masculine power, but in a man. A girlfriend said that without a man, she feels "like a rudderless boat." Similarly, a man without a woman feels like a rudder without a boat.

FEMINISTS SUBVERT HETEROSEXUALITY

Teaching women to challenge masculine power prevents them from getting the love they really seek. A man cannot love a woman who is competing with him for power. Masculinity is defined by power; such a woman is challenging his identity.

Relationships between so-called "equals" are like mergers or roommates. Psychiatrist Irene Claremont de Castillejo calls them "brother-sister" marriages (*Knowing Women: A Feminine Psychology,* 1973). They cannot achieve the intimacy as when a woman surrenders her will to a man, and a man returns this trust with wholehearted love. Some psychiatrists say sexual satisfaction is also linked to this ability to trust and surrender power completely. (See below *"The Power of Sexual Surrender"*)

Feminine women are creatures of God. In love, they sacrifice their "selves" in return for love. In many religions, this is the key to transcendence.

In her classic *The Psychology of Women: A Psychoanalytic Interpretation* (1944), Helen Deutsch described this in "masochist-narcissist" terms. Women sacrifice themselves in return for being cherished and loved. The majority of women fulfill themselves in this way, by becoming wives and mothers. Of course, this is what nature intended.

Women cannot love men with whom they compete. Women are "hypergamous." This means they seek men of higher status than themselves. Even the most ardent heterosexual feminist only can love someone more powerful than she. Needless to say the higher she rises, the slimmer the pickings.

The struggle for power is poisoning male-female relations. It is the death of love. Men cannot give up their defining characteristic and expect to be men. Women cannot criticize and challenge men and expect to be loved. When finally I comprehended this, I felt liberated. I established a healthy relationship with a female complement, and married her.

CONCLUSION

The universal complaint is that men don't know how to be men, and women how to be women. It helps to see heterosexual love as a mystical dance. In a dance, the male leads the female follows. You can't have a graceful dance without each partner playing his or her part.

The dance is love. The male is always considering his mate's wishes because he loves her. In a ballroom dance, who can say which role is more important? Both partners are of equal value. The dance requires both the dynamism of the male, and the beauty, grace and love of the female.

RECLAIMING MALE POWER

In the Viagra Age

YOU'VE HEARD OF THE "STONE AGE," the "Iron Age" and the "Information Age." This is the "Viagra Age," the era of male impotence.

Television commercials state that 1/3 of all men suffer from "erectile dysfunction" due to high blood pressure, prostate cancer or diabetes. I suspect the culprit is often feminism.

Women should empower men but for a long time they have been doing just the opposite. Instead of taking the little blue pill, men need to reclaim their masculine power.

Feminism has created a power struggle as women covet the male role and want men to take the female one. A friend describes his married friends as "wolves circling one another."

The problem is always the same: women want to supplant their husbands. In the workplace, a man can accept leadership from a competent woman. But in the home, a man who takes orders from a woman is not a man, and usually can't perform like one. He feels like a child.

Power is synonymous with masculine identity. Impotence literally means "powerless." We would never say a woman is "impotent." Rather, she is "infertile" or "frigid" implying her natural receptivity. A man cannot love if he does not have power. He expresses his love by exercising his power. Women take away male power and wonder why they aren't loved.

I felt liberated when I understood that power is what being a man is about. I decided to look abroad for a traditional woman. After a misstep in the Philippines (described in my book *"A Long Way to go for a Date"*), I married in 2001 an educated intelligent Mexican woman from a secular Jewish background similar to my own. For the first time in my life, I found happiness and stability.

We have an almost frictionless relationship. She tells me what she's thinking but she never tells me what to do (i.e. control.) She never complains, criticizes or competes. (These are the four C's to avoid in women.) In the past, women constantly blackmailed me by acting distant or making childish scenes. In the first year of this marriage, I still cringed in expectation of this.

Don't think my relationship is rigid. I do all the shopping and cooking and do my best to make her happy. If you love someone, you want her to be happy.

POWER FOR LOVE

The gesture of a man opening a door for a woman illustrates how men and women should relate. We all know a woman can open a door herself. But when a man does it, he is affirming her femininity, beauty and charm. When she accepts this gesture, she is validating his masculine power. *This trade, a woman surrendering physical power in exchange for a man's protection (i.e. love) is the essence of heterosexuality.* In order to develop emotionally, men and women need this mutual validation as much as they need sex itself. Sex is an expression of it.

Under the toxic influence of feminism, women open their own doors. Neither sexual identity is validated; neither sex matures emotionally. Men feel redundant and impotent; women feel rejected and unsexed.

REGAINING MALE POWER

The following are some practical tips to help men restore their power.

• The best way to select a woman is to make a demand. If she salutes smartly and says, "Oui, mon Capitaine," she's hired. OK I'm exaggerating but you get the point. On a summer day, I met a young woman who was roller-skating. I asked her to take off her sunglasses so I could see her face. She obeyed. That was a positive sign. Pursue women who accede to reasonable requests. Forget the others. You will spare yourself a lifetime of misery.

• Courtship is the process by which a man earns a woman's trust (love) so that she will do what he asks. A man expresses love in terms of benevolent power and perceives a woman's acceptance of his wishes as love. Of course, a woman needs to choose a man she can trust with her life, one who makes her feel secure. A man must aspire to be worthy of this trust.

• Feminism deceives men into pursuing "independent" women and rejecting the women they actually need. Marriage is not about being independent. If a woman says, "Are you man enough for me?" or "I'm high maintenance," decline the challenge. Men are not designed to fight women. Marriage is about two people becoming one and that only happens when a woman surrenders her will to a man in exchange for love. Men should focus on women who look up to them and accept their leadership. If you're looking for your "equal" you're probably still looking for yourself.

• Men often give away their power in hopes of getting sex. For a while she is flattered, but ultimately a woman cannot respect a man she can control. She wants to be enlisted not petitioned. She wants a man to have a wholesome vision of his life, one in which she has an important place. This vision need not be elaborate or complicated. It could involve a life focused on mutual values and interests like children, music, church or the outdoors.

• There is a book entitled: *Why do I Think I am Nothing Without a Man* (1982) The author, Dr. Penelope Russianoff, tries to help women overcome this feeling. The truth is, this feeling is grounded in reality. Self-fulfillment for a woman is when the "self" is her husband and children. Women are God's creatures, they sacrifice self and nurture; in return, they are deservedly cherished. If the "self" is her personal satisfaction and career, she is already full of herself and filled. Her husband and children are secondary.

In conclusion, a man can reclaim his identity by recognizing that his power is not negotiable. It represents his ability to love, the essence of his masculinity. A man should focus on finding a woman who is receptive to him. She may be standing behind a counter rather than sitting behind an executive desk.

A single man should be aggressive and quickly sift without fear of rejection. If he knows what he wants, what she wants is less of a worry. The Internet is a godsend in this respect. He must be prepared to offer the right woman a profound relationship. She is not interested in "hooking up." Women are designed for courtship and marriage. Single men are so passive and juvenile single women today are climbing the walls.

MAN'S LOVE

Mirrors God's Love for Creation

> *"And the earth was without form, and void; and darkness was upon the face of the deep. And the Spirit of God moved upon the face of the waters."*
> *--Genesis 1-2*

EVERY YOUNG GIRL imagines being swept off her feet by Prince Charming and living "happily ever after." But imagine if the prince had sex and dumped her. Her whole being would revolt. It would feel like God had abandoned her.

In his book, *Feminism and Freedom* (1987), philosopher Michael Levin links feminist anger to the sexual revolution. In the liberated 1960's, New Left ladies slept with their boyfriends without first establishing committed relationships. After they were dumped, they expressed their sense of violation by referring to sex as "rape," vilifying "the patriarchy" and denying gender differences altogether. Women would become like men and vice-versa. (309)

As a result of the sexual revolution, millions of people today cannot marry and are in a state of arrested development. To end the chaos created by feminist propaganda, men and women need to understand who they are in relation to God, and to each other.

Marriage and family is a God-given path necessary for our fulfillment as human beings. In my view, Man represents the God Principle, woman the Creation Principle.

A measure of the subversion of society is how Marxist standards of class warfare have been applied to gender, and women duped to believe men oppress them. There is no war. God is in love with Creation and vice-versa. This mystical union is mirrored in the love of man and woman.

"Making love" is a physical expression of this mystical alchemy. It illustrates how each principle works. The Male Principle penetrates, possesses and plants the seed. The seed carries her husband's spirit and genetic code. It is the spark of creation. The female yields, receives and combines his essence with her own resulting in organic growth.

By being possessed, she also possesses. Look at the imagery. The penis is totally engulfed by the vagina. The man belongs to the woman who belongs to him.

Another metaphor is the relationship between a farmer and his land. The verb "husband" means to cultivate and manage prudently. The land gives birth and nurtures new life.

Femininity is by nature *instrumental*. Woman is a bridge to the future. She is a medium. When she is fertilized, she grows large and gives birth, transforming herself and her mate into their child. The couple is recreating itself and projecting itself into the future.

A girlfriend once told me, "I want to be used." In a way, a man channels God's love to a woman by making her a wife and a mother.

If a woman isn't chosen and used for this higher purpose, she remains unfulfilled. If she is discarded after having sex, the sting is even sharper. In her soul, the sex act is a living metaphor for the love of God. She feels rejected on a metaphysical plane. This may explain the elemental wrath of the scorned woman.

Love in a woman is synonymous with trust, openness and acceptance. Indeed, this is what a man craves most from a woman. He needs someone to believe in him. Her belief makes anything possible for him. Her faith provides the space into which the male expands. She is Creation.

A woman wants to be nurtured, used and shaped by a man's love. When a woman loves a man, she accepts his leadership. She is content to be consulted and considered.

Men forget that most women aspire to be wives. Dating is an interview. Courtship is probation. Marriage is a Sacred Covenant. Women find their bliss by being indispensable to husband and children.

A single man should have a clear sense of what his goals are, and the role he wants his wife to play. This is what many women actually want and respond to. They do not respond to men who have no plan, and are just starved for sex and love. Nor are they satisfied with men who want them to remain independent, two parallel rails that never meet.

In conclusion, having failed to create a class war between capital and labour, Illuminati Marxists created one between men and women in the guise of "feminism." The aim is the same: divide and conquer. They are creating conflict where none exists. They pervert something that is mystical and divine. They present sick behaviour as healthy. They stand between millions of people and happiness.

Men represent the God principle. Women the Creation principle. Man and woman, God and Creation need each other for completion and propagation. The way to stop the spread of feminism is for men to start acting like men, so that women may trust them enough to accept their leadership.

Men Must Champion Feminine Women

(Or Lose Them)

A FEMININE WOMAN has the effect of a sunrise on a man's soul. In the words of novelist Alex Waugh, she draws a man "into a magic circle where everything is fresher, cleaner; where there is peace, warmth, comfort. She produces in him the desire to be his best."

Nothing on earth is so fine. On this continent, increasingly nothing is so rare.

The Official State Gender Ideology, feminism, has decreed that femininity is a "stereotype" invented by men to oppress women.

Feminism is no longer about equal opportunity for women. It is a thuggish, devious synthesis of Marxism and lesbianism used by ruling elites to weaken individuals and society by undermining heterosexuality. It is to society what AIDS is to the body.

But men are also to blame. We have accepted the feminist lie that women should be independent and pursue careers. We have abandoned the many gentle loving women who instinctively want to build their lives around a man. Many men are happy to evade the responsibility of supporting and leading a family. They pursue busy, neurotic overachievers who guarantee heartbreak and divorce.

For heterosexuals to find fulfillment, each sex must assume its natural part. The sex act is a metaphor: The man's spirit pervades the female and they become one. The male spirit must be active and the female receptive.

Many men ignore willing, feminine women who can complete them. We cannot thrive unless we recognize, defend and love them.

What is a feminine woman?

1. A feminine woman is motivated by love of husband and children. She is devoted to their well-being. This is her career. A woman who is preoccupied with another demanding career must pay less attention to her family. Love is mainly *paying attention.* There is a *New Yorker* cartoon where a child wearing a welder's mask is writing, "I need love" on the wall with a blowtorch. His mother says to her friend, "He's just doing that to get attention."

A feminine woman may have another career but it is her second priority. She is not driven by personal ambition. I liked the movie *"Legally Blonde"* because the heroine showed that she could excel in the work world but why bother? She had a more important goal: a husband and family.

Career is a feminist lie. Since when are careers the source of human fulfillment? What is so great about being an Assistant Loan Manager at a bank? Or even a dentist? How many women can be brain surgeons or astronauts? Is society expected to provide legions of eager feminists "fulfilling" careers to compensate for their loveless lives?

2. Feminists are teaching women to be "strong and independent." This is not feminine. Men respond to a woman's vulnerability. We want to rescue the damsel in distress and win her favours. This archetype is also innate in women. She wants to be saved and enlisted by a man.

A feminine woman depends on a man. This doesn't mean she is an emotional waif. She is competent but she doesn't pretend to be independent. Men and women need each other to be whole. As long as I have my wife, I am self-sufficient. So is she.

3. Just as the woman is the heart of the family, the man is the head and shoulders. A feminine woman is her husband's partner. They make decisions together but he has the last word. Men must be the visionaries, the navigators, and the captains. A woman's most important decision is the man she chooses to love (i.e. trust).

4. A woman wants to be loved more than anything in the world. She wants to be "known" in all her divinity. This happens when she is truly loved. The Bible uses the word "know" as in Abraham "knew" Sarah, to speak of sexual intercourse. All women are beautiful when they are loved.

Women's liberation has taught women to pursue sex for its own sake, as though they were men. This is not feminine. If a man prefers a new car, why would he marry a "used" woman? He doesn't want a car that's been driven by other men. He doesn't know what damage has been done. "A man wants to be a woman's first lover; a woman wants to be his last," my wife says.

I'm not saying women must save their virginity until marriage but certainly sex should be reserved for long-term loving relationships. Men need to stop looking for sex and start looking for the right woman. That's the best guarantee of good sex anyway.

If men chose wives with the same attention as they choose cars, more marriages would succeed. Women are the vehicles to the future, in terms of emotional fulfillment and family. If men knew where they wanted to go, they would choose the women who would get them there. They would not be blinded by sex.

5. A feminine woman *tries to please the man she loves.* Pleasing a man has not been outlawed; it just seems that way. A feminine woman generates love by giving love. She empowers her man by believing in him. Love is expressed in actions and effort. Baking a pie is an act of love. So is making the home inviting. Are we so blind, impoverished and demoralized that we cannot appreciate this? Why have we allowed feminists to stigmatize homemaking? Women would be more than happy to be wives, mothers and homemakers if they received the recognition and appreciation they deserved.

A feminine woman has grace, beauty and wisdom. These all come from staying in touch with her spirit and not pursuing an exhausting career requiring brutish masculine qualities.

On the "Oprah" Show, I saw three 20-something women interviewed about the "quarter-life" crisis. They were having trouble getting their careers on track, and because of their families' high expectations, they were *falling apart.*

Oprah urged these girls to "follow their instincts." No one suggested that this might entail *having a baby.* No one is following their instincts any more. They are doing what feminists tell them to do.

It's time men started listening to their instincts too. We want to be the masters of our domain. We want to love and possess ("pay attention," "know") our wives. We want to create families that are loving, lively and happy according to a positive vision of life.

It's time we embraced the quiet, unassuming beautiful women who want to be our helpmates.

MARIE ROBINSON'S "THE POWER OF SEXUAL SURRENDER"

Why Feminists Often Are Frigid

MARIE N. ROBINSON MD, a Cornell educated psychiatrist devoted her New York City practice to the treatment of frigidity. Her book, *The Power of Sexual Surrender* (1958) is very important but it's out-of-print. Why? It is politically incorrect.

Dr. Robinson says that millions of American women suffer from frigidity. Although she explores various causes, she notes that *frigid women universally adopt the feminist view.* This view, that men exploit women and a career as a wife and mother is demeaning creates an "emotional logjam" which obstructs sexual response and psychological development.

Dr. Robinson writes that a woman's identity lies in an "essential feminine altruism." Her self-expression and power are based on making her husband and children her first priority. Similarly, her sexual satisfaction and spiritual fecundity depend on self-surrender. Robinson says men and women are different by nature. Men are designed for mastery of the external (physical) world, and women for mastery of the internal (spiritual) world and the home. These are not social stereotypes, as feminists argue.

"Women are designed for duties different from those of the marketplace, another kind of stress entirely," writes Robinson. They "tend to lose their essential womanliness if they stay [in the marketplace] by choice." (149)

According to Robinson, modern women have an identity crisis because they think they are no longer needed as women. Before the industrial revolution, the home was the centre of all life with a woman at its heart. She nursed and trained the children, prepared clothing and food, and helped with farm tasks.

The industrial revolution seemed to make women obsolete. Children were not needed and were even considered a liability. Everything could be bought in stores. The home was empty. Children went to school, husbands to work.

Woman's response was to turn against her own femininity. Mary Wollstonecraft wrote a feminist manifesto *Vindication of the Rights of Women* (1792) that proclaimed women were identical to men and promoted maleness in women.

According to Robinson, "the feminist credo thoroughly discredited feminine needs and characteristics and substituted male goals for female goals."(53)

The other response to the industrial revolution was not feminist, but "Victorian." Robinson says Victorian women took "revenge" on men by denying women had any sexual feelings. They "were amazingly successful in convincing men in general and even the scientists of the day that frigidity was indeed a basic attribute of the female." (54)

Thus, feminists and Victorian women both laid the foundations for modern female neurosis.

"The depreciation of the goals of femininity, biological and psychological, became part and parcel of the education of millions of American girls. Homemaking, childbearing and rearing, cooking; the virtues of patience, lovingness, giving ness in marriage, have been systematically devalued. The life of male achievement has been substituted for the life of female achievement." (55)

FEMININE DEVALUATION AND SELF-HATRED

The feminist-Victorian antagonism to men was handed down from mother to daughter so that "to millions of women, hostility towards the opposite sex seems almost a natural law. Although many a modern women may pay lip service to the ideal of a passionate and productive marriage to a man, *underneath she deeply resents her role, conceives of the male as fundamentally hostile to her, as an exploiter of her. She wishes in her deepest heart, and often without the slightest awareness of the fact, to supplant him, to exchange roles with him.*" (Emphasis mine, 56)

Robinson says that if feminism had brought women happiness, the game might have been worth it.

"But it hasn't been. The game has brought frigidity and restlessness and a soaring divorce rate, neurosis, homosexuality, juvenile delinquency all that results when a woman in any society deserts her true function." (56)

Dr. Robinson writes that once the emotional "log jam" is removed, a woman's natural instincts will flow and health will be restored. Essentially this involves "allowing herself to trust her husband in a very deep sense. It means that she finally realizes that she no longer has to fear or oppose his strength, but that she can rely on it to protect her, to give her the secure climate necessary for the full flowering of her femininity." (153)

For a profound vaginal orgasm, Robinson writes, "the excitement comes from the act of surrender. There is a tremendous surging physical ecstasy in the yielding itself, in the feeling of being the passive instrument of another person..." (158)

On the other hand, the woman who mistrusts her husband's love and her own femininity has a "difficult, painful, frenetic" approach to life. She is at war with herself. In bed, she has to feel "in control all the time."

Robinson regards the clitoris as a masculine vestige. She implies that a woman may still be frigid even if she is sexually active and mechanically adroit. Feminine sexuality depends on "absolute trust" in a man, which allows a woman to fully receive and fully respond.

Dr. Robinson says there is nothing in life more important than love. She believes marriage is the key to human development. The power of love is felt in the world through this relationship.

"Love means, in its very deepest sense union; union between individuals...It is the most basic and profound urge we have and its power for good is illimitable... the lover partner becomes as important as oneself...This fact is why real love never leads to domination or to a struggle for power..." (129)

FEMINISM AS ELITE DEPOPULATION PROGRAM

The significance of *The Power of Sexual Surrender* is profound.

By coercing women to abandon their femininity and usurp the male role, feminism has thrown a spanner into humanity's natural heterosexual mechanism. Millions of women are condemned to loneliness and frustration. Similarly, men are deprived of the role of protector and provider and the love essential to their development and fulfillment.

The triumph of such a wrongheaded ideology, and the suppression of the truth, signifies that control in the world has passed over to a malevolent force.

As I have shown elsewhere, the immoral money power fosters feminism as part of a long-term agenda to dislodge Western Civilization from its religious and cultural moorings and replace it with a pagan plutocratic Orwellian police state. Feminists who oppose the NWO and globalization are in fact its unwitting agents and dupes.

THE EFFECT OF SEXUAL DEPRIVATION ON WOMEN

(Women Need Loving)

WE LIVE IN A CULTURE that doesn't admit that women need sex every bit as much as men, if not more.

Conservatives like to put women on a romantic pedestal. Women are virginal and sexless. Feminists deny women need men for *anything.*

"Women are made to feel guilty for needing men," my wife said. "We're told we're weak, co-dependent or lacking in self-esteem."

My 15-year-old son also inculcated this message from TV: "Women don't need sex," he said. "They're just doing men a favor." Sex and love have become horribly confused. When religion held sway, they were inseparable (i.e. marriage.)

But today "sexual liberation" has freed sex from love. It has taken love's place. Millions of men and women behave like addicts. They use sex to assuage a desperate craving for intimacy that only love and marriage can satisfy.

DESPERATELY SEEKING LOVE

In the movie, *"The Business of Strangers"* writer/director Patrick Stettner explores how American women have traded love for the sterility, banality and inhumanity of corporate culture.

While on a sales trip, two women are stranded overnight at an airport hotel. Stockard Channing plays "Julie Styron," a successful divorced 45-ish sales VP whose best friend is her secretary.

Julia Stiles plays Paula Murphy, a tough 25-ish "writer" who handles the overhead.

The movie shows how career has supplanted family for women

like Styron. Feminism promised that women could have both, but in many cases this was a cruel hoax.

Styron is fired without warning. But when she immediately lands an even better job as a CEO, she is oddly indifferent.

ODE TO WASTE & FRUSTRATION

In the hotel bar with Styron, Murphy recognizes Nick Harris, a corporate head-hunter who raped her best friend years ago at a frat party. Murphy lures him to Styron's suite and puts tranquilizers in his drink.

After he passes out, the two women indulge in an orgy of hatred over his unconscious body. They undress him, cover him with obscene graffiti, smear blood and strike him. Both women clearly despise men. Murphy confides it was actually she whom he raped.

However, later it emerges that Nick is a rapist in her mind only. Styron learns that he had never been to the city where the assault supposedly took place.

Men are "rapists" because they are not giving women the love and validation they require. The result is resentment against men and self-loathing. First feminism makes women and men incompatible; then it exploits women's frustration and rage.

"WHAT DOES WOMAN WANT?"

Freud was unable to answer this question despite "thirty years of research into the feminine soul."

Chaucer's "Wife of Bath" knew the answer: *Woman wants to be loved.* She'll do anything for love, even if it means becoming a feminist.

What she really wants is for one man she respects to love her, and to be loyal and devoted.

Many Western women today are dysfunctional because they are getting contradictory messages. Society tells them to be "strong and independent," but men don't like these women. Their behaviour is masculine and makes men feel redundant. Women are doing what society tells them to do; yet they are not getting the male approval they expect and need.

Women are loved *when they put their husband and children before themselves.* It is feminine to self efface. Men love these women because they are willing to become part of them.

GETTING DATING STRAIGHT

A single friend characterized a typical date this way. He describes his work and seeks affirmation and respect. She describes her work and seeks affirmation and respect from him. They never see each other again. Already they are competing.

This is NOT how heterosexuals mate. On a date, a man reveals himself and his vision of life. She decides if she's interested in him or not. If she is, she affirms him by her acceptance and encouragement. In marriage, she demonstrates her love by trusting him to take care of her interests.

He also affirms her by seeking *her* acceptance. Yes, he also wants her to be capable and successful. But this recognition and nurturing come later.

All successful organizations are hierarchical. The heterosexual family is male dominated. If you wanted to destroy it, you promote equality. As someone said, "Only a monster has two heads."

THE FEMINIST TRAP

It is mind-boggling but our politicians, media and educators are deliberately sabotaging society. Feminism like its Communist forebear dogmatically denies human sexual differences, such as the fact that men have 10 times the testosterone levels of women.

There are over 900 Women's Studies Programs in the United States teaching impressionable young women to deny their femininity. According to *"Issues in Feminism: An Introduction to Women's Studies"* femininity is "patriarchal mind control." The "best slaves are the ones who don't even know they are slaves." Who authorized this indoctrination in lesbian dysfunction?

Heterosexual society has been under sustained psychological attack designed to prevent marriage and family and arrest personal and social development. Feminism undermines marriage by encouraging women to deny their femininity and challenge men.

Feminine women are characterized by selflessness. They are not hunters. They are not killers. They are a little vulnerable in a worldly sense. How do men respond to them? By wanting to nurture and protect them. This is how men love. This is what women want.

In *"The Business of Strangers"* both women have become hunters. As a result, they hate men but worse they hate themselves. They need a man's love in order to love themselves again.

BIKINI VS. BURKA

The Debauchery of American Womanhood

O N MY WALL, I have a picture of a Muslim woman shrouded in a burka.

Beside it is a picture of an American beauty contestant, wearing nothing but a bikini.

One woman is totally hidden from the public; the other is totally exposed. These two extremes say a great deal about the clash of so-called "civilizations."

The role of woman is at the heart of any culture. The war in the Middle East is about stripping Arabs of their oil, religion and culture, exchanging the burka for a bikini.

I am not an expert on the condition of Muslim women and I love female beauty too much to advocate the burka here. But I am defending some of the values that the burka represents for me.
For me, the burka represents a woman's consecration to her husband and family. Only they see her.

It affirms the privacy, exclusivity and importance of the domestic sphere.

The Muslim woman's focus is her home, the "nest" where her children are born and reared. She is the "home" maker, the taproot that sustains the spiritual life of the family, nurturing and training her children, providing refuge and support for her husband.

In contrast, the bikinied American beauty queen struts practically naked in front of millions on TV. A feminist, in theory she belongs to herself. In practice, paradoxically, she is public property. She belongs to no one and everyone. She shops her body to the highest bidder. She is auctioning herself all of the time.

In America, the cultural measure of a woman's value is her

sex appeal. (As this asset depreciates quickly, she is neurotically obsessed with appearance and plagued by weight problems.)

As an adolescent, her role model is Britney Spears, a singer whose act approximates strip tease. From Britney, she learns that she will be loved only for sex. Thus, she learns to "hook up" rather than demand patient courtship and love. As a result, dozens of males know her before her husband ever does. She loses her innocence, which is a large part of her charm. She becomes hardened and calculating. Unable to trust, she is unable to love and unfit to receive her husband's seed.

SEX DIFFERENCES

The feminine personality is founded on the emotional relationship between mother and baby. It is based on nurturing and self-sacrifice. Masculine nature is founded on the relationship between hunter and prey. It is based on aggression and reason.

Feminism teaches woman that she is oppressed as a result of being feminine and should emulate male behaviour instead. The result: a confused and aggressive woman with a large chip on her shoulder.

This, of course, is the goal of the social engineers at the New World Order: undermine sexual identity and destroy the family, create social and personal dysfunction, and reduce population. In the "Brave New World," women are not supposed to be "nest" makers, or progenitors of the race. They are meant to be neutered, autonomous creatures that indulge in sex for physical pleasure, not for love or procreation.

At a press conference, Donald Rumsfeld said that Iranian women and youth were restive under the rule of the Mullahs. He implied that the US would soon liberate them. To Britney Spears? To low-rise "see-my-thong" pants? To the mutual masturbation that passes for sex in America?

Parenthood is the pinnacle of human development. It is the stage when we finally graduate from self-indulgence and become God's surrogates: creating and nurturing new life.

The New World Order does not want us to reach this level of maturity. Pornography is the substitute for marriage. We are to remain stunted: single, sex-starved and self-obsessed.

We are not meant to have a permanent "private" life. We are not meant to get our identity from our masculinity or femininity. We are to remain lonely and neutered, worker drones, dependent on pop culture or products for our character.

This is especially destructive for woman. Her sexual attraction is a function of her fertility. As fertility declines, so does her sex appeal. If a woman devotes her prime years to becoming "independent," she is not likely to find a permanent mate.

Her long-term personal fulfillment and happiness lies in making marriage and family her first priority.

Feminism is another cruel New World Order hoax that has debauched American women and despoiled Western civilization. It has ruined millions of lives and represents a lethal threat to Islam.

I am not advocating the burka but rather some of the values that it represents, specifically a woman's consecration to her future husband and family, and the modesty and dignity this entails.

The burka and the bikini represent two extremes. The answer lies somewhere in the middle.

DEMANDING LOVE

How Marriages Go Off the Rails

"I'll kick your butt," my wife said. "You'll be crying like a little girl!"

Even in jest, those were fighting words!

IT WAS SUNDAY EVENING and we were walking past a Jiu Jitsu school. My wife imagined she would become a black belt and teach me a lesson. She often feels resentful on Sundays because I spend them with my son.

Why do women act more unlovable when they feel unloved? They assume independent airs, and put up barriers. They don't need you any more. It's feminism in miniature.

My first reaction was, "Ok, fine. Do your thing. See if I care."

But then I realized that this is how marriages go off the rails. Women demand love, and if men can't respond on cue, they get resentful. Then men get fed up. It's a vicious circle.

I had to nip it in the bud.

When we got home. I hugged my wife.

"Look, you can't demand love. I don't respond to that."

"Don't make an issue of love. Be patient, adaptable and have faith. That's what I respond to."

"Be as independent as you like when it comes to your job and your interests. But when it comes to me, you must obey. You belong to me."

Believe it or not, this is what she wanted to hear.

A real woman is designed to finally shed her "independence" and become one with the man she loves.

This view is not popular because for decades feminists have taught that women must be equal and independent. If you are happy in a feminist marriage, I congratulate you. But if marital happiness eludes you, consider what I have to say.

Feminism is based on political notions that ignore and defy human nature.

Most women are passive by nature. They want to be *possessed* and *used* for a worthwhile purpose. I suspect that many women want *more* control from their husband, not less. The feeling of "neglect" arises from not being needed, sexually and otherwise.

Men have been conditioned not to lead and make demands. They are taught to be cool, laid back and have no plan. Women lose interest in these men.

Women are so formidable these days; men don't know how to approach them. But the essential dynamic hasn't changed. It is about a man convincing a woman to do what *he* wants.

For course, that's easier if he wants the same thing that she does. Generally, women want a lot more than casual sex. Most want a family.

I love that my wife doesn't have a constant set of expectations. With other women, I always felt like I was second-guessing them.

A woman shows she loves a man by obeying him. Nothing makes a man happier than a woman who is acquiescent.

A woman is not going to be loved permanently for her appearance, which is transitory, or for her accomplishments. Love is not like that. We love the people who sacrifice themselves for us. That proves they love us.

Men also sacrifice by working to support their families and providing love and direction. Happiness can only be found in love, not self-seeking. Love is self-sacrifice. Human beings were designed to look after each other.

Sexually, women are excited by male power, men by female vulnerability. Female pornography is full of acts of welcome sexual transgression.

WOMEN ARE "OUT OF CONTROL"

Time for Men to be Men

"**M**ODERN MEN see women as 'castrating, vengeful, power-hungry and obsessed by men's sexual performance,'" a recent study by the French Edition of *Elle Magazine* concluded.

The study based on four 12-man focus groups found that Frenchmen believe that women are out-of-control. They feel belittled by the constant overvaluation of women and dazed by demands to adopt feminine traits yet somehow remain virile.

The 25-35 age group felt that women "consume men and abuse them sexually." The magazine characterized this age group as "subjugated and feminized."

How the French have fallen! I recently watched Truffaut's 1968 film classic *"Stolen Kisses"* and marvelled at Antoine Doinel's girlfriend Christine. She is so irresistibly pert, gracious and pretty. French women were among the most stylish and feminine in the world, accounting for the country's reputation for love.

Of course the complaint of French men is universal. I received this e-mail recently from a young American male who wonders if women haven't become "sociopathic."

"They tend to not give a rip about others and 'break it off' rather suddenly," he wrote. "They just laugh and say 'That's what I do.'"
I replied to this young man:

"Tune out all the mad women. The key is not to barter your power for love. No compromises. Keep looking until you find a woman who obeys you and reward her with loyalty and love."

He replied: "Gee, I never thought of that. Thanks!"

It's time for men to be men again. It's time to serve notice to women that if they want a relationship with a man, if they want a family, then they must learn to obey their husbands. Otherwise, they are welcome to be roommates with "liberated men" or become lesbians.

The essential difference between masculine and feminine can be put in a nutshell: woman exchanges her power for a man's love. This is what makes her feminine.

When men barter their power for love, they become women. Men trade love for power.

The fatal mistake of the men's movement is accepting feminism's bogus assumptions and complaining that the women aren't treating them as "equals."

SOCIAL ENGINEERING

Recently 20 high school graduates toured a science department at the local university. Nineteen of the students were women. The chairman of the department raised the problem at a faculty meeting.

"Seventy per cent of our students are female," he said. "The males in my department are mostly foreign students. We need an affirmative action program for white males."

The chairman was met with stunned silence from the rest of the committee. The proposal was not even discussed.

Don't kid yourself. This is a deliberate policy of social engineering that is authoritarian and sinister. It was never put to a vote. Rockefeller-funded organizations dictate it to state and provincial governments and to universities.

Feminists said they wanted equality but this was a typical Communist ruse. It was a way of putting their acolytes into power and dominating society. The hidden agenda is to destroy the nuclear family. Women who devote their prime years to getting a career will find it harder to become wives and mothers later. Men who are shut out of universities will not become breadwinners and family leaders. The discrimination against white males is also intended to undermine America's European character.

I walk the halls of this university and see bored young women in white lab coats staring distractedly out the door wondering why they are memorizing formulae instead of obeying their natural instincts and having children. Like millions of people duped by Communists, they will be high and dry when there is a depression and they have neither careers nor families.

WHY MEN ARE LOSING INTEREST IN WOMEN

Castrated Men Can't Love

ABC'S FLAGSHIP NEWS PROGRAM "20/20" Friday was devoted to the "biggest secret of American marriage."

"As many as 20% of American marriages are sexless," host Barbara Walters intoned. "It's not women who don't want sex as you might expect, it's the men!"

The program focused on two couples. In both cases, feminist mind control is responsible for their problem but the TV program wouldn't admit it.

One man was married to an attractive 30-something woman who is a stripper. Reporter John Stossel thought this made her husband's indifference even more astonishing. The show's marital therapist, Michele Weiner-Davis, ignored this as a possible explanation for the man's impotence.

Feminist groupthink says a woman's sexuality is the same as a man's, hers to enjoy (or sell). In this essentially lesbian mindset, the male's response to such women is considered irrelevant.

I beg to differ. The stripper's husband is impotent because he is a cuckold. Sex is an act of possession. The husband cannot possess his wife because she gives herself to hundreds of other men every day. She makes part of *their living* this way. How can this man have any self-respect left? No wonder he cannot assert his power.

A woman thrives in the context of a loving marriage. Despite what feminism says, most women want to belong to one man, their husband.

THE SECOND COUPLE

Here the wife criticizes and nags.

"I can't be myself," the husband says. "I'm walking on eggshells all the time."

The wife is emasculating her husband. He compensates by riding a Harley and volunteering at the local fire department.

The therapist suggests that the wife stop nagging and the husband listen. She doesn't notice that the husband responds only *after the wife starts to cry.*

Men respond to *vulnerability* in a woman not power. As I have said, heterosexual love involves the exchange of power for love. Men want power. Women want love. The female surrenders and allows the male to protect and possess her.

FOR EXAMPLE

In 2003, a young Israeli died protecting his girl friend from a knife-wielding Palestinian. The police said he absorbed the attacker's blows with his body, ultimately collapsing on top of his girlfriend who was unscathed physically.

The young man made the supreme sacrifice. His was the supreme act of love.

Men instinctively protect their own. But feminists don't belong to any man and make a point of being independent. If you were married to one, would you sacrifice your life for her? If society put your children under her jurisdiction, would you die for them?

The answers have broader implications. Would you support her if she were incapacitated? Would you do unpleasant work day-after-day to support her children? If not, would there be any point in dying for your country? Feminism clearly sabotages the social contract, which is heterosexual by nature.

If you want to get a man's attention, give him power. A man will not sacrifice himself for woman or family unless they belong to him, i.e. are part of him.

PENIS EQUALS POWER

In the film *The Crying Game* (1992), director Neil Jordan captured the modern male experience: The protagonist discovers his girlfriend has a penis. He runs gagging from the room and vomits.

In contrast, most female impersonators today (i.e. feminists) are anatomically women. By encouraging young women to be "strong and independent", feminism has outfitted them with a mental phallus.

They have become men and made men redundant. Then they try to coerce men to love them as if men were their hand puppets.

In reality, a woman's power consists in being *without penis,* being *everything a man is not.* Not aggressive, forceful, dynamic, muscular and driven. Some weak men are attracted to "dynamic" women but they are really looking for themselves.

Feminine power consists of persuasion rather than force. A real woman relies on moral authority and her *attraction*: beauty, grace, charm, love and devotion. These women are very rare and in great demand.

Men and women are different. Jonathan Swift remarked that women love flattery but men are embarrassed by it. This is because men are active by nature and women are passive. The universe is held in balance by positive (active) and negative (passive) principles. Marriage is the way heterosexuals achieve this balance.

MEN NEED TO TAKE CHARGE

A man told me that after he has worked all day on home renovations, he is afraid his wife will "go ballistic" if he asks why she didn't even do the dishes.

An Australian man recently wrote to me: "For too long I have made girlfriends insecure by not telling them what I wanted because of a fear of appearing overbearing."

Men need to assert their just leadership and dump the women who don't like it. There are plenty of fish in the sea and they are biting. With patience and firmness, some feminists can be saved. The rest can be thrown back.

Generally speaking, men need to figure out what they want to do with their life. You might ask what God wants you to do. Then define the role you want your wife to play and find a woman happy to do it.

This is what women really want. They are attracted to a dynamic man whom they cannot control. He must have a wholesome vision where she is valued and cherished for her contribution.

LOOKING TO DOGS FOR FAMILY

Love Makes Life Sweet

PEOPLE USED TO GET DOGS FOR THEIR CHILDREN," my wife observed. "Now they get dogs *instead* of children."

"Instead of husbands and wives as well," I added.

Marriage and family have been sabotaged by feminist social engineering. People are turning to dogs for love, belonging and a sense of family.

A month ago we adopted "Raffi", a one-year-old Spaniel-Lab mutt from the pound. My wife always had a dog. I didn't realize how they could instantly create a family atmosphere.

We chose Raffi because he wasn't barking and he still doesn't. He just whines or looks sorrowful when he wants something.

HAVING A DOG MEANS NEVER BEING A LONE WOLF

Dogs are pack animals like their wolf ancestors. They hunt and fend off enemies together. They have an innate sense of hierarchy and group solidarity that we have forgotten.

Raffi likes to be with me all of the time. He sits vigil when I go out and is ecstatic when I return. I am the alpha wolf. I feed and look after him. He jumps in the air and kisses my cheek. How many people are this happy to see us?

When I neglect to walk him, he doesn't get all sour and resentful. When I finally get to him, he doesn't say, "It's about time. I want an extra ten minutes." He's just happy to be going out.

No longer are we a childless couple. We are a wolf pack. The house is our den. A couple of bones are strewn on the carpet. Raffi sleeps under the bed. Sometimes he snores or dreams tiny barks and growls. When there is a noise outside, he scrambles to investigate.

We have become a family. Raffi is like our child. We discuss his diet, buy him toys and take him for walks. I treat him to bones.

EVERY BOY SHOULD OWN A DOG

Owning a dog would have taught me stewardship and prepared me for becoming a father and husband. You learn to love a creature that is entirely different from you. You learn that when basic needs are met and some guidance is provided, nature takes care of the rest. Stewardship is easy.

You learn there's a part of his life he shares with you (affection) and a part that is his alone and private (rolling in filth, burying bones, sniffing, chasing cats and rodents.)

Raffi brings out my parental instincts. I take pleasure in his happiness, vitality, and shiny black coat. I admire his speed and grace. He is the "Seabiscuit" of mutts.

I am training him to obey my commands so I can keep him out of trouble. I have disciplined him when he growled at us, or insisted on pursuing other dogs.

Raffi knows I love him. I pat and hug and praise him. "They don't make dogs like you anymore Raffi. They threw away the mould."

This is what fatherhood should be. A father prepares his children for life. He imposes his vision and will. He teaches them values, goals and self-discipline. He wins their assent by virtue of example, strength of character and fairness. He praises them and assures them of their worth.

Dogs, women and children have a few things in common. They need to belong to someone. They need a home. They need to be led, loved, nurtured and given responsibility.

Similarly, men have a strong instinct to "look after" the creatures they love.

We were brought up to believe that "if you love something, set it free. If it's yours, it will come back. If it doesn't, it never was."

This is nonsense. It's necessary to assume responsibility for the creatures that depend on you. This is masculine. You are not his friend. You are his owner. *If you really love something, you do not put it at risk.* Better realise that before it is too late.

FEMINISM DEPRIVES WOMEN OF FATHER'S LOVE

Girl's Need Validation

MOST GIRLS do not receive adequate love from their fathers. Because of this, as women they are insecure, distrust men and feel they must be independent. They can't respond sexually and their marriages often end in divorce. Their daughters continue the vicious cycle of fatherless-ness.

This is the conclusion of Victoria Secunda's book *Women and their Fathers: The Sexual and Romantic Impact of the First Man in Your Life* (1992). It is based on interviews with 150 daughters, 75 fathers, and dozens of authorities.

Because she is not an academic, Secunda has written an honest and useful book. Because she is a feminist, it slipped through the feminist censors and was well received. This is ironic because feminism is largely responsible for the father-loss and consequences she describes.

FATHERS AND DAUGHTERS

Girls base their male romantic ideal on their relationship with their father. "When I grow up, will I ever find a man as sweet and good and kind as my daddy" is how one woman expressed it. (p.105)

A three-year-old girl wants to marry her Daddy. A good father helps her to understand that he is spoken for and prepares her for her future husband. But if he leaves, her idealization of her father can be frozen in time. (197)

Women's romantic attachments are "mirror images" of how they related to their fathers as girls. They often instinctively repeat what they experienced in childhood, even if it was bad. It's what they know. They are trying to have one more shot at childhood, one more chance to rectify their emotional histories. (224)

Little girls must have their father's approval and love. This is like sun and water to a flower.

One woman said: "Whenever I'd worry about ever getting a boyfriend, he'd laugh and say, 'Are you kidding? I'll have to beat them off with a stick. You'll see.' *His whole approach was to make me feel good about myself.... I think if fathers do nothing else, that's a great thing."* (221) (Emphasis mine)

Another woman said: "*It's my dad who made me believe in myself.* I remember my mom once telling me, 'Don't act too smart; boys won't like you." My father responded, 'Hogwash. She'll get smarter boys." (225)

These women naturally feel positively about men and are able to find partners who mirror the devoted father of childhood. A man looking for a mate is safe if he chooses a woman who has a good relationship with her parents, especially her dad.

"FATHERLESS" WOMEN

Conversely a woman with "father issues" is a risk. If she didn't have a loving dependable father, she may feel unlovable and select men who treat her accordingly. She may recoil from male love altogether. (224)

These women may try to get love by becoming sexually active prematurely. Or they may fear intimacy. The common theme is "an inability to trust, to believe that a man won't go away."

Secunda says women whose fathers were emotionally or physically absent during childhood often have trouble achieving orgasm. (31) Understandably, a woman needs to trust in order to "let go." Women with absent fathers feel rootless and aren't sure they belong anywhere. They close up emotionally and tend to have rocky relationships. "Most of these daughters tend to test the men in their lives by starting fights, finding flaws, expecting to be abandoned, or looking for excuses to walk out themselves." (214)

Another pattern is anxiety about supporting themselves or of being financially dependent on men. This is where feminism comes in.

"It seems that the less masculine attention they got in childhood, the more they seem to identify with and imitate men, keeping their feelings hidden, preferring casual teasing and unemotional banter to the intimacies of feminine soul bearing." (212)

Denied their fathers, women become more masculine. This is a way of bringing daddy back. They become the thing they are missing. (212)

In other words, a good father affirms his daughter's innate femininity by telling her how beautiful and smart she is. But if he is absent, she compensates by becoming masculine. This of course undermines her future relationships with men.

THE ORIGINS OF FEMINISM

Feminism is a self-perpetuating form of father-loss. Its goal is to "overthrow the patriarchy." The word originates in the Latin "pater" or father.

Many leaders of second-wave feminism are themselves products of broken homes. "My father didn't ever exist as a presence in my life.... He didn't care about us," said Marilyn French, author of *The War Against Women.*

"My father was living in California," said Gloria Steinem. "He didn't ring up but I would get letters from him and saw him maybe once or twice a year."

Germaine Greer: "My father had decided pretty early on that life at home was pretty unbearable...it gave my mother an opportunity to tyrannize the children and enlist their aid to disenfranchise my father completely." (From Susan Mitchell. *Icons, Saints and Divas: Intimate Conversations with Women who Changed the World,* New York: Harper Collins, 1997.)

THE HAVOC WREAKED BY FEMINISM

Since the onslaught of second-wave feminism in the 1960's the divorce rate has tripled. Almost 50% of white women who married then have divorced. In contrast, a single generation earlier (1940's), only 14% eventually divorced.

Between 1970 and 1992, the proportion of babies born outside of marriage leapt from 11% to 30%. Now it is almost 50%.

Three times as many children (per capita) are now living in single parent households. In 2000, 22.4% of all children under 18 (16,162,000 children) lived in mother-only households. In 1960, the figure was 8%.

A study which tracked 1000 children of divorced parents from 1976 until 1987 found that nearly half of these children had not seen their fathers in the previous year. (203)

As far as women's psychological development and happiness, feminism is a self-perpetuating disease.

FATHER-DAUGHTER: A HETEROSEXUAL PARADIGM

These days' men and women are kept in a state of arrested development, frozen in the courtship stage. If people are distracted and starved for sex, it's easier to sell them products and control them.

The mass media encourages us to obsess on sex and postpone marriage and family indefinitely. When you are married, sex is readily available and less important.

Young men are taught to judge women on appearance and ignore more important qualities. The media presents makes men think beautiful women are superhuman and unapproachable. Possibly the following will be of use.

If women form their ideal of male from their father, present or absent, perhaps men should be more "father-like" in their approach to women. Typically, women choose men who are five years older because they seek to replicate their own family, with husband providing the physical and emotional security of the father.

Many men want a daughter-figure, someone who will demonstrate the loyalty, trust and innocence that a girl feels for her father. A man wants to be affirmed in his authority as husband and father, not mothered like a child.

Of course a man also wants his wife to be strong, sophisticated and effective because this makes her more desirable as a mate. But she should retain those daughterly qualities that he finds so attractive. When a woman trusts her husband's leadership, she can focus on her feminine side. It allows her to retain her youthfulness and attraction into old age.

Victoria Secunda's book confirms that some men occasionally have sexual feelings for their daughters. She says this is normal. Men get spooked by this and avoid their daughters. They shouldn't. There is a world of difference between arousal, which is involuntary, and actually wanting, let alone doing. (16)

A father's responsibility is to build his daughter's trust in men, and prepare her for another man. This involves confirming her in her sexual identity, as a capable attractive partner for a future husband. Obviously, if a father crosses the line with his daughter, he will destroy that trust and ruin her life.

CONCLUSION

In my lifetime the popular image of the father has undergone a transformation from the dignified Robert Young in *Fathers Knows Best* to the bumbling fool Homer Simpson. This is not a coincidence or a "sign of the times." It reflects a sophisticated psychological warfare program designed by the Illuminist elite to emasculate men, degrade and destabilize society.

The people who own and run the planet do not want us to become mature beings able to perceive the truth. Their main instrument is the mass media, which makes trends like feminism appear spontaneous.

A healthy father-daughter relationship in a nuclear family is essential to a woman's psychological development and future happiness. Despite its pretensions, feminism undermines women by depriving them of this.

I want to be clear that women are equal to men in terms of their right to dignity and self-fulfillment. But feminism is not really about these things. It spreads a lesbian developmental disorder that destroys society by attacking its basic social unit, the heterosexual family.

The dysfunction created by the destruction of the family has spawned a predatory class of feminist professionals: politicians, educators, writers, law enforcers, lawyers, counsellors and health care professionals. This class becomes the elite's political constituency. Thus mankind is kept in a state of arrested development.

It's time for men to step up to the plate. We also suffer from father loss. But there is a father that we can know. I am talking about God. We are made in God's image and His image is in our soul. Man in Latin, "vir", has the same root as virtue. It's as simple as doing the *right* thing.

SELF-CONTROL

Managing the Male Sex Drive

AT AGE 12, in 1961 I saw the movie Spartacus. In one scene the camera focuses on Kirk Douglas' face as Jean Simmons sheds her gown. His face is full of wonderment and awe, lighted by the mystical glow seeming to emanate from her naked body but actually from the fire.

The scene made a profound impression on me, a boy just entering puberty.

Our pagan (a.k.a. "modern") Masonic culture programs us to worship sex in the form of the fertile young female.

Romantic love is our ersatz religion. Sexual intercourse is the holy sacrament. Sex is considered the most pleasurable and profound experience life has to offer.

I subscribed to *Playboy* and devoured nudes with Kirk Douglas-like adoration. Henceforth I judged females primarily on the basis of sex appeal; all others were invisible. I also equated sexual desire with love, and love with religion. In essence, I became dysfunctional, unable to relate to real women.

This subversive verse from Paul Simon's *"Kathy's Song"* (1965) became the anthem of my generation:

"So you see I have come to doubt/ All that I once held as true/ I stand alone without beliefs/ The only truth I know is you."

We were taught to be "alienated" from society and to seek fulfillment in romance. Uprooted from our true historical and spiritual context, we were told life is meaningless: find it in sex.

"An erotomania is abroad through our civilization," Francis Parker Yockey wrote in 1948. It is "the identification of 'happiness' with sexual love, holding it up as the great value, before which all honour, duty, patriotism, consecration of Life to a higher aim, must give way." (*Imperium*, 297)

This message has not changed and it is pervasive. The pagan goddess is used to sell everything from cell phones to insurance. In one commercial, she says, "even I get constipation" as if she were supernatural.

As if this weren't enough, lately she has become an Amazon warrior anxious to avenge centuries of imagined oppression. As result, she is either frostily unapproachable or a demanding pleasure-seeking slut.

These factors have poisoned male-female relations. We are fearful and cannot form a permanent bond. Many men have turned to pornography, which has become a multi billion-dollar industry and national pastime.

PROCREATION OR RECREATION?

In Plato's *Republic* Socrates says that when he finally lost his sex drive in old age, he felt as if he had been " released from the jaws of a wild beast."

Sex is not intended to be a lifelong obsession. It is part of the courtship and procreation phase. We are meant to marry young, have children and *outgrow sex* to some extent. We were intended to focus our energy on more important things.

For men, the goal is to control our sex drive rather than to be controlled by it (and by women.) How do men do this if they cannot find a compatible mate?

Obviously most masturbate and many use pornography as an aid. Most men would be thinking of nothing else if they didn't relieve the pressure in this way.

But, as a sensible teenager said to me recently: "If I need to look at pictures, well then I don't really need to do it." His focus is on managing his sex drive not on dissipation. By masturbating every few days, he can be "cool" with girls.

HARD CORE PORN: THE UNDEFINED HATE CRIME

If a pipe were spewing untreated sewage into our streets, we would stop it. But hard-core pornography does this on a psychic level on a much larger scale, and somehow we are helpless.

A swastika graphitti or the epithet "nigger" are considered "hate crimes" yet every day millions of men receive offensive email offers to extend their penises or watch 14-year-old Sue get sodomized.

That is considered "free speech."

Hard-core porn is anti human. It is hate. But anything that is prohibited assumes an undue importance. I'd rather curious males investigated and were disgusted and bored.

There is a difference between hard-core porn, which is tedious and sick, and tasteful female nudity, which can be a temporary substitute. The key is to grow beyond it. The temporary substitute should not become a permanent one. It should not interfere with finding a mate.

Pornography makes us see women in purely sexual terms and obviously this affects how we treat them and how they respond to us.

ANOTHER OPTION

When men dehumanize women, we dehumanize ourselves.

Men and women are demeaned when they seek sex merely as physical release. Let's face it. Most of us have been demeaned.

This is the goal of the New World Order, which centres on the question: Is human life sacred or are we merely animals? The New World Order wants to prove we are cattle so we can be herded, enslaved or slaughtered.

Resistance begins at home. Attack the programming head on. Let's stop looking at women as sex objects. Let's humanize sex by insisting that it belongs in a loving long-term male-led relationship.

The sex act is the sacred ritual of creation. The man plants his seed, which contains his essence, his genetic code. The woman receives and nourishes this seed into a creature capable of knowing God.

Let's look for compatible mates rather than sex partners. This would save us a lot of hardship, rejection and wasted time. Women would instantly become more approachable and available.

In societies that respect marriage vows, married men and women are able to be friends with other men and women without anyone feeling threatened.

SUBLIMATION

Being human is a spiritual discipline. It means holding our behaviour accountable to our ideals and evolving morally. Let's catch ourselves when we look at women lasciviously. There is a difference between that and admiring their sex appeal, beauty and grace.

Holding ourselves accountable requires will power. We are the product of our thoughts. The thought is father of the deed. We must control our thoughts and the stimuli we allow.

One acquaintance doesn't masturbate very often. "Why stoke the fires?" he says. He keeps his mind off sex and focuses on more exciting pursuits.

This is called sublimation. The prodigious American writer Upton Sinclair (1878-1968) wrote in his *Autobiography* (1962):

> *My chastity was preserved at the cost of much emotional effort... What did I get in return for this? I got intensity and power of concentration; these elements in my make-up were the product of my effort to resist the tempter.*
>
> *I learned to work fourteen hours a day at study and creative effort because it was only by being thus occupied that the craving for woman could be kept out of my soul. I recited the Wisdom of Solomon: "he that ruleth his spirit is greater than he that taketh a city." (p. 46)*

According to Sinclair, and many religions, the energy goes right to the spiritual bottom line:

> *"Imagine anyone wanting a lot of money or houses and servants or fine raiment if he knew how to be happy as I did! Imagine anyone becoming drunk on whiskey if he might become drunk on poetry and music, sunsets and valleys full of clover!" (56)*

Go to Julian Lee's website www.celibacy.org for a wealth of information and inspiration on how abstinence can make men strong.

CONCLUSION

The masculine sex drive is a powerful creative force that needs to be controlled and steered. We can do this by applying and then releasing the brake. Every man is different and must find his own formula.

Slavery begins with the mind. We can resist by not being controlled by sex.

ANXIETY

Men Don't Need to Perform

MANY PERFECTLY HEALTHY MEN apparently are using "performance enhancing" drugs, supposedly intended just for erectile dysfunction.

Reports include, "It's like having a jackhammer between your legs" and "You can swing the bat all night long."

To continue the baseball metaphor, I ask: Isn't this cheating? Isn't it like using steroids to hit a home run?

Should these men be treated like heroes or impostors? Do women feel they have been with a real man or a lifelike dildo?

These drugs completely automate an act that already is too impersonal and mechanical. Is this really necessary?

A young man of my acquaintance described how Viagra removed his performance anxieties.

I don't think men should feel obligated to perform. It's not the measure of a man. What a quaint vestige from our primate days! We become a man by serving a higher ideal, not by keeping an erection.

An erection is a measure of arousal, like the needle on a gauge. Ninety degrees suggests acute interest; 270 degrees suggests the chemistry is wrong. The woman or the relationship is equally to blame.

In my experience, a woman's response is a major factor. Arousal and love mirrored on a woman's face, is the biggest turn-on.

If the gauge reads 270, we need to fix the problem, not mess with our body's natural feedback.

We live in an age where we are lied to continually. Do we want to lie to ourselves?

A READER REPORTS

A reader "Bud" wrote that he took Viagra right after his second divorce.

"I found much to my delight that women were easy. Real easy! [Only] my heart, s oul and body were not as easy as most of the women I met. BUT being a "Man" I thought that I "Needed a woman" and further that I "Needed" to please them.

Well the Viagra worked to fix a part of me that was telling me by not working that I didn't "Need" sex.

Here was the bizarre part, with the Viagra, Yes I had a glowing erection, yes I had her all "going" as well, but after even a minute or two of Sex, I WAS BORED.

I mean I was bored, and distracted and found the whole situation meaningless.

So, to counter my distraction I used of course, booze and "perversion."

I tried to keep my interest in seeing what "I could get her to do". The answer was "everything" as modern American women are prone to do. But what didn't change was the boredom.

I'd rather wanted to listen to music. I'd rather think about how I missed my children. I'd rather take a walk.

And ALL while having this "great "Viagra sex! But it was not great.

It actually made me sad!

So actually Viagra was a great wake-up for me, as it helped me become more aware of my body and my needs. Sex just wasn't one of those needs."

SEX IS OVERRATED

We live in a culture that regards sex as a mystical experience, necessary for our fulfillment. In the movies, the sex act is treated like a holy sacrament.

Why is this? Modern Western culture is Masonic in character. That's their pyramid symbol on the US dollar bill. Freemasonry originated as a pagan sex cult. We are brainwashed to think that sex has some inherent value, that it is necessary for our identity, health etc. Are we secretly being initiated into depraved occult sex practises?

Without love, sex is hardly better than masturbating. And masturbating is just another excretory function.

Sex in our occult-ure replaces love and family. The ultimate goal is to dissolve the family and create a society of anonymous mutual masturbators, who cannot form permanent bonds.

It's a long time since I read Aldous Huxley's "Brave New World" but these drugs remind me of SOMA, a drug used to distract the masses from their slavery.

BIOLOGY AS DESTINY

To divorce sex from love and reproduction is unnatural and inhuman. For most of us, our natural development requires marriage and family. This applies to both sexes.

The reproductive act determines a woman's destiny. If she offers herself to all and sundry, her husband will be another in a long line of casual lovers. She will not know how to be monogamous.

Similarly, men have been brainwashed to see women as sexual receptacles. "I'd hit that," young men are fond of saying. Or "Would you do Britney Spears?"

No wonder men and women are confused. So many people are "do" able, especially with Viagra.

Too often we mistake sexual attraction for love. Real love is based on a willingness to devote oneself to another person. True love humanizes sex. With love, sex assumes its real significance as the sacred ritual of human reproduction. By creating Life, we imitate God.

THE TREADMILL OF SEX & ROMANCE

Elite Exploits Nature's Con

A T 57, I am no longer of draft age. I'm referring to the press gang of nature. I am not required to father a child.

My sex drive is not what it once was. I can "perform" but I don't need to as much. Far from being alarmed, I am relieved.

As the hormonal fog evaporates, I have moments of clarity that I'd like to share with younger males still on the treadmill of sex and romance.

After survival, the reproductive urge is our most powerful natural instinct.

Most men don't realize how they are routinely victimized by this instinct. When they are attracted to a female, they rarely think, "Oh, that's nature calling, wanting me to breed."

Instead, they are fascinated, even awe-struck, by any comely young (i.e. fertile) female regardless of her character, personality, ability, or intelligence. Men invest her with great mystery and usually she won't correct them.

Like so many things we idolize, Gertrude Stein's comment about Oakland applies. "There's no THERE there." Nature is peddling a hoax and popular kulture is exploiting it.

Over time, very few women (or men) live up to their billing.

Jung said that when you take God away, men create false Gods. In place of God, the Illuminati gave us a bogus religion of sex and romantic love, which they din into our heads using movies and popular music.

There is nothing mystical about sex. It's mostly about reproduction.

Ninety per cent of what we call "love" is sexual attraction. Nature gave us hunger so we will eat, lust so we will propagate. This is why we are rarely attracted to women beyond childbearing age.

Romantic love is a form of idolatry. Thanks to birth control and porn, sex has become a largely sterile mass entertainment and addiction.

A woman is peripheral to a man who knows his business, and subconsciously women know this. They shun men who put them on a pedestal.

The romantic inflation of woman causes arrested development in males. (This is why the media empowers and idealizes women.) Any man who thinks a particular woman has anything he cannot live without is destined to remain a child.

A young man should choose a wife who will help him achieve his goals. Ideally, one of these goals will be a family. Children represent our natural growth; they project us into the future. They are our offering to God, an Act of Faith. A young man should find a woman who complements him and will be a good mother.

Subconsciously, women want men who serve God. Men (and women) were created to be God's agents. We know God by doing His will, by serving Him through our actions. Women serve God by serving husband and children, and are loved and honored in return. When women serve themselves, they end up alone and bitter.

THE EROSION OF CIVILIZATION

The hallmark of civilization is the limitation of sex to love and marriage. This humanizes sex and encourages families, which are essential for procreation and societal health.

The alternative is "free love" where man is essentially a dog and woman a hydrant. Throughout my life, I was taught that sex for its own sake is actually worthwhile and profound, that sexual inhibition causes neurosis, and orgasms are mystical etc. Woody Allen summed it up: "For an empty experience, sex is one of the best there is."

Lets put this conflict in historical perspective. As recently as 50 years ago, our sexual mores were governed by religious principles. In 1960, there was still a social stigma against illegitimate children. I don't favor unkindness toward anyone but this stigma was removed by a powerful force determined to destroy the institution of the family.

We shriek at the position of women in Saudi Arabia but in Chicago in 1912, a woman could be fined for showing too much leg. Ben Hecht recalls that the police arrested women for "smoking cigarettes, for shopping without their corsets on...for using profanity...for wearing slacks and shorts, for kissing in public, for wearing a man's hat, for sitting alone in a cafe or drinking in a saloon, for driving an automobile without a male in attendance, for putting too much paint on their faces or cutting their hair too short." (*A Child of the Century*, p.47)

This is a reminder that our civilization was founded on Christian values. These proscriptions were extreme and needed some reform but they had a sound basis. They were designed to channel women into the role of wife and mother as opposed to sex objects. Deprived of their natural role, many young women now are in crisis.

Occult forces are gradually inducting us into their sex cult without our knowledge. "Secular" is their term for satanic. The "freedom" they trumpet is freedom from the self-discipline necessary to follow the Creator's operating manual and grow healthy and happy.

Until we wake up to the fact that mankind is in the grip of a powerful satanic force, we will remain defenceless. Elite social engineers are waging an undeclared war on society. By subverting sexual roles, and separating sex from marriage and procreation, they hope to divert, degrade, sedate and finally control us.

THE DYING ART OF FEMININITY

Fascinating Womanhood

> Femininity is a gentle tender quality found in a woman's appearance, manner and nature. A feminine woman gives the impression of softness and delicateness. She has a spirit of sweet submission, and a dependency upon men for their care and protection. Nothing about her appears masculine, no male aggressiveness, competence, efficiency, fearlessness, strength, or the ability to kill her own snakes." (247)

HELEN ANDELIN'S *Fascinating Womanhood* (1965) is subversive to the New World Order because it upholds the inherent difference between the sexes and the basic laws governing marriage.

Such a book would never be published today. It is only available because it appeared 40 years ago and sold 2 million copies.

If you have any doubt about your sexual identity, I recommend *Fascinating Womanhood.* It is pertinent for men as well as women. I also recommend Andelin's *Fascinating Girl* for single women and her husband's *Man of Steel and Velvet* for men.

I'm not saying you should treat this model as gospel or that it's for everyone. It represents a timeless heterosexual paradigm that works. Every couple is different. Choose what is relevant to you and ignore the rest.

Femininity and masculinity are an art, like playing the piano. They must be learned. We have to know the basics before we can improvise.

People are very malleable. Society is the target of a long-term hate campaign designed to degrade and discredit heterosexuality. Domestic violence and rape are trumpeted to make women fear men, reject femininity and become masculine. The destruction of the family has always been the goal of the financial elite in order to control people.

THE BASICS OF FEMININITY

Andelin says a woman's happiness depends on her husband's lifelong devotion and love. Her book teaches women how to be attractive to men, how to be *feminine.*

Andelin writes that women don't have to be beautiful to be feminine. "Acquire a feminine manner by accentuating the differences between yourself and men, not the similarities. Since the masculine manner is strong firm and heavy, yours should be gentle, delicate and light. Apply this in the way you walk, talk, use your hands and carry yourself." (256)

I can still remember how a girl I knew closed a kitchen cupboard with a motion of her hip. This happened 37 years ago when I was 20!

When Andelin writes that a feminine woman is never "crude, vulgar, harsh, overbearing or critical," it is apparent that the fair sex is being deliberately degraded and neutered by the media. "All your conversation should reflect tenderness, patience, forgiveness, tolerance and love."

A wife's first priority is her husband and then her children. Thus a single woman will consecrate herself for her future husband and children as much as possible. She will not be promiscuous.

Wives tend to put career, friends, parents, success and appearance before their husbands. "If you are a successful career woman, keep your priorities straight," Andelin writes. "Let your husband know by words and actions that he is number one." (95)

The woman's primary role is to be wife, mother and homemaker. The man's role is to be guide, protector and provider. This doesn't mean women can't have careers or men can't cook or change a diaper.

A man needs to feel that he is needed, and that he excels his woman in his role. If she becomes independent, he may question his purpose and his feelings for her "since his romantic feelings partly arise from her need to be protected, sheltered and cared for." (102)

A woman should accept her husband at face value and not try to change him. His pride and freedom are inviolable. She should focus on his good qualities and he will improve naturally in response to her.

Reactions to Andelin are either very positive or very negative. One minister wrote on Amazon:" I have given approximately 250 copies of this book to women I have counselled in the past 5 years. In this period of time, I have yet to see ANY of them NOT improve their marriage by working on what they bring to the marriage."

Many women find the book outdated and laughable. One contentious point is that Andelin advises wives to adopt an endearing childlike petulance when upset with their husband. A lot of women find this demeaning. But in practice, most men will respond positively when their authority is not directly challenged.

Andelin may seem outdated in places but she has the basic principles right. Let us adapt them.

Beautiful women are a dime a dozen but feminine women are exceedingly rare. In my view, jeans are the symbol of the unisex virus. Feminine women should never wear jeans.

The world suffers the loss of feminine spiritual qualities: trust, modesty, grace, innocence, serenity, tenderness, patience and nurturing love. This is behind the male obsession with pornographic sex. Men unconsciously seek femininity and love to balance them. The restless masculine spirit seeks a calm harbor.

THE MONSTROUS HOAX

This weekend yet another movie opens about a woman who is a violent killer. *"Domino"* is the story of a female bounty hunter. The real-life inspiration for this story Domino Harvey died recently of a drug overdose or murder. No wonder young women are confused! Where do they see wives and mothers presented in a positive light? Women are always harried, arguing with men and running off to work.

I get email from feminists who say my articles are "hurtful." It's eerie how they all use that word and repeat the party line. I think it's "hurtful" that the super rich want to take the place of God and nature and enslave humanity.

But these feminists don't get it. They don't get A's for connecting feminism with the Rockefellers, Sept. 11 and Iraq, i.e. NWO Central Banker Dictatorship.

Feminism is designed to make women feel unworthy for devoting their lives to the people they love. It forces them out of the house where their employers can control them. It forces infants into joyless daycares subject to conditioning and who-knows-what-else.

I would never stand between anyone and their idea of fulfillment. But ladies, don't be so gullible! You're being defrauded of a lifetime of love. Have your careers later but don't forfeit your femininity and your chance to have a family.

Defining Your Needs

Love is Based on Mutual Dependence

A HAUNTING NEW STAPLES COMMERCIAL captures the predicament of the modern "independent" woman.

It portrays the modern feminist at leisure.

She is scaling a sheer 1000-foot rock face somewhere in the wilderness.

Her cell phone rings and a co-worker informs her that they have won a contract.

She calls Staples Office Centre and requests that a report be ready by Wednesday. These are her contacts: her co-workers and her suppliers.

Then, something eerie and ominous happens. She drops the phone!

We can almost hear it crashing on the rocks below.

I don't know what Staples means by this. Maybe they think she no longer needs it.

To me, dropping the phone symbolizes the plight of modern woman.

Instead of being dependent on husband and family, she is dependent on her boss and the vagaries of the marketplace and politics.

In other words, she is dependent on the bankers. When they have finished their latest "revolution," the (homo) sexual one, feminists will be disposable.

Take her job away (drop the cell phone) and her vaunted "independence" comes crashing down too. She is left isolated and alone, clinging to a rock face.

ANOTHER VIEW OF LOVE

Romantic love is a pseudo religion. Popular songs are its hymns. Sex is exalted as though it were a mystical experience. We are supposed to love (or "worship") our mate's mystery as if s/he were divine.

Of course, very few people live up to this standard. The sex-driven infatuation and novelty fade as the pressures of daily life intrude. We discover that we married a human being like ourselves with both good and bad qualities.

A marriage is more likely to succeed if it is based on mutual dependence rather than romantic idealization. We are taught that love is based on mutual independence but in reality we marry because our mate fulfills certain needs and vice-versa.

These "needs" may be emotional, spiritual, sexual, familial, and financial or you name it.

A husband might say to his wife: This is what I need from you. What do you need from me? No wife can meet her mate's needs if her own aren't also fulfilled.

Marriage is a contract. You live up to your bargain even when you are not feeling "loving." You play the role. It's a "commitment."

Jonathan Swift said that love and faith eventually become real after constant dissembling.

LOVE MAKES BEGGARS OF US ALL

Our dysfunctional culture promotes the idea that people should be loved for their excellent qualities (especially sex appeal) and achievements (especially power and wealth.)

We are naturally drawn to people who have qualities we admire. But this adulatory love often feels like *envy.* There is something self-negating about it, something vampire-like. We want to possess what they have. We are looking for these qualities *in ourselves.* We are looking for ourselves.

Similarly, people often think they will be loved for their accomplishments.

For example, in the movie *"Something's Got to Give,"* Diane Keaton plays a 60'ish woman. Jack Nicholson is supposed to love her because (gasp!) she is a famous playwright!

Think of the people you truly love. Is it because of their appearance, talent or achievements? Or is it because they give you what you need?

If I am right, independent women are misdirecting their energy to career (which does not bring love.)

They are so busy frantically trying to forget they aren't married and having children, they barely have time or inclination for men.

The older ones who have given up are traumatized. I have been to two offices where women my age actually covered their bare ring fingers while talking to me. The toll in human suffering is incalculable.

GIRL ON A CLIFF

The traditional arrangement went like this. A man took care of a woman's material needs. In return, she took care of his emotional and sexual needs. The man made the house; the woman made the home and family. The woman raised the family's cultural level.

Mutual dependence worked very well until elite social engineers decided to break up the family using the mass media.

They convinced millions of gullible women that feminism was the "latest" thing. The poor dears learned the loving husbands who toiled to support them and died in war were in fact exploiting them!

"Oh foolish man, is there anything you cannot be made to believe?" Adam Weishaupt, the founder of the Illuminati opined. This applies to women as well.

Today, a woman works and supplies her own material needs (making a man redundant.) Often, she is too exhausted and hardened by the marketplace to provide for her husband's emotional and sexual needs. Frustrated, both husband and wife look elsewhere; their marriage collapses and their children lose a healthy environment in which to grow.

Women do not get love and satisfaction from career. They get it from being indispensable to their loved ones and treasured for it.

Men and women were designed to complement each other. Love and marriage are about mutual dependence.

By the time independent women realize their mistake it is often too late. They are between a rock and a hard place.

LILLITH

The Occult Roots of Feminism

FEMINISM has roots in the occult Kabalistic and Gnostic tradition that sees marriage and family as impediments to free sex and occult control of society. (Kabala and Gnosticism are the basis of Freemasonry, and in turn the basis of modern Communism, Socialism, Fascism, Zionism and Feminism.)

According to this occult tradition, Lilith was Adam's first wife, the archetype feminist that every man marries and then divorces.

Lilith and Adam argued constantly because Lilith refused to be under him in the act of love saying they were "equal." This is from "The Story of Lilith" which dates from the between the 8th and 10th Centuries A.D:

God "created a woman for Adam, from the earth, as He had created Adam himself, and called her Lilith. Adam and Lilith began to fight. She said, 'I will not lie below,' and he said, 'I will not lie beneath you, but only on top. For you are fit only to be in the bottom position, while I am to be in the superior one.'

Lilith responded, 'We are equal to each other inasmuch as we were both created from the earth.' But they would not listen to one another. When Lilith saw this, she pronounced the Ineffable Name and flew away into the air. Adam stood in prayer before his Creator: 'Sovereign of the universe!' he said, 'the woman you gave me has run away.'

Lilith's refusal to lie beneath Adam is tantamount to the earth refusing to receive a seed. There is nothing inferior or "unequal" about this, no matter what this text has Adam say. It is part of the yin-yang, the active-passive, masculine-feminine dynamic that is at the heart of nature.

Man serves God. Woman serves family. In this way both are useful and their lives have meaning.

But the Gnostic/Kabalistic tradition wishes to overthrow God and nature and substitute the rule of (some) men. The New World Order is the culmination of this Satanic tradition.

That is why replicas of the Ten Commandments are carted out of courthouses and replaced with "human rights" which are not God given, but defined and applied selectively by politicians.

That is why our young women are raised to be dysfunctional and useless; why young men are not taught to serve God (Truth, Love) and give women a noble purpose.

LOVE HAS TO BE EARNED

The occult roots of modern culture also explain the confusing mystical haze that surrounds romantic love. The notion that men get their meaning from love and marriage is very confusing and wrong. It is also feminine. Men get their confidence from doing work they enjoy and getting recognition and reward for it.

The notion that we are divine and can love the "God within" our mate is a form of idolatry. Most of us are closer to apes than to God.

I would replace the word "love" with two words: "trust and respect." This concept is more realistic and understandable. True love develops over a period of years and is based on trust and respect.

Naturally, we must begin by "earning" our own respect by living up to our ideals and achieving our goals. This is the source of self-confidence and attraction.

Then a man must "earn" a woman's trust and respect through slow and patient courtship. For a woman, love is an act of self-surrender, which renders her vulnerable. Her happiness depends on her careful choice of husband.

I have a hunch that the most satisfying aspect of sex is not physical but *emotional*: total possession for the man, and total surrender for the woman. This depends on earning a woman's trust so she can let down her defences.

The popular misconception that we are entitled to love is partly responsible for our arrested development. Instead of becoming more worthy, and more useful, we seek the magical "someone" who will love us just as we are.

WHAT WE CALL LOVE

What we call love is usually sexual infatuation. Young women behave as if sex appeal is all they need, and young men tend to confirm this error. The movies show men going gaga over women who have very little to offer, other than being pretty and quirky.

That's good for ten minutes, what about the rest of life? In the past, women had practical skills as wives and mothers. They learned to cook and sew and make the home beautiful and inviting. They became cultured and mastered a musical instrument. They knew about child rearing.

But more important, they developed a mental attitude. They were going to join their lives with a man and be "on his team" for better or for worse. They were going to bear his children and project his spirit into the future. That's what a woman's love really means. That's what binds a man to a woman.

My wife who is Mexican still has something of the Old World. We met five years ago over the Internet. She sent me a link, which she said was a gift. When I opened it, I saw she had designed a great new web site for my book, *A Long Way to go for Date.*

Love at first web site, her gesture told me that she was prepared to be useful, to *help* me.

A woman helping a man! What a strange concept these days when an ancient satanic conspiracy nears culmination.

NOTE: I am indebted to **DAVID LIVINGSTONE,** author of *The Dying God: The Hidden History of Western Civilization,* for bringing *The Story of Lilith* and the relationship of Feminism to Kabala to my attention.

POLITICALLY INCORRECT

Advice for Young Men

M Y LIFE WAS DYSFUNCTIONAL until the age of 50 because I naively accepted the feminist assumptions purveyed by the mass media. I never imagined the financial elite is engaged in a war to undermine society by trashing heterosexual roles. This hateful government attack on the traditional family continues unabated today. The purpose is to create a totalitarian New World Order where mind control replaces jackboot.

Like millions of men, I was let "off the hook" by sexual liberation and feminism. Instead of becoming a husband and father, I was free to have sex and search for my "identity."

Often sex and identity were confused. I didn't understand that men mature and find direction and purpose by embracing their traditional role, not shunning it. As a result, I suffered from arrested emotional development and missed my opportunity to have a family.

What follows is an antidote to elite feminist propaganda. I don't want young men to fall into the same trap as i did.

1. We rarely hear this but strong healthy children are a man's highest achievement. The paternal instinct is as powerful as the maternal one, but men mistake it as lust. We are really looking for a woman to carry and nurture our children; a woman whose excellent qualities combined with our own will produce wondrous beings. Family is the natural process by which men (and women) grow over a lifetime. This is how we find love and intimacy. It isn't for everyone but it is the path to happiness for most.

2. Stop listening to the media, your peer group or parents. "Trust thy self," Emerson says in "Self Reliance" (1841): "Whoso would be a man, must be a nonconformist." What are your instincts telling you? For example, I always knew I wanted to rule my own roost but feminism prohibited this. *Obey your instincts.*

3. Make your work your passion instead of women. Work is the backbone of a man. Men gain self-confidence from their skill and the reward it earns. Women will try to come between a man and his work but don't let them. Don't let anyone or anything thwart your gift. Women do not respect men who make them their first priority. Your work will keep you on course and help you avoid temptation.

4. Our society makes sex, love and female beauty into a phoney religion in order to distract and manipulate us. Sex and beauty soon become tedious. When the novelty wears off, you are left with character and personality. Best marry a woman with some talent and life skills, one that can program a DVR, decorate the house and mow the lawn.

5. Do not put beautiful women on a pedestal. They are flawed like everyone else. They are more trouble because of their sense of entitlement. Do not marry someone based on sexual infatuation. I recount this error in my book *"A Long Way to go for a Date."* Never show weakness. In courtship, don't appear eager. Women interpret this as weakness. Keep your dignity. *Nothing earns her respect quicker than rejecting her.* Men think they will be loved for their sterling qualities. This is not so. Women are looking for men who make them feel secure. They want men who exude strength and confidence. If you're insecure, build your confidence by meeting your personal goals. Don't despair. Woman's middle name is insecurity. Find someone whose self esteem is lower than yours.

6. Now that I have emerged from the hormonal haze at age 55, I can see that sex is mostly nature's way of ensuring the species' survival. But sex is used to distract and control us. People wouldn't need to search for it if they got married at a young age as they did in the 1950's and started families. Women should marry and have kids *before* going to university. After beginning their careers, men should seek mates five years younger. Sexually, an unmarried man is a live electrical wire. He needs to plug that energy into a woman.

7. Do not marry a woman who doesn't make you and her family her *first* priority. Do you want to share your wife with her boss? If you have an aim in life, why would you marry someone who doesn't support it? Or has a *competing* agenda? In the marketplace of love, men have the power. Our fertility lasts three times as long as theirs. We are the buyers. Select a wife by her commitment to you. One hundred per cent of a "Seven" is a lot better than 25% of a "Ten."

8. Real women are self-effacing. They put their husbands and their children before themselves. Avoid women who compete, control, criticize or complain (the 4 c's). Avoid women who are overachievers.

Don't get hung up on unavailable women. They're not as special as they want you to think (or they think.) Choose a wife who complements you and is a good companion. Choose one who will be a good mother.

9. Being possessive is natural. A man wants to possess a woman. Women want to be possessed. In the act of love, we say a man "possesses" a woman. For total power, a woman gets total love (i.e. total possession.) This is not the same as domination. You wouldn't dominate your right arm, would you? Your wife is part of you. Marriage is a partnership based on mutual trust and respect.

10. Think of your semen as your unique spirit and essence. It is our genetic code. Would you entrust your seed to a vulgar or mediocre woman just because she is attractive? Ideally we would only have sex with a woman we would want to mother our children. This is why sex was reserved for marriage.

11. The media is doing a number on us regarding children. How often do we see children portrayed in a truly positive light? As the angels they often are? We are rich in proportion to the things we love. The highest love is between husband and wife, and parents and children.

12. Don't waste your time "looking for God." We find God by serving Him, and obeying Him. God speaks through our sense of right and wrong, and ideals of absolute truth, justice and love. We are not men if we refuse to sacrifice our "selves" to God (i.e. obey). Truth is liberating even if the truth is about our present bondage.

Much of this was common knowledge when I was a child in the 1950's. Over the years the elite has gradually undermined our understanding of the natural order

An establishment that sows fear and confusion between the sexes, and promotes promiscuity and family breakdown does not have the country's best interest at heart.

HOLLYWOOD SEXUALIZES GRANNIES

Illuminists Compound the Hoax

HOLLYWOOD'S CHRISTMAS FARE includes yet another crude assault on women.

Opening Dec. 19 is "Calendar Girls", a heart warming "true" story of Yorkshire women, age 50-60, who raise money by posing nude for a calendar.

It's for a good cause. Mary's husband John needs an operation and National Health doesn't cover it. The women will pose nude for the calendar while performing traditional activities like baking and gardening. A nice jab at traditional women.

The trailer extols Yorkshire women. "The last stage of their growth is the most glorious." They're "changing the world one month at a time."

By "sexualize" I mean treating a person as if her value lies in her appearance and sex appeal. In other words, she must be sexually desirable to be loved.

This has driven women crazy for years. "Role models" like Britney Spears sexualize prepubescent girls. Now postmenopausal women are suffering an epidemic of eating disorders.

The Illuminati run Hollywood. They mess with our psyches by pretending the unnatural is perfectly normal.

Calendar Girls is an outrage. A woman's sexual attraction is a function of her fertility. To pretend otherwise is cruel and insulting, not just to older women but to all heterosexuals.

Sex appeal is related to one stage of life: courtship, mating and procreation. Postmenopausal women should not be made to compete with young women on this basis.

The secret of a successful marriage is that years of mutual devotion more than compensate for appearance when it comes to sex.

A friend married 30 years wrote to me: "Old naked women are repulsive. A wife of age, however, is beautiful because of history; and when a man looks at his wife he sees the young girl he married, not the age and wrinkles, as her eyes light up for him."

Postmenopausal women deserve dignity and respect. They are our mothers, grandmothers and wives. They have served us and deserve our bountiful love. Their beauty derives from their soul. Their importance lies in the love they continue to give their families.

Feminists, like their Communist sponsors, want to redefine nature. Hollywood is pushing the feminist fantasy that women can ignore their biological clocks and behave as though they were men.

A women's sexual window of opportunity corresponds with her peak years of fertility. In contrast, male sex appeal is based on power. Men become more attractive as they get older and more secure.

Hollywood portrays middle-aged women in sexual terms because there's no other reason to love them. They devoted their lives to careers not families, as they were taught. Now millions are alone and desperate. So feminists compound their hoax by pretending these women are still eligible, and can even attract younger men. Just like Luciferians to rewrite nature.

FEMINIST AGITPROP

This is the theme of *"Something's Got to Give"* another "Christmas movie" which apparently includes nude scenes of 57-year-old Diane Keaton. In one case, Jack Nicholson gets an accidental peak at her breasts.

"I've never seen a woman that age naked before," he exclaims in shock.

According to the synopsis:

"Harry Langer (Jack Nicholson) ... has the world on a string -- and a string of beautiful young girlfriends to prove it. During a romantic rendezvous with his newest girlfriend, Marin, at her mother's Hamptons beach house, he develops chest pains and is nursed by Marin's reluctant mother, Erica Barry (Diane Keaton) -- a successful, divorced New York playwright. In the process, Harry develops more heart pangs, the romantic kind, for Erica, a woman who is right for him in every way.

However, some habits die hard. When Harry hesitates to pursue Erica, his charming thirty something doctor (Keanu Reeves) becomes smitten with her. Harry undergoes a true change of heart and fights to win Erica back."

Dream on ladies. Feminists who gave their lives to the rat race do not miraculously transform into tender sympathetic creatures. Their reputed maturity, sophistication and achievements do not compensate for their wrinkles and emotional baggage. This is written and directed by Nancy Myers, who also gave us the movie *What Women Want.* Apparently they want to fool themselves.

Admittedly at 66, Jack Nicholson's face has more stitches than a quilt, but as long as he can attract a fertile woman, he will choose her. It's nature. Ultimately sex is an act of procreation. Men want to procreate too, or at least have the option.

Ultimately we reap what we sow. If women make careers and independence their first priority, they will end up with a pension.

THE BIGGEST MISTAKE MEN MAKE

Men can have successful marriages with younger mates as long as they behave like men. The biggest mistake men make is to sacrifice their power for love.

Most women will test a man to see what he will do for sex. They will see how much abuse he will take, then try to control him.

A woman cannot love a man she cannot respect. She cannot respect a man who *does not respect himself.* Paradoxically the way to win a woman's love is *not* to take *any* crap. Ignore the cold shoulder.

A man must dedicate his life to a higher purpose and obey his inner voice. That's what women respect.

Another example. I know a man whose wife insists on remaining "best friends" with a former lover. This drives him crazy but she refuses to drop her ex. He accepts the situation, but this is a mistake. He should ask her to leave. His marriage is doomed.

You get the picture. Men cannot afford to be with women who do not accept their leadership.

On the other hand, a man must provide leadership. He must provide money, direction and vision. He must take the time to win his wife's assent. He will compromise because he wants his wife to be happy. But on essentials, he must have the final say.

Many men are too selfish. They don't give a woman what she needs. A woman will do anything so long as she is loved in return. A husband must pay attention his wife's needs and tell her how important she is to him.

WEIRD THINGS

The sexualizing of grannies is part of a larger trend to depravity promoted by our Lucifer loving elites. Pagans who think man's animal nature is divine have hijacked our planet.

That's the reason for our increasing adolescent obsession with sex and nudity characteristic of arrested development.

It's the reason why vulgarity and debauchery are presented as "daring;" why music videos and movies resemble sex orgies and satanic bacchanalia. The media is initiating an unsuspecting public into the occult. Many entertainers belong to satanic societies. We are being subverted, degraded to the level of dogs sniffing each other's genitals.

They abolished God in order to control us. Without that reference point, we are defenceless and gullible. We accept *false Gods*: money, sex, experts and entertainers. The media manipulates us. The movies define our social norms.

There is also a political dimension. In the Preface to *Brave New World,* Aldous Huxley wrote:

"As political and economic freedom diminishes, sexual freedom tends correspondingly to increase. And the dictator will do well to encourage that freedom...it will help to reconcile his subjects to the servitude which is their fate."

Mankind is the interface between God and nature. God's Plan is for humanity to become more God-like. Our Divine Spirit is supposed to refine our animal nature. Hollywood should help us to evolve by celebrating what is highest in us. We cannot be God-like without radical self-transformation.

God has imprinted his Plan in our conscience. We must return to that inner voice and proclaim it from the rooftops. Send the Illuminati a message in the only language it understands. Boycott the movies and the mass media.

Book Four

Freemasonry, Brainwashing & The Illuminati

FREEMASONRY

Mankind's Death Wish

"ARCHITECTS OF DECEPTION," a 600-page history of Freemasonry by Estonian writer Jyri Lina offers profound insight into the true character of modern history.

Essentially, a dominant segment of Western society has joined the Jewish financial elite in embracing Freemasonry, a Luciferian philosophy that represents a death wish for civilization. They imagine somehow they will profit from the carnage and suffering caused by their "New World Order."

Incredible, bizarre and depressing as it sounds, Lina writes that 300 mainly Jewish banking families have used Freemasonry as an instrument to subvert, control and degrade the Western world.

This view is consistent with the 1938 NKVD interrogation of an illuminati member who names many of these banking families and confirms that Freemasons are expendable tools. (See the three-part "Rothschild Conducts Red Symphony" below.)

Based on the archives of the powerful French Grand Orient Lodge, captured in June 1940 and later made public by the Russians, Lina details how Freemasonry has conspired for world domination and orchestrated all major revolutions and wars in the modern era. (Lina, p.332)

Masons, often Jewish, are responsible for Communism, Zionism, socialism, liberalism (and feminism.) They love big government because it is the ultimate monopoly. "World government" (dictatorship) is the final trophy. This is the vision behind 9-11 and the "War on Terror."

These "world revolutionary" "progressive" movements all mirror Lucifer's rebellion against the laws of God and nature, which is at the heart of Freemasonry. They ensnare millions of gullible idealists by promising a utopia based on materialism and "reason" and dedicated to "liberty, equality and fraternity," "public ownership" or some other idealistic sounding claptrap. It's called bait-and-switch.

According to Lina: "The primary aim of modern freemasonry is to build the New World Order, a spiritual Temple of Solomon, where non-members are nothing but slaves [and] ...where human beings would be sacrificed to Yahweh." (52)

Lina cites numerous Jewish sources that claim Freemasonry is based on Judaism and is "the executive political organ of the Jewish financial elite." (81-83) Freemasonry extended Judaism to non-Jews, or non-Jews who claim to be Jews. (See "The Jewish Conspiracy is British Imperialism" on my website.)

Lina and others who attempt to alert humanity to its real condition are routinely slandered as anti-Semitic, fascist, and right wing "haters" by people indirectly employed by the bankers.

This tactic shields the conspirators from scrutiny and makes discussion of our grim predicament impossible.

I am a Jew. I am not part of this banking monopoly, nor is the majority of Jews. By way of analogy, the mafia is often considered Italian but most Italians do not belong to the mafia.

Italians don't viciously attack opponents of organized crime and call them "racists" and "hate mongers". That would look awfully suspicious. Jews compromise themselves by their defence of the Masonic bankers and their perverse vision for humanity.

My four grandparents perished in the Jewish holocaust. I demand to know the real reason they were murdered. London-based Masonic bankers and their cronies brought Hitler to power in order to provoke war, control Stalin, and justify the creation of Israel. They betrayed non-Zionist Jews and let them perish. They are using naive Jews in the same way they use Masons and numerous other nations and groups.

THE ILLUMINIST CONSPIRACY

We cannot understand the modern world unless we appreciate that it is the result of the Masonic conspiracy. People scoff yet the evidence stares them in the face every day.

The Great Seal of the United States on every dollar bill is a Masonic symbol. There are 33 steps on the side of the pyramid representing the 33 degrees of Freemasonry. The Masons established the United States as a base to advance their goal of world supremacy.

Similarly, the emblem of the United Nations is also a Masonic symbol. The world is caught in a grid consisting of 33 spaces surrounded by acacia leaves, which signifies intense activity in Masonry. (215)

Three-quarters of US presidents in the twentieth century were high-level Masons. Both Bush and Kerry are Masons (Skull and Bones.) FDR, Churchill, Lenin, Trotsky and Stalin were Masons. Most Zionist leaders were and are Masons. Gerhard Schroeder, Jacques Chirac and Tony Blair are Freemasons. So is Sadaam Hussein, which suggests the Iraq war could be a sadistic charade.

There are over six-million Masons in 32,000 lodges around the world including 2.5 million in the US. In 1929, 67% of Members of Congress were Masons. There are 360,000 Masons in England.

Lina believes, "Freemasonry plays the same role in Western society as the Communist Party did in the Soviet Union. Without belonging to the freemasonry there is no chance of a fast career, regardless of how talented one is."

Keep in mind that Communism was a Masonic enterprise and the puzzle starts to take shape.

Lina says Freemasons not only control politics but also virtually every sector of Western society, including science and culture. "The present cultural life has become virtually unconscious," he writes. "We have witnessed the beginning of cultural senility." (333)

In his pamphlet *"The Open Conspiracy: Blueprint for a World Revolution"* (1929) the Freemason H.G. Wells describes an "open secret society" consisting of society's leading men operating as a hidden force to secure world resources, reduce population through war and replace the nation state with world dictatorship. (340)

MASONIC IDEOLOGY

Human beings are naturally attracted to good and repulsed by evil. Thus evil always represents itself as good. To the public, and its own lower ranks, Freemasonry pretends to be dedicated to "making good men better", humanism, tolerance, Christianity and you-name-it.

If this were true, would they have to extract vows of secrecy from members on pain of slitting their throat? Would they exhort Masons to support their brother even when they are breaking the law? Would they have been condemned by many Popes and banned from numerous countries? (84)

I do not wish to impugn the many good and decent men in the lower "Blue Degrees" who are unaware of Freemasonry's true function and character. But there is abundant evidence and testimony that Freemasonry is a satanic cult dedicated to the worship of the Devil. (134-138)

For example, when the Italian Grand Orient Lodge was evicted from the Palazzio Bourghese in Rome in 1893, the owner found a shrine dedicated to Satan. The Italian freemasons published a newspaper in the 1880's where they admitted time and again, "Our leader is Satan!" (135)

The Masons also admit to having a revolutionary political agenda. Typical of statements Lina cites from Masonic publications is the following from a German magazine in 1910: "The driving thought is at all times focused on destruction and annihilation, because the power of this great secret society can only rise from the ruins of the existing order of society." (272)

CONCLUSION

The Illuminist Conspiracy is responsible for humanity's arrested development. Mankind resembles a person suffering from a serious disease and sinking into a coma.

Juri Lina has written a courageous book to revive us. He says we face "the largest spiritual crisis in the history of mankind...They have taken our history, our dignity, our wisdom and our honor, sense of responsibility, spiritual insights and our traditions."

We are partly to blame, he says: "We have failed to act against the Masonic madness due to our enormous gullibility. We have been totally fooled and ignored the warning signals." (274)

He ends on a hopeful note, saying evil is dysfunctional and inevitably destroys itself. "Freemasonry carries within it the seeds of its own destruction." (563)

Wars, revolutions and depressions are all part of a "revolutionary" process designed to frogmarch humanity to "world government" under the rubric of Freemasonry which is a proxy for an alliance of occult Jewish and gentile financial elites. Their "self-destruction" seems to be our best hope since the public is too feckless and weak to resist.

INDOCTRINATION

How University Betrays Students

I WOULD ONLY SEND MY SON TO UNIVERSITY if he had no talent. He is going anyway, for the social life and the certificate. I warn him that studying the humanities and social sciences will stunt his ability to think independently or absorb information that doesn't fit his programming.

The modern university is not devoted to truth, quite the opposite. Repressive feminism is rampant on campus but this is just a symptom of a much more profound problem.

Modern Western "culture" is based on the fraudulent assumptions of the "Enlightenment," an intellectual movement dating from the Eighteenth Century. This in turn was the product of the Illuminist program to create a new (secular) world order by denying the existence of God and immutable natural and spiritual laws.

In practice this means Arts students study a bunch of atheists who are presented as if *they* were Gods. Their professors act as high priests.

Like deaf men tuning a piano, they try to explain the human condition without any reference to the Creator, Design or man's Divine Spirit.

They portray mankind as a forlorn animal in an amoral world, characterized by a merciless struggle for survival.

They celebrate human "freedom" by which they mean the freedom to reject God's Order, indulge animal appetites, and be alienated and dysfunctional.

Illuminism is the Luciferian doctrine of Freemasonry. The mortar board that university graduates wear is a symbol of Freemasonry. Black gowns symbolize the occult. Arts students are unwittingly being inducted into a Luciferian/Communist cult.

God represents moral and spiritual absolutes like love, truth, goodness, harmony and justice. Belief in their reality is essential for our healthy development. While our culture pays lip service to them (this is how fraud works), it is frankly devoted to their demise.

DYSFUNCTION BY DESIGN

Modern education and culture is designed to make us dysfunctional. *The Protocols of the Elders of Zion* confirms this. The *Protocols* is not an anti Semitic diatribe. (They say that because they don't want you to read it.) It is the blueprint of the New World Order that is now in place.

Someone like Baron Lionel Rothschild wrote it between 1875-1895 for a Masonic Secret Society, the Illuminati. The Illuminati represents a continuation of the feudal alliance of Jewish bankers and European aristocrats. The Illuminati created and financed Nazism and Communism.

The Illuminati is bound by a devotion to Lucifer, the rebellious angel who defied God and said man will define reality. He is called "the bringer of light." Now do you understand the "Enlightenment"? The super rich want to be God and reshape reality to fit their interests. To do this, they need to sever our links with Reality, i.e. God (absolute truth, love and justice.)

Their means are unlimited; so are their ambitions. Here are some relevant statements from Protocol 16.

"In order to effect the destruction of all collective forces except ours we shall emasculate the first stage of collectivism, the universities, by re-educating them in a new direction."

"We must introduce into their education all those principles which have so brilliantly broken up their order."

"Do not suppose for a moment that these statements are empty words: think carefully of the successes we arranged for Darwinism, Marxism, Nietzsche-ism.... it should be plain to see what a disintegrating importance these directives have had upon the minds of the goyim. " (Protocol 2)

"We shall erase from the memory of men all facts of previous centuries which are undesirable to us..."

We shall turn them into "unthinking submissive brutes waiting for things to be presented before their eyes in order to form an idea of them..."

This is consistent with a 1930's Communist manual on brainwashing. "In the United States we have been able to alter the works of William James, and others, ...and to place the tenets of Karl Marx, Pavlov, Lamarck, and the data of Dialectic Materialism into the textbooks of psychology, to such a degree that anyone thoroughly studying psychology becomes at once a candidate to accept the reasonableness of Communism."

"As every chair of psychology in the United States is occupied by persons in our connection, the consistent employment of such texts is guaranteed... Educating broadly the educated strata of the populace into the tenets of Communism is thus rendered relatively easy." ("Soviet Art of Brainwashing" II, Ch. 11)

BOW DOWN BEFORE "GREAT MEN"

At university students encounter "The Cult of Great Men" the pantheon of modern pretenders who have usurped God's place.

Their every utterance is treated as Holy Writ. Scholarly articles are devoted to words that later turn out to be typos. In a graduate seminar, I witnessed a student read a list of filthy obscenities that had been censored from William Faulkner's novel "Sanctuary." After each expletive, the other students gasped with horror as though a religious artefact had been desecrated.

Professors are the overpaid priests of this secular cult. They have a vested interest in maintaining its shibboleths. They initiate students into a lifelong habit of mental servility. All knowledge comes from Great Men. Students can only aspire to analyse their meaning. A professor once told me I had failed because "only great men can say things like that."

The students' state-of-mind becomes passive and disoriented. He struggles to reconcile contradictory world-views.

One day I had an awakening. Don't these "great men" live in the same world? Isn't it the one I live in?

Dare I think for myself?

Dislocation takes place in time as well as space. By continually studying the past, the student thinks nothing remains to be done. No manifestos remain to be written, no Bastilles need to be stormed.

While the world cries out for leadership, the new generation is buried in musty manuscripts writing footnotes to dead men.

EDUCATION SERVES ITS PURPOSE

As you've gathered by now, a humanities education is not intended to uplift or empower. The world is owned and run by an inbred banking cabal and their allies. Its goal, in the words of Cecil Rhodes, is to "gradually absorb the wealth of the world." Naturally it must obscure this plan. They want to make students their tools. Professors who don't play the game are fired.

Universities are not places of invigorating inquiry and debate. They are stagnant backwaters that reek of moral compromise and disillusionment.

Mankind is groping in the dark. "All we know is the wind that blows," Thoreau wrote. Our false confidence is based on material progress and technology, which Thoreau calls "improved means to unimproved ends."

"We have turned the brainless head of the goyim with progress," says the *Protocols*(XIII). With the exception of "material inventions," progress "like a fallacious idea, implies a departure from truth in all cases."

In other words, the Illuminists have infected mankind with the illusion that they are building a humanist utopia based on reason, when in fact they are constructing a neo feudal tyranny. This is the essence of "globalism" and the principle behind world events.

In conclusion, God is a Spirit or state of consciousness where ideals of justice goodness truth and love are self-evident. The Illuminists' first priority is to destroy Christianity and belief in God. They have to sever humanity from its metaphysical moorings in order to substitute a false reality conducive to their rule.

Humanities education today is a placebo, a substitute for a true education. It is a pretext for indoctrination, acceptance of which qualifies you for employment. I would recommend university only for a practical education (i.e. science, commerce, pharmacy, engineering etc.)

The world will not be saved by acts of God but acts of men representing God. Our duty is to take these ideals seriously in our personal lives and bring them into the world. The cost of rejecting God is to become slaves of very bad men.

TAVISTOCK

How the Elite Plays God

LIKE A CAT TOYING WITH A MOUSE, the elite teases us with glimpses of our true predicament. One such peek was the 1998 movie *The Truman Show* directed by Peter Weir.

Truman Burbank, played by Jim Carrey, is unaware his life is a live reality TV show. Everyone, including his wife, is an actor, and everything that happens is staged. In other words, his life is a fraud.

Truman Burbank's predicament describes our own. According to John Coleman, the elite has been writing and directing the script for almost hundred years at the Tavistock Institute of Human Relations based in London.

Coleman, 71, a former British Intelligence officer (MI-6), first exposed the clique that dominates the world is his *Conspirator's Hierarchy: The Story of the Committee of 300* (1992).

As its title suggests, his latest book is a rambling cry of despair: *The Tavistock Institute of Human Relations: Shaping the Moral, Spiritual, Cultural, Political and Economic Decline of the United States of America* (2005).

The book is confirmation that a financial elite engineered every war and depression in modern history and continues to condition our beliefs and behavior.

According to Coleman, Tavistock began life before WWI to convince peace-loving populations of the need to massacre each other.

"Those fresh-faced young American boys from Arkansas and North Carolina were sent marching off to Europe believing they were "fighting for their country" never knowing that the "democracy" [Woodrow] Wilson sent them to "make the world safe for" was a Socialist-International One World Government dictatorship." (42)

Funded by the royal family, the Rockefellers and the Rothschilds, Tavistock pioneered the techniques of propaganda used to justify war. Outright lies about German atrocities in WWI resonate down through the decades to lies about Sadaam Hussein's gassing Kurds and killing babies in Kuwait. Of course the biggest lie of all is that Muslims had anything to do with Sept. 11.

Coleman found that 94% of the key words and phases developed by Tavistock for WWII use "matched up with those used in the Korean War, the Vietnam War and the Gulf War." (153)

Coleman's main point is *we can't trust anything* the mass media or government tells us, especially not the "News." He cites Stalin's propaganda chief Willy Munzenberg: "All news is lies and all propaganda is disguised as news."

Coleman says society is rotten with institutions and organizations directed by Tavistock to deceive and distort. They are called "elite" institutions because of whom they serve.

The conspiracy reaches right down to the local level. According to Coleman, Tavistock has an "invisible army" of actors found "today in the halls of justice, police, churches, school boards, sports bodies, newspapers, TV...town councils, state legislatures, and are legion in Washington. They run for every office..."

Virtually every important corporation, university, think tank or foundation is linked to Tavistock. (See *Conspirators' Hierarchy* pp. 221-253 for a list.) It chooses the entertainers we watch, the pundits we listen to, the politicians we elect. Every US President since Theodore Roosevelt has been under its control. They made examples of rebels like JFK and Richard Nixon.

Tavistock is behind every "spontaneous" social movement of the last century, including feminism, sexual "liberation", the peace movement, the "New Age" movement, environmentalism, homosexuality, and abortion.

"The moral, spiritual, racial, economic, cultural and intellectual bankruptcy we are in the midst of today is not some social phenomenon...that just happened. Rather it is the product of a carefully planned Tavistock program," Coleman writes.

We are constantly studied to see how we will react under stress. Orson Well's Martian invasion in 1938 was designed to demonstrate the power of the "news" to deceive. Coleman doesn't mention it but the power blackout in the Northeast was probably another study of mass behavior. So was New Orleans. Confident of our sedated sheep-like behavior, Coleman says Tavistock went ahead and massacred David Koresh and his followers at Waco after lying about his activities. (240)

Tavistock follows Sun Tsu's maxim of "Kill a few; terrorize many." Coleman calls Winston Churchill's decision to bomb German civilians "a war crime." Dresden was "an outright attack on Christianity, timed to take place during Lent," he says. (188)

According to Coleman, Tavistock is waging war on the Muslim world because Islam represents an obstacle to its control. (151) He claims Russia and China still have a measure of independence.

CONCLUSIONS

We are in this jam because a small group of dynastic families have amassed unlimited wealth by usurping the government's money-creation role.

To maintain this unjust advantage, they need to create a "world government" dictatorship. As in any colonial situation, our national elites are chosen by their willingness to collaborate with the occupying power. Most people will do whatever it takes to be "successful". Many think they are free citizens creating a better world. Like the two Jewish professors who criticized the Israel Lobby recently, they discover the reality when they stray from the script.

The public is constantly under psychological attack. Turn on the news and we see 9-11 cover-up accomplice Rudolph Giuliani shedding crocodile tears with victims' families at patsy Zacharias Moussaoui's show trial. Al-Quaeda hijacker Mohammed Atta "mistakenly keyed the air traffic control microphone instead of the cabin intercom" and is heard talking to the frightened passengers! Sure.

Meanwhile, the bird flu is coming to get us. Someone is burning black churches. Illegal aliens are flooding the country (despite the "heightened security" mandated by the "war on terror.") We're told Jesus asked Judas to betray him. It goes on and on.

People find the Illuminati to be an abstract and elusive enemy. Look no further than your television, your iPod, your radio, movie or newspaper.

Coleman says 450 of the Fortune 500 companies get their marching orders from Tavistock. This may explain why TV commercials seem more concerned with behavior modification than with selling a product.

I saw this gem recently. A little boy besieges a little girl with gifts. Each time she rejects him. Finally she accepts a vase full of flowers but slams the door in his face. She dumps the flowers in the garbage and uses the vase to gulp McCain's Kool-Aid.

What a message to send to children! They are messing people up so we are too divided and dysfunctional to resist them.

Like Truman Burbank, more and more people are recognizing the plot. They are testing the elite's story line and finding it mendacious and perverse. They are walking off the stage to find an authentic life.

MODERN KULTURE

The Judeo Masonic Roots

MODERN "CULTURE" is a product of the Luciferian conspiracy against Christian Civilization.

Relentlessly negative and increasingly obscene, modern "culture" attacks the sources of dignity, decency and hope that define us as human beings rather than animals.

For example, last week the media was hyping a play that opened in London about "sexual love" between a married man and a goat.

In an interview, the playwright Edward Albee said *"The Goat"* challenged this "societal taboo" and hoped that members of the audience would "re-examine their values and attitudes toward bestiality."

"Funny, moving and tragic," raved *Channel 4 News,* a respected and "serious" programme in the UK.

Bestiality has occurred and the play is primarily concerned with the protagonist's confession and inability to deal with the fact that he "feels guilty for not feeling guilty". "We are all animals," he rationalizes. The play deals with the confrontation between the protagonist, his wife and their gay son.

A reader, Jonathan Stonehouse, wrote: "It staggers me to think that there are many who now associate freedom with the normalization of everything formerly regarded as morally repugnant, when the truth is we're building a world in which the majority will be slaves to every whim and fancy, not to mention dark and abhorrent desire, the human imagination can conceive. That's a form of 'freedom' I can well do without."

True culture is based on refining our animal instincts in terms of our spirituals ideals (like truth, justice, goodness and beauty.)

Modern anti-culture is based on demoralizing and destroying society by disparaging these ideals.

Anti culture portrays man in purely naturalistic and material terms. Every sexual impulse and bodily function must be recognized and indulged. This is considered "courageous" while any demur is considered repressive and prudish or fascist.

In one of the final episodes of *"Sex and the City"*, the audience had to endure Carrie getting a bikini wax. Thankfully we were spared a full frontal view.

This is not prudishness. Human dignity requires privacy. Female allure requires modesty and mystery. We have souls, not only bodies.

The exaltation of man's animal nature at the expense of his spiritual qualities is a direct consequence of the deification of man. Our anti culture assumes that man is a finished product and doesn't need to be transformed by God's Love.

A symptom of making man God is that we mystify and worship human beings. We worship a cult of great minds, a cult of great beauty, a cult of great wealth and power.

Modern "culture" reflects the final unfolding of a diabolical conspiracy that rejects God's plan for mankind's development.

THE JUDEO MASONIC ROOTS OF ANTI CULTURE (MODERNISM)

By eating the forbidden fruit, Lucifer promised: "Your eyes will be open and you will be like God, knowing good and evil." (Genesis 3:5)

This means that man will define what is good and evil.

God is Good. When man makes himself God, he really becomes Satan. Good becomes whatever the most powerful man or group wants. Good becomes evil and evil becomes good. This is happening today.

There were a lot of groups who wanted to be God but some believe our anti culture can be traced to the Jewish view of their "chosenness."

Originally Jews had a conception of God as a Universal Moral Force. (This is the Judaism I identify with.)

Apparently in 79 BC there was a Civil War and the Pharisees were victorious. They proclaimed the supremacy of the Babylonian Talmud over the Torah (the first five books of the Old Testament.)

The Talmud teaches that the Jews are chosen by God to lead mankind. In practice this makes them God and gives them the right to redefine reality. It has made them Luciferians. In the words of Harold Rosenthal, "Most Jews do not like to admit it, but our god is Lucifer...and we are his chosen people. Lucifer is very much alive."

According to the author "Rabi": "Christianity is essentially preoccupied with the individual salvation of man. Judaism only contemplates the salvation of the House of Israel, which alone can permit the salvation of seventy nations of the universe." (*Anatomie du Judasime Francaise,* pp.203-204)

Thus the Pharisees rejected Christ because he taught that God is Love and all men are equal in the sight of God.

"The advent of Christ was a national catastrophe for the Jewish people, especially for the leaders," Leon de Poncins writes. "Until then they alone had been the Sons of the Covenant; they had been its sole high priests and beneficiaries.... "

He continues: "The irreducible antagonism with which Judaism has opposed Christianity for 2000 years is the key and mainspring of modern subversion...[The Jew] championed reason against the mythical world of the spirit ...he was the doctor of unbelief; all those who were mentally in revolt came to him either secretly or in broad daylight..." (Judaism and the Vatican, pp.111-113.)

FREEMASONRY AND JUDAISM

In addition to Jewish Messianism, Freemasonry has been the bankers' tool. It was instrumental in the destruction of the Christian monarchies in Germany, Austria and Russia and the decline of the Catholic Church.

In his *Encyclical Humanum Genus* (1884) Pope Leo XIII wrote that the ultimate aim of Freemasonry is "to uproot completely the whole religious and moral order of the world, which has been brought into existence by Christianity...This will mean that the foundation and the laws of the new structure of society will be drawn from pure naturalism."

Again Pope Leo XIII said: "Freemasonry is the permanent personification of the Revolution; it constitutes a sort of society in reverse whose aim is to exercise an occult overlordship upon society as we know it, and whose sole raison d'etre consists of waging war against God and his Church." (De Poncins, *Freemasonry and the Vatican,* p. 45)

Leon de Poncins uses Jewish sources to argue that Freemasonry is closely related to Judaism. For example, Rabbi Elie Benamozegh wrote: "Masonic theology corresponds well enough to that of the Kabbala.,,,(*Israel et L'Humanite,* p.73)

De Poncins cites an article that appeared in 1861 in a Parisian Jewish Review *La Verite Israelite*: "But the spirit of Freemasonry is that of Judaism in its most fundamental beliefs; its ideas are Judaic, its language is Judaic, its very organization, almost, is Judaic... "

De Poncins writes that the goal of both Freemasonry and Judaism is the unification of the world under Jewish law. (*Freemasonry and the Vatican,* p. 76)

CONCLUSION

Judeo Masonic culture hasn't been all-bad. It has allowed us to accept our sexual desires without guilt and given us the freedom to find God again on our own terms. However these benefits are unintended. The ultimate aim is to divorce us from God and enslave us to our sexual and material lusts, i.e. to arrest our development.

Like a scientist who begins with a hypothesis, I am offering this as a paradigm. You must decide if it helps to explain the world. Obviously I am just scratching the surface, and welcome guidance from people who are better informed than I.

But I have no doubt that mankind is being subverted by its political and cultural leaders, beholden to international bankers and their allies, who often are practising Luciferians. They use Judaism (incl. Zionism) and Freemasonry as instruments of organization and control. Obviously the majority of Jews and Freemasons are unaware or do not believe this.

I'm afraid spiritual and psychological enslavement is but a prelude to a political and economic one. Since 9-11, we are sheep grazing in sight of an abattoir.

CULTURAL MARXISM
The Fraudulent Basis of Modern Kulture

THERE SHOULD BE A POISON SYMBOL over the doors of our universities, cinemas and art galleries. There should be a similar warning on our TV, music and videos.

In the 1920's, leaders of the Communist International decided that Western society was too strong to conquer. It was necessary to weaken it by subverting its cultural institutions--family, education, religion, art, mass media and government.

They have largely succeeded. While maintaining these institutions in their familiar format, they have subtly changed the content. It's like lacing a bottle of aspirin with arsenic. The purpose is to gradually poison, paralyse and eventually destroy us.

We are noticing that our political and cultural leaders are mostly cowards, dupes, traitors, crooks, opportunists and impostors rewarded by how much harm they can do.

Our failure to combat Communism is due to a misunderstanding of its real nature. We imagine it is a discredited movement, devoted to social justice, equality and public ownership. Millions of idealists, including myself, were duped.

In fact, Communism is an international phenomenon that invaded Russia and China. It is the creation of a satanic cult (the Illuminati) formed in 1776 by international bankers. It is designed to put all the world's wealth in their hands, and eventually to reduce and enslave the human race. The 5-pointed Red Star of Communism is also the symbol of Satan-worship. A demonic virus, Communism has morphed into countless forms (such as feminism) and is hoodwinking more people than ever.

Western Civilization is built on Christianity, the premise that God is real, in fact the ultimate and only permanent Reality, a spiritual one. Through man's Divine soul, the ordinary individual can discern the Divine Will without mediation from a worldly authority. This is why the bankers hate Christianity.

God is the Truth, Love, Beauty and Goodness to which we aspire. This moral order precludes a small clique monopolizing the world's wealth. So the bankers set out to destroy our belief in a Divine Order by promoting Darwinism, Existentialism etc. They promote war, depression and terror so we will demand their "antidote": the New World Order.

In his brilliant essay, *"The Frankfurt School and Political Correctness"* Michael Minnichino describes how most of the fashionable intellectual and artistic movements in the 20th century, still in vogue today, were actually inspired by thinkers who were Commintern (Communist International) agents financed by the central bankers. Some of them actually worked for Soviet Intelligence right into the 1960's.

He writes: "The task [of the Frankfurt School] was first to undermine the Judeo-Christian legacy through an "abolition of culture" ...and second, to determine new cultural forms which would increase the alienation of the population, thus creating a "new barbarism." ...The purpose of modern art, literature and music must be to destroy the uplifting potential of art, literature and music..."

Funds came from "various German and American universities, the Rockefeller Foundation, the American Jewish Committee, several American intelligence services..."

This subversive movement "represents almost the entire theoretical basis of all the politically correct aesthetic trends which now plague our universities." They are associated with Post Modernism, Feminism, Cultural Studies, Deconstructionism, Semiotics, etc.

Their net effect is to divorce us from truth, social cohesion and our cultural heritage. They assert that reality is unknowable and that writers and artists are in fact depicting themselves. For example, postmodernist Hayden White writes, "historical narratives are verbal fictions, the contents of which are more invented than found...truth and reality are primarily authoritarian weapons of our times." In other words, we cannot know what happened in the past (which is exactly what they want us to believe.)

Postmodernism is part of the authoritarian agenda. Similarly the Frankfurt School championed the notion that "authoritarianism" is caused by religion, male leadership, and family, when these things actually uphold society.

As far as the humanities and social sciences are concerned, universities are enemy territory and professors usually are obstacles to genuine learning.

THE MASS MEDIA

The same applies to the mass media, which the central bankers own and control. We imagine that books, movies and music are commercially or artistically motivated. This is not true. Elite brainwashers discovered they could sell almost anything as long as it is hyped and adheres to a familiar format. Thus the hidden agenda of entertainment is social engineering, Satanism, sex and violence. Musician Wes Penre says stars are selected not for talent but because they advance the elite agenda. He writes:

"Their task is to demoralize our youth, to create a society where no one is able to think for themselves (contrary to what the pop culture is trying to teach us about the "rebellious" rock music). The Art Industry creates "Icons" with degrading and satanic messages, who are supposed to take the place of God. The musicians are also often acting degraded and high or low on drugs, so their fans start acting the same. The purpose is to create apathy and decay. Quite a few artists also put subliminal backward messages in their music, like Led Zeppelin, Michael Jackson, The Eagles, and more...."

Many musicians died young due to "drug overdoses" because they tried to buck the agenda.

This also explains the obsession with romance in popular music. Love and sex are intended to distract us from everything else.

Increasingly, there is a lesbian message in popular music. For example, the Dixie Chicks scorn men and celebrate female independence. In one song, women self-righteously murder a man who gave his wife a black eye. Young women sing these songs and identify.

A friend noticed his Dixie Chick-singing girlfriend has been psychologically neutered. She thinks becoming a wife and mother will cramp her style.

Ever wonder why there hasn't been a truthful movie about real American heroes like Henry Ford, Charles Lindbergh (Post "The Spirit of St. Louis"), Huey Long, Louis McFadden and Whittaker Chambers? They opposed the banker agenda.

CONCLUSION

Just as we need healthy food and exercise, our mind and soul needs truth and beauty. We need to see life portrayed honestly, with the real forces identified. Instead, we are deliberately deceived and poisoned by a small financial elite with a diabolical plan.

Whether it's school or mass media, we are bombarded with propaganda designed to produce alienation and dysfunction. We must protect ourselves from this poison before it is too late.

The good news is that modern culture, based on the premise there is no inherent purpose or positive design in human life, has been exposed. It is a long-term Illuminati psy-op designed to demoralize us. It will fail.

CREEPY

Is Local Legislature a Disguised Pagan Temple?

Not five miles from my Winnipeg home is the Manitoba legislature. In November, the Winnipeg Free Press ran a 15-part series revealing how the legislature building is similar in numerous ways to a pagan Egyptian temple.

For example, Researcher Frank Albo found that the Lieut. Gov.'s reception room has precisely the same measurements as the "Holy of Holies," the sacred chamber in Solomon's Temple, which housed the Ark of the Covenant. It is symbolic of the Master's Lodge where the most sacred rites of Freemasonry are performed. The Entrance Hall is 66.6 ft by 66.6 ft and boasts three sets of 13 steps each. etc.

Albo discovered that nearly everyone involved in the construction from 1914 to 1920, was a Freemason, including the Paris-trained architect, the contractor, the Premier and almost his whole government. The temple, replete with colonnades, murals, sphinxes and statues of famous Masons cost three times as much as other provincial legislatures.

In 1911, the Manitoba Free Press commented that the architectural competition smacked of a "frame-up with some ulterior object in view." (Dec. 9, 1911) (In fact a scandal over costs and corruption which erupted in 1915 cost the Premier his job and sent the contractor to jail.)

If the legislature is indeed a disguised pagan temple, the implications are staggering:

This building ostensibly represents the public. It seems that, even in 1912, an occult secret society, the Freemasons, controlled society with relative impunity and dispensed patronage.

They built a temple instead of a legislature. Did they contemplate the overthrow of democracy and the installation of an authoritarian pagan theocracy, presumably the Masonic hierarchy?

Built for the ages, is the legislature intended to become a religious center in the New World Order, perhaps after a nuclear war? Is the temple going to be the seat of government? Obviously I want to be wrong about all of this.

However, experts like lawyer Constance Cumbey says that the money elites are preparing exactly this kind of "New Age" government and religion. http://www.newswithviews.com/Cumbey/constance1.htm

BACKGROUND

Freemasonry is empowered by the London-based central banking cartel as a way of corrupting and controlling society. Privately they refer to Freemasonry as "a madhouse but at liberty."

Does Freemasonry serve the devil? Does a benevolent society have to be secret? Does it threaten to cut the throat of initiates who talk? Does it demand its members assist each other even when they are breaking the law or being immoral?

Freemasonry pretends to be concerned with moral uplift. Given its incredible power, is the world becoming a better place? "Know them by their fruit."

In fact, the Illuminati literally represent a malevolent supernatural force that is waging pitiless war on humanity. It is gradually creating Hell on earth.

It wages war-using war. It turns us against each other by deceiving and dividing us. The enemy is not ordinary people, many of whom have based their identity on falsehoods. We need to unite against the puppet masters and their agents.

"IN PLAIN VIEW"

The Freemasons have a philosophy of "hiding in plain view." Theirs is an "open conspiracy." That means they'll talk about it openly but then deny or prevaricate if there is any heat. Their Luciferian power is rising before our eyes but if someone notices, he is attacked and called "paranoid."

Illuminati symbolism is on the US Great Seal and the US dollar bill. It is in the logos of countless corporations. CBS, AOL, Exxon, Shell. The horned goat satanic symbol is becoming omnipresent, especially among youth. They are using it to advertise Yahoo Messenger now. Of course, they'll say it represents something else. That's how it works.

I can't go anywhere without seeing the new logo of the city of Winnipeg. It has Illuminati motifs. A dot in a circle evokes the original Illuminati symbol , representing the Eye of Horus, or the sexual act. This is over a swoosh representing the sunrise, i.e. the Sun, or Lucifer the light bringer.

This logo is on all City of Winnipeg buses and trucks. Winnipeg always has been an occult headquarters. At the center of the continent, apparently part of the earth's "energy grid" runs right through the legislature. Recently the province adopted the motto "Spirited Energy."

After attending a séance here in 1923, Sir Arthur Conan Doyle wrote, "Winnipeg stands very high among the places we have visited for psychic possibilities."

(Between 1870 and 1970, Manitoba had 12 Premiers who were masons. Several city mayors were also masons, including Francis Cornish, Winnipeg's first mayor. Between 1870 and and 1924, over 140 masonic lodges were established in Manitoba and, between 1875 and 1970, 86 masonic corner stones were laid in public buildings throughout the province, including city hall, many churches and many schools.)

There are probably a lot of public buildings that have been surreptitiously co-opted by the Freemasons. The Israeli Supreme Court immediately comes to mind.

There are too many occult symbols in the Manitoba Legislature to mention. The most obvious is the statue of the "Golden Boy" on the dome. Manitobans have been told that he represents "Spirit of Enterprise."

In fact he is Hermes, the god of alchemy, patron of the occult and messenger to the underworld. Sculptural groups representing the noble elements Earth Water Air and Fire, (the materia prima of the Hermetic alchemist) surround him on the dome.

Hermes promises to lift man to god-like status by virtue of "secret knowledge" rather than by self-purification and devotion to God, (justice, truth and Love.) He is facing north, which apparently also has ominous connotations.

REACTION

When the Free Press series ran in November, there was a lot of interest from Manitobans but few no objections. No people seemed to mind that a public institution representing freedom and prosperity for Manitobans was taken over by an occult society for its own bizarre purpose, at taxpayers expense.

In Letters to the Editor, only two commented on the fact that the political heart of an ostensibly Christian society, (at least in 1912) should be represented by heathen symbolism.

The Freemasons seem happy to hide in plain sight. Ronald Stern and Bob Stern, local textile tycoons, bought the Winnipeg Free Press in 2001. Shortly after, the Bnai B'rith, a Jewish Masonic Order, honored them. The newspaper would not have run this series if Freemasons were afraid to reveal their handiwork.

CONCLUSION

We live in a world where a large segment of the leadership class has sold itself, if not to Satan, to people who worship Satan..
This is what happens when we eschew genuine religion in favor of diversity and secularism. We don't get religious neutrality, tolerance and freedom. We get paganism and Satanism. In hindsight, the "separation of church and state" was a tactic by which dark forces have discredited God and taken control of society.

Satan's success is partly due to our failure to revitalize our image of God. God is the principle of our own development. We can no more deny our need for Him than our need for oxygen. As far as humanity is concerned, God represents our spiritual ideals: peace, harmony, beauty, truth, goodness, justice and love.

God depends on us to do His work. He is not a magician. He is the Creator. He works through us. Worshiping God is as simple as telling the truth and doing the right thing.

Prophesies of tribulation and doom can be self fulfilling. The Messiah may not appear. We need to use our common sense. The port is reached mostly by avoiding the rocks.

JOHN KERRY

& The Soviet Art of Brainwashing

THE NEW WORLD ORDER increasingly resembles a '50's Sci-Fi movie where the protagonist discovers his family and neighbors have been brainwashed and he begins to question his own sanity.

If you watched the Democratic National Convention, you might be feeling the same way.

Fifty per cent of Americans, and probably 80% of Democrats, believe Iraq is a tragic and unnecessary blunder, yet John Kerry promises more of the same, only better.

Democracy is about giving the people a real choice. Yet no one questioned this.

There was hardly a dissenting voice at the convention. Everyone applauded on cue. Even Howard Dean seemed lobotomized. He now liked the war. He'd learned his lesson.

Protestors were stuck in a cage three blocks away.

Is this America's vaunted "Freedom"? Nuremberg with straw hats and balloons?

Democrats chanted like first-graders: "We can do better." "Help is on the way."

They were treated like simpletons and they stooped to the challenge. The appeal was to mawkish sentiment not to intellect or reason.

Hallelujah! Kerry is going to cure cancer! Believe in him!

And the weird thing is, you want to! But this man can't even be candid about his Jewish ancestry, that of his wife, and his membership with George W. Bush in the satanic *Skull and Bones.*

In a slip of the tongue, Kerry pledged more forces for "terrorist work."

He quickly corrected himself: "anti-terrorist work."

Americans are told they are under siege and must give up the protection of the Bill of Rights and Constitution.

It doesn't matter that there hasn't been a terrorist attack in the US for almost three years. There have been no reports of apprehended attacks, arrests and trials. This is right out of the textbook on how dictatorships operate.

BRAINWASHING

In the future, sanity will be based on your willingness to accept lying platitudes such as those peddled by John Kerry and George Bush.

Future? It's already happening. Those who expose the elite conspiracy are "right wing fanatics," "anti Semites", "hate mongers" and "conspiracy nuts."

Now, I refer you to *"The Soviet Art of Brainwashing,"* a textbook that was used in Communist training schools both in the USA and Russia starting in the 1930's.

Remember Communism was never a "working class revolt." It was created by the Illuminati (Kabalistic bankers and British-American bluebloods like Bush and Kerry) to control the common man and enact their one-world dictatorship.

The textbook suggests that we are currently the subjects of mass hypnosis, which relies on trauma through the application of terror.

"In order to induce a high state of hypnosis in an individual, a group, or a population, an element of terror must always be present on the part of those who would govern." (Part II, Ch.6)

But if we say so, we are "paranoid."

"The by-word should be built into the society that paranoia is a condition "in which the individual believes he is being attacked by Communists." It will be found that this defence is effective." (II- Ch 10)

"The populace must be brought into the belief that every individual within it who rebels ... against the efforts and activities to enslave the whole, must be considered to be a deranged person ...and... be given electric shocks, and reduced into unimaginative docility for the remainder of his days." (II-Ch.12)

THE ELITE ART OF BRAINWASHING

Communists (elite Satanists) view man as (I quote) "a mechanism without individuality." He is "basically an animal" with a "civilized veneer." Like an animal, he can be forced to believe and do anything given the right combination of terror, deception, drugs and brute force.

The goal of "psycho politics" is to "produce the maximum chaos in the culture of the enemy," and to "leave a nation leaderless." The textbook advocates the use of doctors, social workers, psychiatrists and the whole field of "mental healing" to bring about the Satanic goal.

Mental healers are not suppose to heal anyone, and are instructed to drive out competent people.

"Mental health organizations must carefully delete from their ranks anyone actually proficient in the handling or treatment of mental health." (II Ch. 9)

"The psycho political operative should also spare no expense in smashing out of existence, by whatever means, any actual healing group, such as that of acupuncture, in China; such as Christian Science, Dianetics and faith healing in the United States; such as Catholicism in Italy and Spain; and the practical psychological groups of England." (II-9)

The textbook claims Communists took over the Freudian movement and the field of psychoanalysis, which has been "made fashionable," and is useful because of its "stress on sex." This serves the purposes of "degradation" and "defamation of character" i.e. blackmail. (II-9)

"Recruitment into the ranks of "mental healing" can best be done by carefully bringing to it only those healing students who are, to some slight degree, already depraved, or who have been "treated" by psycho political operatives. Recruitment is effected by making the field of mental healing very attractive, financially, and sexually."

"The promise of unlimited sexual opportunities, the promise of complete dominion over the bodies and minds of helpless patients, the promise of having lawlessness without detection, can thus attract to "mental healing" many desirable recruits who will willingly fall in line with psycho political activities." (II-13)

Alfred Kinsey is a prime example of the "psycho political operative." In *"The Kinsey Report"* (1948) Kinsey influenced heterosexuals to adopt homosexual behaviour by lying about his surveys. Hollywood celebrated him in the movie starring Liam Neeson.

Clearly "psycho political operatives" have infiltrated all institutions: military, religion, law, mass media, education and business. They have infiltrated all religions and political parties of every stripe. In the US, they are coordinated by the CFR, CIA, the Rockefeller network of Foundations, NGO's, think tanks, professional associations and Freemasonry.

Here are some more instructions for these operatives:

"You must work until "religion" is synonymous with "insanity. You must work until the officials of city, county and state governments will not think twice before they pounce upon religious groups as public enemies." (II-14)

"Movements to improve youth should be invaded and corrupted, as this might interrupt campaigns to produce in youth delinquency, addiction, drunkenness, and sexual promiscuity." (II-15)

Seek out " the leaders in the country's future, and educate them into the belief of the animalistic nature of Man. This must be made fashionable. They must be taught to frown upon ideas, upon individual endeavour. They must be taught, above all things that the salvation of Man is to be found only by his adjusting thoroughly to this environment. ...Nations, which have high ethical tone, are difficult to conquer." (II-8)

As you can see, the gradual degradation of Western society, the obsession with possessions, pleasure, sex (pornography), violence and trivia, is not random or commercial in nature. It is a deliberate preparation for destruction and tyranny.

TV Commercials

Corporations Have Subversive Social Agenda

NESTLE IS USING CANDY TO PEDDLE LESBIANISM (or vice versa) in a deceitful socially destructive television campaign.

Their Aero chocolate bar commercial is the best example.

Two severe-looking young women (in masculine dress with cropped hair) are in the office lunchroom. With obvious allusions to oral sex, one instructs the other on how to let the Aero bar melt in her mouth slowly.

She places it in her friend's mouth.

"Put it on your tongue."

"Don't bite it."

"Can you feel the bubbles?" "The bubbles are melting."

They have an orgasmic experience. "Pure chocolate pleasure."

The scene naturally draws the attention of a nerdy male. They ignore him and he goes away. The male is redundant.

Nestle is currently targeting teenage girls with a revised version. The girls are young and feminine so the lesbian message is even more reprehensible.

Imagine if the commercial were different. Imagine that a handsome male is instructing a comely adult female on the sensual properties of this chocolate bar. She blushes, aroused.

Imagine that a butchy female is attracted to the scene. She is ignored.

I'm not advocating the use of sex to manipulate people but you get the point. Commercials like these contribute to the lesbian chic sweeping Western countries. Considering that 97% of the market is heterosexual, they are clearly designed to sabotage the social fabric which is based on heterosexuality.

The Nestle ad is typical of scores of commercials that attack heterosexuals by patronizing women and denigrating men.

A SURVEY OF OTHER ADS

In an award winning 2002 ad for Heinz Microwavable soups, a man rolls off a woman after having sex. The unsatisfied woman goes to the kitchen where a microwave has been set for two minutes. She removes and eats her soup. The blatant message: soup, not men is the source of happiness.

Now picture this commercial if her sex partner had been another woman. That would be "intolerance" and "hate." (Human rights are applied selectively in the NWO.)

The academic literature in this area is predictable. It complains that commercials enforce traditional gender roles. In fact, today traditional gender roles are usually undermined. Women's groups would be howling if ads portrayed women the way men are portrayed.

For example, there is a commercial for Alfredo sauce where a father is making supper.

His 10-year-old daughter keeps needling him, "Are you sure mommy isn't mad at you?"

He keeps denying it, but finally her question gets under his skin.

"Did she say anything?" he asks timidly.

This man is abused. Imagine if the ad portrayed a woman living in fear of her husband's wrath. Imagine the daughter repeating, "Are you sure Daddy isn't mad at you?"

"Did he say anything?"

This ad teaches men to be wimps and girls to manipulate males by having tantrums.

A Swanson's TV Dinners commercial completely unsexes the father:

"Working mom asked for a big bowl she can eat on the run. Swanson responded. [Mom rushing off to work.]

Kids wanted something for after school. Swanson responded.

[Happy kids enjoying snack.]

Dad wanted to wear mom's frilly under things! We didn't know how to respond." [Father shown with goofy embarrassed smile.]

Message: Mothers are responsible providers. Fathers are sexually ambiguous twits.

In this context, I should mention the "Whiskas" cat food campaign that encourages young women to substitute cats for male leadership. "Only cats can be cats," is the message.

Each commercial shows men emulating cats: clawing at the curtains, playing with yarn or lying on the couch.

Well they finally did it. They now have a commercial that shows a man taking a dump in a litter box. Can you imagine if they degraded a woman in this way?

Bruce Miller, director of marketing for Whiskas, said the company's consumer research showed that cats are in charge. "We had women in the focus group say, 'If my husband behaved that way, I wouldn't put up with it. But my cat does, and I love him for it.' "

In other words, women are in charge of the male-female relationship. "Only cats can be men."

GENERAL MOTORS

Have you seen this General Motors commercial? The young male has to race his girlfriend down 20 floors for the right to drive the car first! Or the one where the woman orders the man out of the car after he makes a remark about "women drivers." Message: Women kick male butt.

This 2007 Cadillac commercial (entitled "Khakis") depicts white males scurrying like mice at the appearance of the office cat. To a chorus of "Here Comes Success" a young woman strides confidently through the office intimidating the young slackers who are in various states of idleness.

In one office, a man smells his armpit. Another man is doing Tai Chi. Another takes his feet off his desk. Another is eating. Another throws up his arms in submission. There is no way to impress her; she is unattainable. While they include minorities, there is not one women in the ranks of these slackers!

The young goddess finds herself alone in an elevator with a male co-worker. When she says, "Hi Chris," the pen in his pocket spurts ink, suggesting he cannot contain his excitement. Premature ejaculation = impotence.

The goddess notices and smirks. In the next scene, she is driving away in her Cadillac. She thinks about Chris and laughs triumphantly. It is not enough that she is "successful"; the satisfaction is in lording it over men.

The message on the screen is "Enjoy the Driver's Seat." Then the Cadillac emblem appears with another message "Life, Liberty and the Pursuit of [Success]". But where is she going? Home to an empty apartment? What man would put up with her?

This commercial demonstrates that female empowerment is really about degrading and emasculating men so they will accept subjugation in the New World Order.

MORE NESTLE'S PYCHOLOGICAL WARFARE

The Swiss-based food giant with annual sales in excess of $60 billion fosters sexual dysfunction for both commercial and political reasons.

Dysfunctional women gorge on candy. When women's natural instincts and desires are frustrated, they make a beeline for chocolate.

In a third Nestle ad, this time for Kit Kat Chunkies, two male teenage slackers ponder the question, "How do we know we are taking a break when we are never doing anything anyway?" By eating Kit Kat Chunkies, of course.

These commercials shape the way young males and females view themselves and interact. They reinforce feelings of male impotence and female power, independence and androgyny. Men can't humiliate themselves enough for these sexless unapproachable God-like females. These attitudes may prevent healthy relationships from developing.

A reader points out that Nestle's political agenda is called the "UN Global Compact." He writes: "If one views the websites of most large corporations it becomes evident they are getting their values and policies from the same source."

The constant inflation of women and disparagement of men produces sexual dysfunction that undermines the family and renders men politically impotent.

Nestle is a leader in elite social engineering designed to breed a slave race.

THE "RED SYMPHONY" SERIES

Part One: Rothschilds Conduct "Red Symphony"

INCREDIBLE AND BIZARRE AS IT SOUNDS, humanity is indeed the victim of a diabolical conspiracy.

War, depression and genocide in the past century were not accidental or inevitable but the result of malevolent design.

Shocking evidence is a 1938 Stalinist police (NKVD) interrogation of a founder of the Communist International, Christian G. Rakovsky, 65, who was facing execution for plotting to overthrow Stalin.

The 50-page transcript of his interrogation, dubbed *"The Red Symphony,"* was not meant to become public. It confirms that the Rothschild-Illuminati planned to use Communism to establish a world dictatorship of the super rich.

This is perhaps the most explosive political document in modern history. It reveals why the Illuminati created Hitler and then sought to destroy him, and why Stalin made a pact with Hitler in 1939.

Christian Rakovsky was a veteran Communist insider. Born Chaim Rakeover in 1873, he studied medicine in France before becoming a revolutionary. He was the leader of a terror group that attacked government officials.

In 1919, Lenin put him in charge of the Soviet Ukraine government. He successfully kept the area for the Bolsheviks during the Civil War. Stalin appointed him Russian ambassador to Paris in 1925.

Rakovsky belonged to the powerful Trotskyite faction that took their orders from the Rothschilds. Many of this group were shot in Stalin's 1937 Communist Party purge.

MIDNIGHT INTERROGATION

The circumstances of the midnight interrogation Jan. 26, 1938 were very dramatic.

What could Rakovsky possibly say to save his life?

Rakovsky appears to use the tactic of "deceiving with the truth." He wins trust by revealing the truth but leaves some of it out. He tries to impress his interrogator that he and Trotsky represent an invincible power he calls the *"Capitalist-Communist Financial International."*

He confirms that the "revolutionary movement" was designed to enlist support by pretending to serve mankind's moral and collective ideals. The real aim however is to give total world power to the bankers by dividing society and undermining established authority.

"Revolution" really means, "overturning" Western Civilization.

"Christianity is our only real enemy since all the political and economic phenomena of the bourgeois states are only its consequences," Rakovsky, says. (Griffin,247)

Peace is "counter-revolutionary" since it is war that paves the way for revolution.

Rakovsky, whose tongue was loosened by a mild inebriant in his wine, refers to the Illuminati as "they" or "them." He is a member although not part of the inner circle.

He explains that the "Illuminati" is a Masonic secret society dedicated to Communism. Significantly, its founder Adam Weishaupt took the name from "the second anti-Christian conspiracy of that era, gnosticism." (249)

HOW THIS GRIPPING ACCOUNT SURFACED

The interrogator was one of Stalin's cleverest agents, Gavriil Kus'min known as "Gabriel."

Apart from him and a hidden sound technician, a doctor Jose Landowsky was the only other person present.

Conscripted by the NKVD to help "loosen the tongues of detainees,"

Dr. Landowsky was sickened by the many tortures he witnessed.

The interrogation of Rakovsky, however, was cordial. Dr. Landowsky doubts if the mild euphoric he put in Rakovsky's drink had much effect.

The interrogation, conducted in French lasted from midnight until

7 a.m. After, Kus'min ordered Landowsky to translate the interview into Russian and make two copies.

The content was so mind boggling that Landowsky made an additional carbon for himself. "I am not sorry that I had the courage for this," he wrote. (279) (The Bolsheviks had shot Landowsky's father, a Tsarist colonel, during the 1917 revolution.)

A Spanish Fascist volunteer later found the manuscript on Landowsky's dead body in a hut on the Petrograd front during World War Two. He took it back to Spain where it was published as "Sinfonia en Rojo Mayo." in 1949.

Peter Myers put the complete text of "The Red Symphony" online. http://users.cyberone.com.au/myers/red-symphony.html

The transcript was published in English in 1968 as "The Red Symphony: X-Ray of Revolution." You can find it in Des Griffin's "Fourth Reich of the Rich." (1988) I recommend this book and everything this fine man has written.

REVELATIONS

Rakovsky gives his interrogator an astonishing inside view of modern history in order to prove that his sponsors control the world.

"Money is the basis of power," Rakovsky says, and the Rothschilds manufacture it thanks to the banking system.

The "Revolutionary Movement" was an attempt by Meyer Rothschild and his allies to protect and extend this monopoly by establishing a totalitarian New World Order.

According to Rakovsky, "The Rothschilds were not the treasurers, but the chiefs of that first secret Communism...Marx and the highest chiefs of the First International ... were controlled by Baron Lionel Rothschild, [1808-1878] whose revolutionary portrait was done by Disraeli the English Premier, who was also his creature, and has been left to us [in Disraeli's novel 'Coningsby.']" (250)

Lionel's son Nathaniel (1840-1915) needed to overthrow the Christian Romanoff Dynasty. Through his agents Jacob Schiff and the Warburg brothers, he financed the Japanese side in the Russo Japanese War, and an unsuccessful insurrection in Moscow in 1905. Then he instigated the First World War (Trotsky was behind the murder of Archduke Ferdinand); and financed the 1917 Bolshevik Revolution. Rakovsky says he was personally involved in the transfer of funds in Stockholm. (251-252)

The Jewish labour movement or "bund" was Rothschild's instrument. The Bund's "secret faction" infiltrated all the socialist parties in Russia and provided the leadership for the Russian Revolution. Alexander Kerensky, the Menshevik Prime Minister was a secret member. (253)

Leon Trotsky was supposed to become the leader of the USSR. Trotsky, a Jew, married the daughter of one of Rothschild's closest associates, banker Abram Zhivotovsky and became part of the "clan."

Unfortunately "national" Communists like Lenin (one-quarter Jewish) got in the way. Lenin overruled Trotsky and made peace with Germany (Treaty of Brest Litovsk, 1918.) This was not the Rothschild's plan.

World War I was supposed to end the way the Second World War did. Russia was supposed to overrun Germany in 1918 and assist local "revolutionaries" in establishing a "peoples' republic."

Trotsky was responsible for an attempt to assassinate Lenin in 1918 but Lenin survived. When Lenin had a stroke in 1922, Trotsky had Levin, Lenin's Jewish doctor, finish him off.

At this critical moment, the unexpected happened. Trotsky got sick and Stalin was able to take power. At this crucial juncture, the Trotskyites pretended to support Stalin and infiltrated his regime in order to sabotage it.

Rakowsky characterizes Stalin as a "Bonapartist," a nationalist as opposed to an International Communist like Trotsky.

"He is a killer of the revolution, he does not serve it, but makes use of its service; he represents the most ancient Russian imperialism, just as Napoleon identified himself with the Gauls..." (257)

CONTAINING STALIN

In order to control Stalin, international finance was forced to build up Hitler and the Nazi party. Rakowsky confirms that Jewish financiers backed the Nazis although Hitler was not aware of this.

"The ambassador Warburg [James Warburg] presented himself under a false name and Hitler did not even guess his race... he also lied regarding whose representative he was... Our aim was to provoke a war and Hitler was war...[the Nazis] received...millions of dollars sent to it from Wall Street, and millions of marks from German financiers through Schacht; [providing] the upkeep of the S.A and the S.S. and also the financing of the elections..." (259-260)

Unfortunately for the bankers, Hitler also proved intractable. He started to print his own money!

"He took over for himself the privilege of manufacturing money and not only physical moneys, but also financial ones; he took over the untouched machinery of falsification and put it to work for the benefit of the state... Are you capable of imagining what would have come ...if it had infected a number of other states and brought about the creation of a period of autarchy [absolute rule, replacing that of the bankers]. If you can, then imagine its counterrevolutionary functions..." (263)

Hitler had become a bigger threat than Stalin, who had not meddled with money. Rakovsky's present mission was to convince Stalin to make a pact with Hitler and turn Hitler's aggression against the West. The purpose was for Germany and the Western nations to exhaust each other before another front was opened in the East.

[According to Walter Kravitsky, the head of Soviet Military Intelligence in Europe who defected to the West and was later assassinated in 1941, Stalin was determined to make a pact with Hitler as early as 1934. He had no desire to fight the Nazis. Is it possible Rakovsky and his sponsors did not know this? Kravitsky *On Stalin's Secret Service* (1939)]

Rakovsky urged the Russians to use the tactic of "deceiving with the truth." The Russians were to impress Hitler with their genuine desire for peace. Hitler was not to suspect that he was being set up for a war on two fronts.

Stalin was given a choice. If he agreed to divide Poland with Hitler, the West would declare war on *only one* aggressor, Germany. If he refused, the bankers would allow Hitler to depose him.

Kus'min demanded some high level confirmation. Rakovsky told him to see Joseph Davies, the US ambassador in Moscow, a fellow Freemason and representative of the International Communist Roosevelt administration.

Someone was sent to Davies who confirmed that "much would be gained" if Rakovsky got an amnesty. On March 2, 1938, a powerful radio message was sent to Moscow in the cipher of its London embassy.

"Amnesty or the Nazi danger will increase," it said. Davies attended Rakovsky's trial and gave him a Masonic greeting. On the same day, March 12, 1938, Hitler marched into Austria.

Rakovsky's death sentence was commuted. Some believe he

lived out his years under an assumed name. Another source has him shot in 1941.

Secret negotiations were begun with Hitler. The result was the Ribbentrop-Molotov pact signed in August 1939 just one week before the invasion of Poland.

The interrogation seems to have created an accord between Stalin and the Illuminati.

RUSSIA STRUGGLES IN ROTHSCHILD CLUTCH

Europe and the United States long ago succumbed to Rothschild Illuminati control. In Russia, there are still some death spasms.

In 2003, Vladimir Putin arrested Mikhail Khordordovsky, the head of Russia's largest oil company "Yukos" and "the richest man in Russia."

Putin announced that Russia would seize his $12 billion 26% stake in the oil company, one of many national assets plundered in the reorganization of Communism 15 years ago.

Then we learn the shares already had passed to none other than banker Jacob Rothschild under a "previously unknown arrangement" designed for such a circumstance. The two have known each other for years "through their mutual love of the arts."

Rakovsky told Kus'min that the Illuminati never take political or financial positions. They use "intermediaries."

"Bankers and politicians are only men of straw.... even though they occupy high places and appear to be authors of the plans which are carried out..." (248-249)

Obviously Khodordovsky is an "intermediary" for Rothschild. So are Richard Perle, Henry Kissinger and Ariel Sharon who each spoke out against Putin's action. Perle, the architect of the Iraq war, called for the expulsion of Russia from the Group of Eight. Sharon expressed concern about "persecution of Jewish businessmen." Khodordovsky is Jewish as is Simon Kukes his successor. And Perle and Kissinger.

Many Jews serve the Illuminati and that is a cause of anti-Semitism. But Tony Blair and George W. Bush serve it too and are not Jewish. The membership of the Bilderbergers and the *Skull and Bones* is mostly not Jewish. The Illuminati is an alliance between the Rothschilds, and the world's super rich united by Freemasonry, whose God is Lucifer.

Mankind, God's magnificent experiment, has been subverted and compromised. From the U.S. soldier in Iraq, to the taxpayer who pays the national debt, we are all pawns.

THE RED SYMPHONY PART 2

Terminated! Freemasonry's Final Revelation

FREEMASONS "have to die at the hands of the revolution which has been brought about with their cooperation," according to C.G. Rakovsky, a founder of the Communist International.

"The real secret of masonry is the suicide of Freemasonry as an organization, and the physical suicide of every important mason."

This disclosure is from a 1938 Stalinist police interrogation entitled *"The Red Symphony."* (Transcript in Des Griffin, *Fourth Reich of the Rich,* p. 254)

"It is clear that I know of this not as a Freemason, but as one who belongs to 'Them,'" [the Illuminati] says Rakovsky, a colleague of Leon Trotsky arrested for plotting against Stalin.

'PROTOCOLS OF ZION' AND 'RED SYMPHONY'

Freemasonry is the world's largest secret society with over five million members, including three million in the US. It is instrumental in the totalitarian conspiracy. In *The Protocols of the Elders of Zion,* the author (who I believe is Lionel Rothschild) writes,

"Gentile masonry blindly serves as a screen for us and our objects, but the plan of action of our force, even its very abiding place, remains for the whole people an unknown mystery....Who and what is in a position to overthrow an invisible force?" (Protocol 4)

Again he writes, "we shall create and multiply free Masonic lodges... absorb into them all who may become or who are prominent in public activity, for in these lodges we shall find our principle intelligence office and means of influence.... The most secret political plots will be known to us and will fall under our guiding hands...We know the final goal...whereas the goyim have knowledge of nothing..." (Protocol 15)

In his interrogation, Rakovsky says that millions flock to Freemasonry to gain an advantage. "The rulers of all the Allied nations were Freemasons, with very few exceptions."

However, the real aim is "create all the required prerequisites for the triumph of the Communist revolution; this is the obvious aim of Freemasonry; it is clear that all this is done under various pretexts; but they always conceal themselves behind their well known treble slogan [Liberty, Equality, Fraternity]. You understand?" (254)

Masons should recall the lesson of the French Revolution. Although "they played a colossal revolutionary role; it consumed the majority of masons..." Since the revolution requires the extermination of the bourgeoisie as a class, [so all wealth will be held by the Illuminati in the guise of the State] it follows that Freemasons must be liquidated. The true meaning of Communism is Illuminati tyranny.

When this secret is revealed, Rakovsky imagines "the expression of stupidity on the face of some Freemason when he realises that he must die at the hands of the revolutionaries. How he screams and wants that one should value his services to the revolution! It is a sight at which one can die...but of laughter!" (254)

Rakovsky refers to Freemasonry as a hoax: "a madhouse but at liberty." (254)

In Russia in 1929 every Mason who was not Jewish was killed along with his family, according to Alexey Jefimow "*Who are the Rulers of Russia?*" (77)

Like masons, other applicants for the humanist utopia master class (neo cons, liberals, Zionists, gay and feminist activists) might be in for a nasty surprise. They might be tossed aside once they have served their purpose.

WHO ARE "THEY"?

When the interrogator presses Rakovsky for Illuminati notables to approach with an initiative, Rakovsky is sure of only two who are now deceased: Walter Rathenau, the Weimar foreign minister, and Lionel Rothschild. He says Trotsky is his source of information.

Others he insists are speculation:

"As an institution, the bank of Kuhn Loeb & Company of Wall

Street: [and] the families of Schiff, Warburg, Loeb and Kuhn; I say families in order to point out several names since they are all connected ... by marriages; then Baruch, Frankfurter, Altschul, Cohen, Benjamin, Strauss, Steinhardt, Blom, Rosenman, Lippmann, Lehman, Dreifus, Lamont, Rothschild, Lord, Mandel, Morganthau, Ezekiel, Lasky....any one of the names I have enumerated, even of those not belonging to "Them" could always lead to "Them" with any proposition of an important type." (272)

By allowing bankers the privilege of creating money, we have created an insatiable vampire. If you could manufacture money, imagine the temptation to own everything!

COVERT REVOLUTION

Rakovsky refers to the 1929 Crash and Great Depression as an "American revolution." It was deliberately precipitated by the Illuminati for profit, to break the "classical American," and to take political power.

"The man through whom they made use of such power was Franklin Roosevelt. Have you understood? ...In that year 1929, the first year of the American Revolution, in February Trotsky leaves Russia; the crash takes place in October...The financing of Hitler is agreed in July, 1929. You think that all this was by chance? The four years of the rule of Hoover were used for the preparation for the seizure of power in the United States and the USSR: there by means of a financial revolution, and here [Russia] with the help of war [Hitler, World War Two] and the defeat which was to follow. Could some novel with great imagination be more obvious to you?" (273)

Rakovsky proposes that Stalin cooperate with the Illuminati, (which he subsequently did.) The first condition is that he stops executing Trotskyites. Then "several zones of influence" will be established dividing "the formal Communism from the real one." There will be "mutual concessions for mutual help for a time while the plan lasts...There will appear influential persons at all levels of society, even very high ones, who will help the Stalinist formal Communism..." (276)

Rakovsky outlines the Illuminati plan to blend Communism and Capitalism. In each case, the Illuminati will control all wealth and power.

"In Moscow there is Communism: in New York capitalism. It is all the same as thesis and antithesis. Analyse both. Moscow is subjective

Communism but [objectively] State capitalism. New York: Capitalism subjective, but Communism objective [central banker ownership]. A personal synthesis, truth: the Financial International, the Capitalist Communist one. 'They.' " (276)

THE RED SYMPHONY PART 3

Central Bankers Seek Totalitarian Control

THE "WAR ON TERROR" is a ruse by central bankers *to control every aspect of your life.*

Rereading *"The Red Symphony"* recently, I was shocked to read an insider's statement that the bankers are not content with infinite wealth, but want *unlimited power.*

The human experiment is endangered by private interests who have usurped the function of money creation. Modern history reflects the gradual process by which they transfer all wealth and power to themselves, destroying Western Civilization and creating a world police state.

Rakovsky, whose real name was Chaim Rakover, was sentenced to death in Stalin's purge of the Trotskyite faction of the party. Leon Trotsky wrote in his autobiography, *My Life:* "Christian G. Rakovsky... played an active part in the inner workings of four Socialist parties-- the Bulgarian, Russian, French, and Rumanian--to become eventually one of the leaders of the Soviet Federation, a founder of the Communist Internationale, President of the Ukrainian Soviet of People's Commissaries, and the diplomatic Soviet representative in England and France..."

Rakovsky tried to convince his interrogator that Stalin should cooperate with the bankers who "are just like you and me. *The fact that they control unlimited money, insofar as they themselves create it, does not...determine the limits of their ambitions . . .*The bankers, have the impulse towards power, towards full power. Just as you and me."

They created the Communist state as *a "machine of total power"* unprecedented in history. In the past, due to many factors, *"there was always room for individual freedom.* Do you understand that those who already partially rule over nations and worldly governments *have pretensions to absolute domination? Understand that this is the only thing which they have not yet reached."* (Emphasis mine)

A pernicious force paralyses our national life. Rakovsky identifies it: "Imagine to yourself, if you can a small number of people having unlimited power through the possession of real wealth, and you will see they are the absolute dictators of the stock exchange and [economy]...If you have enough imagination then...you will see [their] anarchical, moral and social influence, i.e. a revolutionary one...Do you now understand?"

The Revolutionary Movement, which defines modern history, was a means to increase banker power by destroying the old order.

In the French Revolution power subtly passed to the bankers who weren't constrained by Christian niceties, Rakovsky says. "The supreme Royal power was taken over by persons, whose moral, intellectual and cosmopolitan qualities did allow them to use it. It is clear that these were people who had never been Christians, but cosmopolitans."

Communism, far from distributing wealth, is designed to concentrate it in the hands of the world's wealthiest people. (The State owns the wealth and they own the State.) And Marxism, "before being a philosophical, economic and political system, is a conspiracy for the revolution."

Rakovsky scoffs at the "elementary Marxism...the demagogic popular one" that is used to dupe the intellectuals and the masses. [Whatever its intrinsic merits, Socialism seems designed to bribe and make people dependent on big government, which the bankers control.]

As for Freemasonry: "Every Masonic organization tries to create all the required prerequisites for the triumph of the Communist revolution; this is the obvious aim of Freemasonry," says Rakovsky, a high-ranking Mason himself.

The aim of the Revolution is no less than to redefine reality in terms of the interests of the bankers. This involves the promotion of subjective truth over objective truth. If Lenin "feels something to be real" then it is real. "For him every reality, every truth was relative in the face of the sole and absolute one: the revolution."

Rakovsky marvels that "the benches on which sat the greasy usurers to trade in their moneys, have now been converted into temples, which stand magnificently at every corner of contemporary big towns with their heathen colonnades, and crowds go there ...to bring assiduously their deposits of all their possessions to the god of money..."

He says the Soviet five-pointed star represents the five Rothschild brothers with their banks, who possess colossal accumulations of wealth, the greatest ever known."

Isn't it strange that Marx never mentions this fact? Rakovsky asks. Isn't it strange that during revolutions, the mobs never attack the bankers, their mansions or banks?

War is the means by which the central bankers advance their goal of totalitarian world government. Rakovsky says Trotsky was behind the murder of Arch Duke Ferdinand (which sparked WWI.) He recalls the phrase used by the mother of the five Rothschild brothers: "'If my sons want it, then there will be no war.' This means that they were the arbiters, the masters of peace and war, but not emperors. Are you capable of visualizing the fact of such a cosmic importance? Is not war already a revolutionary function? War, the Commune. Since that time every war was a giant step towards Communism."

After the murder of [Illuminati member Weimar Foreign Minister] Walter Rathenau in 1922, the Illuminati give political or financial positions only to intermediaries, Rakowsky says. "Obviously to persons who are trustworthy and loyal, which can be guaranteed a thousand ways: thus one can assert that those bankers and politicians [in the public eye] - are only men of straw . . . even though they occupy very high places and are made to appear to be the authors of the plans which are carried out."

In 1938, Rakovsky outlined three reasons for the upcoming Second World War. The first is that Hitler began to print his own money. "This is very serious. Much more than all the external and cruel factors in National-Socialism."

Secondly, the "fully developed nationalism of Western Europe is an obstacle to Marxism...the need for the destruction of nationalism is alone worth a war in Europe."

Finally, Communism cannot triumph unless it suppresses the "still living Christianity." He refers to the "permanent revolution" as dating from the birth of Christ, and the reformation as "its first partial victory" because it split Christianity. This suggests that the "conspiracy" also contains a racial or religious factor.

"In reality, Christianity is our only real enemy since all the political and economic phenomena of the Bourgeois States. Christianity controlling the individual is capable of annulling the revolutionary projection of the neutral Soviet or Atheist State."

Now the Central Bankers are promoting World War Three as in "The Clash of Civilizations." Substitute Islam for Christianity above.

CONCLUSION

Our beliefs must adjust to the truth and not vice versa. Apparently, the truth is that a relatively small clique of Jewish banking families and their non-Jewish allies in the leading families of Europe and America have usurped control of money creation, and with it the destiny of the world.

This overclass owns or controls most of the world's largest corporations, media organizations, intelligence agencies, secret societies, universities, politicians, foundations, think tanks and NGO's. It also appears to dominate organized crime.

Sept. 11, the War on Terror and Iraq are part of an inexorable process by which this overclass increases its wealth and control. The end goal is a world police state in which the masses will be deprived of their wealth, freedom and possibly their lives.

Neo Cons are really Neo Com-munists. They jeopardize the security of their fellow Jews (as well as all Americans) by their evil machinations. Jews should follow my example and repudiate them.

The overclass wants us to see it as a "Jewish problem." This way it can deflect blame onto innocent Jews and then dismiss opposition as "hatred" and "prejudice." The problem is mainly one of money creation (credit) that has led to an untenable concentration of wealth and power in a few hands.

Almost everyone who is "successful" in society, Jewish or not, is forced, wittingly or unwittingly to align themselves with the overclass. Our religious, cultural and political institutions have been subverted. This explains the false quality of social life in the West.

Let's remember Christ's message: God is Love. God is more powerful than the satanic force that holds mankind in its thrall. But His will cannot be done unless men do it.

Whatever the cost, doing nothing will cost more. The affluence we now enjoy is part of an age-old plot to ensnare and enslave humanity

SVALI

Illuminati Defector Details Pervasive Conspiracy

I F YOU DETECT THE DEVIL'S HAND in current events, you may be closer to the truth than you think.

A woman who was raised in the Illuminati cult describes a powerful secret organization comprising one per cent of the U.S. population that has infiltrated all social institutions and is covertly preparing a military takeover. Her revelations cast the "war on terror" and "homeland security" in their true light.

"Svali" is the pseudonym of the woman in her late 40's who was a mind "programmer" for the cult until 1996. She was the sixth head trainer in the San Diego branch and had 30 trainers reporting to her. She has risked her life to warn humanity of the Illuminati's covert power and agenda.

She describes a sadistic Satanic cult led by the richest and most powerful people in the world. It is largely homosexual and pedophile, practises animal sacrifice and ritual murder. It works "hand in glove" with the CIA and Freemasonry. It is Aryan supremacist (German is spoken at the top) but welcomes Jewish apostates. It controls the world traffic in drugs, guns, pornography and prostitution. It may be the hand behind political assassination, and "terrorism," including Sept. 11, the Maryland sniper and the Bali bomb blast.

It has infiltrated government on a local, state and national level; education and financial institutions; religion and the media. Based in Europe, it plans a "world order" that will make its earlier attempts, Nazism and Communism, look like picnics. One other detail: these people are not happy.

Svali's courageous testimony explains why our children are no longer taught civic values, why they are being habituated to homosexuality and violence, and why our "culture" is descending into nihilism and sexual depravity. It raises the possibility that George W.

Bush and his Administration are Illuminists and much of the world "elite" is engaged in a mind-boggling criminal conspiracy.

Here are some highlights of Svali's testimony:

PERVASIVE PRESENCE

Svali: "The Illuminati are present in every major metropolitan centre in the United States. The Illuminati believe in controlling an area through its: banks and financial institutions (guess how many sit on banking boards? You'd be surprised) Local government: guess how many get elected to local city councils? Law: children are encouraged to go to law school and medical school. Media: others are encouraged to go to journalism school, and members help fund local papers.

BELIEFS

Svali: "The Illuminati is a group that practices a form of faith known as "enlightenment". It is Luciferian, and they teach their followers that their roots go back to the ancient mystery religions of Babylon, Egypt, and Celtic druidism. They have taken what they consider the "best" of each, the foundational practices, and joined them together into a strongly occult discipline. Many groups at the local level worship ancient deities such as "El", "Baal", and "Ashtarte", as well as "Isis and Osiris" and "Set".... I do know that these people teach and practice evil."

WEISHAUPT

Svali: "Weishaupt did not create the Illuminati, they chose him as a figurehead and told him what to write about. The financiers, dating back to the bankers during the times of the Templar Knights who financed the early kings in Europe, created the Illuminati. Weishaupt was their "go fer", who did their bidding."

MILITARY TAKEOVER

Svali: "Briefly, each region of the United States has "nerve centres" or power bases for regional activity. The United States has been divided up into seven major geographical regions. Each region has localities within it that contain military compounds and bases that are hidden in remote, isolated areas or on large private estates.

These bases are used intermittently to teach and train generational Illuminati in military techniques, hand- to- hand combat, crowd control, use of arms, and all aspects of military warfare. Why? Because the Illuminists believe that our government, as we know it, as well as the governments of most nations around the world, are destined to collapse. These will be planned collapses, and they will occur in the following ways:

The Illuminati has planned first for a financial collapse that will make the great depression look like a picnic. This will occur through the manoeuvring of the great banks and financial institutions of the world, through stock manipulation, and interest rate changes.

Most people will be indebted to the federal government through bank and credit card debt, etc. The governments will recall all debts immediately, but most people will be unable to pay and will be bankrupted. This will cause generalized financial panic, which will occur simultaneously worldwide, as the Illuminists firmly believe in controlling people through finances.

Doesn't sound pleasant, does it? I don't know the exact time frame for all of this, and wouldn't want to even guess. The good news is that if a person is debt-free, owes nothing to the government or credit debt, and can live self sufficiently, they may do better than others. I would invest in gold, not stocks, if I had the income. Gold will once again be the world standard, and dollars will be pretty useless (remember after the Civil War? Our money will be worth about what confederate money was after the collapse).

Next there will be a military takeover, region by region, as the government declares a state of emergency and martial law. People will have panicked, there will be an anarchical state in most localities, and the government will justify its move as being necessary to control panicked citizens. The cult trained military leaders and people under their direction will use arms as well as crowd control techniques to implement this new state of affairs. ...Military bases will be set up, in each locality (actually, they are already here, but are covert). In the next few years, they will go above ground and be revealed. Each locality will have regional bases and leaders to which they are accountable. The hierarchy will closely reflect the current covert hierarchy.

About five years ago, when I left the Illuminati, approximately 1% of the US population was either part of the Illuminati, sympathetic to it, or a victim of Mind Control (and therefore considered useable). While this may not sound like many, imagine 1% of the population highly trained in the use of armaments, crowd control, psychological and behavioral techniques, armed with weapons and linked to paramilitary groups."

LEADERSHIP

Svali: "The national council [consists of] influential bankers with OLD money such as: The Rockefellers, the Mellon family, the Carnegie family, the Rothschild family etc. I know I shouldn't name names, but I will.

The "Supreme World Council" is already set up as a prototype of the one that will rule when the NWO comes into being. It meets on a regular basis to discuss finances, direction, policy, etc. and to problem-solve difficulties that come up. Once again, these leaders are heads in the financial world, OLD banking money. The Rothschild family in England, and in France, have ruling seats. A descendant of the Hapsburg dynasty has a generational seat. A descendant of the ruling families of England and France have a generational seat. The Rockefeller family in the US holds a seat.

This is one reason that the Illuminati have been pretty "untouchable" over the years. The ruling members are very, very, very wealthy and powerful. I hope this information is helpful. How do I know this? I was on a local leadership council (a head trainer), but I talked to those on regional. Also, every Illuminati child is taught who their "leaders" are, and told to take an oath of allegiance to them and the "New Order to come"."

ROYALTY

Svali: "The Illuminati leadership state that they are descended from royal bloodlines, as well as unbroken occult heritage.

See, there were two definitions of "royalty" used. Open royalty that is currently seen now, and "hidden royalty" of royal lineage and extreme occult power. Sometimes the two were concurrent, such as with the Prince of Wales.

I never thought of which country/line held the most power, since I was just a peon busily doing my job. But my understanding was: The Hanoverian / Hapsburg descendants rule in Germany over the Bruderheist. They are considered one of the strongest lines for occult as well. The British line is just under them, with the royal family. Definitely, they rule the UK branch under the Rothschilds in the occult realm, even though parliament rules the country openly.

In France, again, descendants of the royal families are also in power in the occult realm, but the French Rothschilds hold the reigns over all of them."

RANK OF THE US

Svali: "The U.S. is considered lower, and younger, than the European branches. ...Germany, France, and the UK form a triumvirate that rules in the European cult. The USSR is considered important, and has the strongest military groups. The USSR has been promised fourth position in the New World Order, BEFORE the role the U.S. would have, because the USSR has been more helpful and cooperative over the years with furthering the agenda.

The descendants of the former ruling families there are also involved in the occult leadership, along with the newer ones. There is no Marxism in the cult. China will be ranked after the USSR, then the U.S. But a lot of the current U.S. leadership will be in Europe when the change occurs, and many have homes there. They will be "changing nationalities" overnight, as it were. This is the little that I do remember. Wish I had been a better student of this stuff, but I was too busy trying to stay alive when I was in it.

Russia will be the military base and powerhouse of the group, since their military commanders (Illuminist) are considered the best in the world, and very, very disciplined. China, because of its roots in oriental occultism, and its large population, will also be considered a higher power than the US. But again, the real power will reside in Europe, according to what I was taught when part of the group.

THE UNITED NATIONS

Svali: "The UN was created early in this century in order to help overcome one of the biggest barriers to a one-world government ...That barrier is the one of nationalism, or pride in one's country. This is why it was NOT a popular concept when first introduced, it took years of country bashing in the media and the destruction of any sense of national pride by a (not so subtle) media campaign over the years.

The UN is a preparation, but it is not the real power in the world, and will be relatively unimportant when the NWO comes into being. The real councils will then step forward. But as a means of getting the general public to accept the idea of a "global community" and the "one world community" the UN is a stepping stone in their working towards the NWO."

ISRAEL

Svali: "The conflict in the Middle East is only to the advantage of the Illuminists. They HATE Israel, and hope one day to see it destroyed, and are biding their time. One of the olive branches offered by the UN when it takes over is that they will prevent war in the Middle East, and this will be greeted with joy by many.

At the same time, the Illuminati covertly supply guns and funds to BOTH sides to keep the conflict fuelled. They are very duplicitous people. They used to funnel guns through the USSR to Palestine, for example, in the name of promoting "friendliness" between the USSR and this state and other Arab nations. Then, the US Illuminists would help funnel guns to Israel, for the same reason.

These people love the game of chess, and see warfare between nations as creating an order out of chaos. The USSR is going to get stronger again. It has too strong a military both openly, and covertly (ALL Illuminati military trainers have visited Russia to learn from them) to sit quietly and quiesciently to the side. In the NWO, they will be stronger than us."

IS THE ILLUMINATI A JEWISH CONSPIRACY?

Svali: "Absolutely not. In fact, Hitler and his people (especially Himmler and Goebbels) were top Illuminists. The Illuminati are racist in the extreme, and as a child, I was forced to play "concentration camp" both on my farm in Virginia, and also in Europe in isolated camps in Germany.

The Jews historically fought against the occult (see Deuteronomy and the Old Testament for how God through the Jewish people tried to cleanse the land of the occult groups that were operating there, such as those who worshipped Baal, Ashtarte, and other Canaanite and Babylonian gods.

(from an email to Henry Makow) Yes, there are some very powerful Jewish people in this group. For instance, the Rothschild family literally runs the financial empire in Europe (and indirectly the States), and are a well-known Jewish family. I have also known people whose parents were Jewish diamond merchants in the group, and at every level. But to rise to power in the Illuminati, a Jewish person at night would be forced to renounce their faith, and to give their first allegiance to Lucifer and the beliefs of the Illuminati. In return for this betrayal, they believe that power (financial) and rewards come; and in one sense they do, but at too high a price (losing their eternal soul).

The nazi/concentration camp mentality is very strong, though, and I was told that Hitler, Himmler, Goebel, and others were high-ranking German members of the group (Himmler was higher than the other two), and Mengele their paid puppet as well, who later worked as a high trainer of the American branch between his periods of hiding in South America. They honestly believed that they were acting as agents of their 'gods' to exterminate the Jewish race, and I am so, so sorry that this group has enacted so many horrors on the earth (and so, so glad that I left it).

I hope this helps you. I have always wondered this, though, why some of the highest ranking financial families in the group (baron Rothschild of France is one of the 13 European lords, or "kings" that run the group in Europe, and sits on the World Council) are Jewish, yet the group espouses hatred of their own race."

ARE THEY RACIST?

Svali: "Lots of Illuminists have Fourth Reich programming inside. The Illuminati are racist, and have a very "Aryan" outlook. They believe strongly in the rule of the "pure" and "intelligent" by their definitions, and in their ceremonies, there will occasionally be minorities killed in ceremonies.

They are trying to breed a "genetically superior" race to rule, with their children and descendants. They are also followers of Plato's Republic, and believe that they will be the ones to usher in this "Utopian" rule with the NWO in their opinion. In their Utopia, the intelligentsia will rule, and the sheep like masses will follow their leaders (that is their view of the world; that the occult leaders are "enlightened' and intelligent, while the average person is a "sheep" to be led by the nose)."

FREEMASONRY

Svali: "The Freemasons and the Illuminati are hand in glove. I don't care if this steps on any toes, it's a fact. The Masonic temple at Alexandria, Virginia (the city itself was named after Alexandria, Egypt, and is a hotbed of Illuminati activity) is a centre in the Washington, DC area for Illuminati scholarship and teaching. I was taken there at intervals for testing, to step up a level, for scholarship, and high ceremonies. The leaders in this Masonic group were also Illuminists.

This has been true of every large city I have lived in. The top Freemasons were also top Illuminists. My maternal grandparents were both high ranking Masons in the city of Pittsburgh, Pa. (president of the Eastern Star and 33rd degree Mason) and they both were also leaders in the Illuminati in that area.

Are all Masons Illuminati? No, especially at the lower levels, I believe they know nothing of the practices that occur in the middle of the night in the larger temples. Many are probably fine businessmen and Christians. But I have never known a 32 degree or above who wasn't Illuminati, and the group helped create Freemasonry as a "front" for their activities."

CIA FBI ARE ALL INFILTRATED. SO ARE MORMONS ETC.

Svali: "Many of the administrators and directors at the FBI are also Illuminists. The CIA helped bring over German scientists after WWII. Many of these were also Illuminati leaders in their own country, and they were welcomed with open arms by the U.S. group. They also funnelled all information they were learning to the Illuminati.

The Mormons affiliated years ago in a meeting with Illuminati leadership in the 1950s. The same with the Jehovah's Witnesses."

THE COLD WAR

Svali:"Russia was never really a threat to us. Marxism was funded by the Illuminati, and espoused as a counterbalance to capitalism. The Illluminati believe strongly in balancing opposing forces, in the pull between opposites. They see history as a complex chess game, and they will fund one side, then another, while ultimately out of the chaos and division ..., they are laughing because they are ultimately beyond political parties. A top western financier will secretly meet with an eastern or Russian "adversary" during those years, and have a good laugh at how the "sheep" were being deluded. I am sharing here what I was taught, and also observed.

They are truly an international group, and the group's agenda supersedes any nationalistic feelings. There is also a lot of trading back and forth of members in these groups. A Russian trainer might come to the US for awhile, complete a job, then go back, or vice-versa."

ASSASSIN TRAINING

Svali: "Here is how it is done (how it was done to me):

1. When the child is 2 years old, place them in a metal cage with electrodes attached. Shock the child severely.

2. Take the child out, and place a kitten in its hands. Tell the child to wring the kitten's neck. The child will cry and refuse.

3. Put the child into the cage, and shock them until they are dazed and cannot scream any more.

4. Take the child out, and tell them again to wring the kitten's neck. This time the child will shake all over, cry, but do it, afraid of the torture. The child will then go into the corner and vomit afterwards, while the adult praises them for "doing such a good job".

This is the first step. The animals get bigger over time, as the child gets older. They will be forced to kill an infant at some point, either a set up or VR, or in reality. They will be taught by age 9 to put together a gun, to aim, and fire on target and on command. They will then practice on realistic manikins. They will then practice on animals. They will then practice on "expendables" or in VR. They will be highly praised if they do well, and tortured if they don't comply.

The older the child or teen, the more advanced the training. By age 15, most children will also be forced to do hand to hand combat in front of spectators (high people who come to watch the "games" much as the ancient gladiators performed). These matches are rarely done to the death, usually until one child goes down. They use every type of weapon imaginable, and learn to fight for their lives. If a child loses a fight, they are heavily punished by their trainer, who loses "face". If they win, they are again praised for being "strong' and adept with weapons. By the time they are 21, they are well trained combat/killing machines with command codes to kill and they have been tested over and over to prove that they WILL obey on command. This is how children in the German Illuminati are brought up, I went through it myself."

TRUST IN FAMILY

Svali: "They tell their children as they are torturing them, "I am doing this because I love you." To them, the greatest love is to make a child strong, and fit to lead or to move higher in the group, by whatever means it takes.

If a leader sees a child, and wants it as a prostitute, the loving parents will give it away, happy that their child will rise in status. Also, again, they view betrayal as the greatest good. They will do set up after set up to teach their children to never openly trust others.

I remember hundreds of agonizing set ups and betrayals, and hearing when I was betrayed or wounded, "And such is the heart of man." Those doing this to me thought they were teaching me something of value, that would help me. And because of the vicious and political nature of the group, in one sense they were right; the naive get stepped on and wounded. I have known parents who tried to spare their children some of this out of love, but often they were overruled by other family members, who viewed these parents as "weak" and "unfit" to teach their child."

MORALE

Svali: "Most of them are wounded, abused victims, who don't realize that it is possible to leave the group. There is a lot of discontent in the ranks, and there would be a mass exodus if the members believed it were really possible to get out (and live). Many of the trainers I knew (I know, wicked, torturing pedophiles) were NOT happy with what they did. They would whisper quietly, or give a look, to show that they disagreed with what they had to do. They would resignedly do their jobs, in the hope of advancement.

Know what one of the biggest carrots offered to those who advance up in the group is? That you don't have to hurt people anymore, and that you can't be abused (it's true: only those higher than you in the group can abuse you, so everyone wants to move up, where the pool of candidates becomes smaller). Of course, people can choose to abuse anyone beneath them, and that motivates.

The Illuminati are a very political and back stabbing group, a "dog eat dog" mentality; everyone wants to move up. These are NOT nice people and they use and manipulate others viciously. They cut their eyeteeth on status, power, and money.

They never openly disclose their agenda, or their cult activities, as often they are amnesic to them. These are well-respected, "Christian" appearing business leaders in the community. The image in the community is all-important to an Illuminist; they will do anything to maintain a normal, respected facade, and DESPISE exposure. ....

None of the Illuminists that I have known, had unkind, or evil appearing, persona in their daytime lives, although some were dysfunctional, such as being alcoholics. The dissociation that drives the Illuminists is their greatest cover ... Many, if not most, of these people are completely unaware of the great evil that they are involved in, during the night."

TV

Also, remember those studies that stated that "TV violence doesn't affect children's behaviour" years ago? Guess who funded them? They are a bunch of bullcrud. What a person watches DOES influence them, and this is well known by the behaviourists in the group. In fact, they know that TV is a tool that they purposely use to influence "the masses". It cannot create a total personality change in the average citizen, but it can desensitize us increasingly to violence, pornography and the occult, and influence the perceptions of young children.

ROCK MUSIC

I believe that Brittany Spears, Eminem, and others are being used by them to sing lyrics they like (ever notice that he wears a Neo-Nazi look and sings hate lyrics? This is NOT by chance). In fact, many of the top pop singers come from an internship with the "Mickey Mouse club" (yep, good old Walt the Illuminist's Empire) and I believe they are offered stardom in exchange for allegiance or mind control.

How many lyrics advocate suicide, violence, despair, or New Age spirituality in pop/rock today? Or just get a copy of the words and read (but be aware that many are possibly triggering to survivors of mind control).

ILLUMINATI WEAKNESSES

Svali:

"1. Their arrogance (I think I mentioned this before) is their weakness. These people think they are untouchable, and this could make them careless.

2. If by a miracle, enough people took this SERIOUSLY and started organizing in some way to stop the Illuminati take over, with prayer and God's guidance, perhaps they could be stopped. I hope so, with all of my heart.

3. Stopping pornography and child prostitution and drug smuggling and gun running would take out a huge chunk of their profits. Maybe they would slow down. But honestly, stopping the above would be as difficult as stopping the group."

PUBLIC'S DENIAL MECHANISM

Svali: The evidence is there, but in my opinion, the average person does NOT want to know, and even when confronted with it, will look the other way.

The Franklin case is a point. How much evidence has come out? Or the MK-Ultra documents that have been declassified, shown as real, and people ignore it.

Okay, I'll get off my soapbox. But I believe that the media that downplays ritual abuse is feeding into a deep need in the average person to NOT know the reality. In fact, how can a person face the fact of great evil in mankind, unless they have either a strong faith in God, or are faced with insurmountable evidence? We as human beings want to believe the BEST of our race, not the worst, IMHO.

I really don't believe people will do anything about the Illuminati even if they know. Sorry for the cynicism, but it is based on a lifetime of experience.

The Illuminists don't care who prints this stuff, or if they are "exposed" because they are counting on the majority not believing it, having done a pretty good job with a media blitz campaign (seen any articles in Newsweek or Time lately that addresses this other than as a laughable conspiracy theory? Guess who owns Time-Warner?).

I have heard them laughing about this very thing in leadership meetings five years ago, and I doubt their attitude has changed much since then. If people DID believe this, if action could be taken, then I would be very surprised and quite happy."

Since alerting mankind to its danger, "Svali" has either gone underground or has been captured or murdered. She cannot be reached.

EPILOGUE

What Can Be Done?

WE LIVE IN A DECADENT ERA that wants easy answers.

There is no quick fix to this mess. Rich and powerful forces have been subverting the human race for at least 300 years. The satanic central banking cartel is gradually degrading and colonizing us. Generally speaking, our "leaders" are complicit in our enslavement. The people selected to advance in culture, politics and big business often are traitors criminals and perverts at worst, opportunists and dupes at best. Our present prosperity is designed to keep us complacent and docile.

This is a battle for the mind and soul of mankind. The front lines are family, race, religion and nation. We have to educate our families, friends and neighbors. Our fellow citizens are well meaning people who have been deceived. They represent a sleeping giant that needs to be awakened. Let's defend our collective identity and resist tyranny by all legal means. If they try to ban the truth (e.g. "hate speech") we will be defiant. The truth is all that matters; the truth is the only thing that will save us.

The Luciferians are dependent on deception. The events of 9-11 have blown their cover. Millions are learning the horrible reality. Courageous people are standing up. Defectors are appearing. Finally we have a protest movement that is not elite sponsored. Eventually there will be a groundswell that will make the enemies of God and man reconsider.

Each of us has a special gift. Do your part.

Made in the USA
Las Vegas, NV
21 December 2024

15000965R00142